A GUIDE TO WELSH LITERATURE

A GUIDE TO
WELSH LITERATURE
c. 1530–1700
VOLUME III

Edited by
R. GERAINT GRUFFYDD

UNIVERSITY OF WALES PRESS
CARDIFF
1997

British Library Cataloguing in Publication Data

A catalogue record for this book is available from the British Library

ISBN 0-7083-1400-7

Published with the financial support of the Arts Council of Wales

Cover illustration: title-page from the Welsh New Testament, 1567, reproduced by permission of the National Library of Wales

Cover design by Olwen Fowler
Typeset at the University of Wales Press
Printed in Wales by Dinefwr Press, Llandybïe

For Eluned, Siân, Rhun and Pyrs

CONTENTS

PREFACE

This volume seeks to take forward the story of Welsh literature from the point at which it was left, in the early sixteenth century, by its precursor in this esteemed series. It begins, as did the first two volumes in the series, with a general historical introduction to the period and ends with a discussion of the complex relationship between manuscripts and printed books as means of disseminating literature at this time. In between, the main aspects of the writings of the period, including poetry, prose and scholarship, are discussed by experts in their various fields. The chapters are not of uniform length because some aspects of the subject clearly demanded closer attention than others: the second chapter is an obvious example. There is inevitably some repetition between one chapter and another, but too forceful wielding of the editorial knife would have resulted in imbalance within an individual contribution; in any case, some things bear saying twice.

I am most grateful to the contributors to the volume for agreeing to undertake a difficult task, and for honouring their agreement in so competent a fashion. My thanks are also due to the founders of the series and editors of the first two volumes, Professor A. O. H. Jarman and Dr Gwilym Rees Hughes, for their active assistance and encouragement. Finally, the Director of the University of Wales Press and its staff could not have been more supportive and helpful. The faults of the volume must therefore, I fear, be laid wholly at my door.

R. Geraint Gruffydd

A NOTE ON CONTRIBUTORS

Dr Geraint Bowen was formerly a H. M. Inspector of Schools.

Mr Cennard Davies is a Lecturer in Welsh Studies at the University of Glamorgan.

Professor R. Geraint Gruffydd was formerly Director of the University of Wales Centre for Advanced Welsh and Celtic Studies at Aberystwyth.

Mrs Branwen Jarvis is a Senior Lecturer in Welsh at the University of Wales Bangor.

Professor Gareth Elwyn Jones is Research Professor in the Department of Education at the University of Wales Aberystwyth.

Professor Ceri W. Lewis was formerly Professor of Welsh at the University of Wales Cardiff.

Dr Nesta Lloyd was formerly Lecturer in Welsh at the University of Wales Swansea.

Mr Charles Parry is an Assistant Librarian at the National Library of Wales.

Mr Graham C. G. Thomas is a Senior Assistant Archivist at the National Library of Wales.

The Revd Dr Isaac Thomas was formerly a Senior Lecturer in the Department of Biblical Studies at the University of Wales Bangor.

Professor M. Wynn Thomas is a Professor of English at the University of Wales Swansea.

CHAPTER 1

WALES 1550–1700
THE HISTORICAL BACKGROUND

GARETH ELWYN JONES

GOVERNMENT DEFINED

While the notion of a 'mid-Tudor crisis' is now held to apply more aptly to demography than to affairs of state, mid-century Wales was still in the throes of an administrative revolution by which its former constitutional status of 'Principality' and 'Marches' had been legislated out of existence. It now formed part of a state of 'England and Wales', a nomenclature which still serves as a reminder of the equivocal position of country and inhabitants through the centuries.

Legally and politically, mid-Tudor Wales was defined by that series of Acts passed between 1536 and 1543 known collectively as the Acts of Union. The conquest of Wales had, of course, been accomplished in 1282–3 and had been followed by the duality of control exercised by king and marcher lords. Thereafter, the Principality of Wales shared a system of shire government with England but the marcher lordships continued a quasi-independence which grew increasingly anachronistic. Economic and social changes in the fifteenth century, particularly the consolidation of gentry estates, made some accommodation inevitable.

There is controversy as to the motives of Henry VIII and Thomas Cromwell in undertaking, very tentatively, a reform of Welsh government and administration of justice but, in Principality and marcher lordship alike, there was serious, longstanding, lawlessness affecting people and property. Violent assault, ambush, cattle-stealing, perversion of justice, suborning of juries and misuses of traditions such as *arddel* and *comortha* were commonplace. A series of piecemeal measures, from individual executions to Acts of Parliament, immediately predated comprehensive measures which brought the whole of Wales broadly into line with English structures. Tentatively in 1536, more decisively in 1543, the government of Wales was given a shape which remained substantially unmodified throughout this period, except during the Commonwealth and Protectorate. The Acts of Union created the counties of Brecon, Radnor, Montgomery, Denbigh and Monmouth, carved out of former marcher lordships, and enlarged the erstwhile counties palatine of Glamorgan and Pembrokeshire, to supplement the shires of the Principality. The territory of Wales now consisted of the twelve or thirteen counties which were to last until the local government reorganization of 1974.

The position of the thirteenth county, Monmouthshire, was equivocal in that it was not included in the judicial system established by the Act of 1543. Four circuits of justices, each covering three counties, comprised the Great Sessions, courts held twice yearly. Monmouthshire, like the English counties, was under the jurisdiction of the Westminster courts. The courts of Great Sessions constituted a unique judicial arrangement which lasted until the nineteenth century. Another unique tier, crucial to both government and justice, was the Council in the Marches, located at Ludlow, a town which became, as a result, a surrogate social and political capital. The Council was established on a statutory basis by the Act of 1543.

The shiring of Wales allowed the English system of county administration and justice to be implemented in modified form. By the reign of Elizabeth, large English counties had their individual lords lieutenant but there was one only for Wales. This office was combined with that of lord president of the Council in the Marches and placed the holder at the apex of social, administrative and political influence, especially during the second half of the sixteenth century. By 1586 each of the Welsh counties had its own deputy lieutenant(s), responsible for military security and for controlling the Roman Catholic recusancy which was a matter of such concern to Tudor monarchs in the wake of the Reformation. It was a prestigious office held by the élite gentry families.

The increasing importance of the office of deputy lieutenant resulted in the displacement of the sheriff as the county's most influential official. The sheriff's office was ancient, and continued to be significant in the years after Union in that it involved providing juries for the courts of Quarter Sessions and Great Sessions and seeing that court sentences of fines and gaoling were implemented. Although the sheriff's military duties were eventually taken over by the deputy lieutenant, Union legislation relating to Welsh representation in Parliament resulted in continuing shrieval influence.

The Acts of Union gave the Welsh counties parliamentary representation on a more restricted basis than in England. Wales was granted one knight for each shire, other than Monmouthshire which, like English counties, was to have two, and one member for the ancient boroughs within each county other than Merioneth, which was to have no representation. Haverfordwest was granted its own member. Elections were to be avoided if possible since they involved expense and disastrous loss of face for a defeated candidate. This was particularly so since the issues over which elections were fought were local rather than national, and were usually an extension of deep-seated family rivalries within counties. If contests did take place, voting was open. As returning officer the sheriff was able to decide on the exact location, timing and casting of votes. Elections in Tudor Wales furnish numerous examples of partial sheriffs in league with a county faction and prepared to use illegal influence.

Extending elements of the English structure of county government into Wales, even before the Acts of Union, had seen the introduction there of the ancient office of justice of the peace. Under the Act of 1536 eight justices were to be nominated for each of the Welsh counties; numbers which soon proved totally inadequate and were substantially exceeded. The justices were the vital element in county administration of justice, being responsible for implementing orders from the Privy Council and the Council in the Marches as well as statutes of the realm. By apprehending, interrogating and bringing to the courts offenders of all kinds their role in controlling crime was crucial. Once more, it was the more important landowning families of the counties who filled this office. Reward for undertaking such onerous duties came in the form of prestige and influence within the county.

The Acts of Union established a comprehensive system of administration in Wales. County office-holders, drawn from the ranks of the gentry, operated through a system of local and national courts and administrative bodies to enforce the myriad statutes relating to law and order, military arrangements and religious observance, including all-important disputes over land and other property. The theory of good government remained far removed from its proper practice, however. The personal interests of office-holding gentry often clashed with their official duties. The gentry played a key role at all levels. They took depositions relating to cases heard in the London courts of Star Chamber, Chancery, Exchequer and Requests, as well as the Council in the Marches. As deputy lieutenants, sheriffs and justices of the peace they were crucial to the conduct of courts of Great Sessions and Quarter Sessions. But all these duties were unpaid; it is therefore not surprising that the records of the Council in the Marches, for example, are dotted with complaints that reports were inadequate or not completed at all and that orders were ignored. More of a problem was that there were so many examples of gentry office-holders breaking the law which they were responsible for upholding.

The Acts of Union did not, therefore, inaugurate an era of exemplary good order and government in Elizabethan Wales, despite the attempts of men such as George Owen of Pembrokeshire to stress, in the 1580s, the transformation wrought by Tudor legislation. Both the scale of lawlessness in Principality and March in the second half of the fifteenth century, and the efficacy of post-Union judicial processes, have been exaggerated. Yet in Elizabeth's reign the system of administration and justice, for all its imperfections, did work.

UBIQUITOUS LANDOWNERS

The reorientation, in Glanmor Williams's word, brought about by the Acts of Union was made possible by the existence of owners of landed estates in the Welsh counties. Changes in government recognized the realities of economic and social power and, in turn, consolidated them. The structure of land-holding in Wales had been transformed over the two centuries before 1550 as a result of dramatic political and economic change. The Edwardian conquest, the effects of the Black Death and the Glyndŵr revolt all contributed to modifying both the Norman manorial structures of the lowland areas of Principality and March and the Welsh system of land tenure, *cyfran*, or partible inheritance. The Acts of Union recognized the existence of landed estates which had already passed intact from generation to generation by endorsing primogeniture as the legal method of inheritance. During the sixteenth century these estates were often extended by acquisition of crown land, or monastic land after the dissolution of the monasteries in the 1530s. Indeed, the process of estate building, through purchase, acquisition of a tract of a former monastic estate, gradual engrossment, or marriage to an heiress continued throughout the sixteenth century and beyond in a fluid land market.

The greatest of the landed estates in Wales, as in England, were those of the few aristocrats. In the Tudor period the earls of Worcester and Pembroke owned and leased vast acreages in counties and boroughs in Wales and England. Although the earls of Worcester were based at Raglan and had extensive estates in Gower, the main aristocratic influence was exercised from England. The earls of Pembroke had considerable power over the gentry and inhabitants of Cardiff and Glamorgan but, in our period, were resident in England. The earl of Leicester, who had a substantial power base in north Wales, had far less connection with Wales. It was the gentry, particularly the élite among them, who predominated in wealth, social influence and political power in the counties of Wales for three centuries and more from 1500. They constituted a group with sufficient surplus wealth to invest in homes, lavish to varying degrees, in fine furniture and furnishings, recreation, superior food and wine, scholarly interests such as the collection of books and manuscripts, the best available education for their families, patronage of bards and musicians and travel, as well as the time and resources to fulfil their unpaid role in government and the administration of justice.

If the predominance and permanence of landed estates are the most significant features of Tudor and Stuart Wales, this does not imply a static or undisturbed gentry hegemony. Sixteenth-century inflation told on even the wealthier families and explains some of the constant litigation between landowners and tenants over encroachment and enclosure, as well as legal and illegal clashes between gentry factions. Such disputes, together with the jockeying for positions of influence in the counties, produced regular conflicts of interest between landowning families in their role as law-enforcers. The records of the Westminster courts of Star Chamber, Requests and Chancery, as well as the courts of Great Sessions in which the gentry had a more direct role, are studded with examples of their use of force, subterfuge, jury-rigging and bribery.

Nevertheless, the position of the landed gentry at the apex of county society remained unassailable: the key to the political, administrative, cultural and religious life of Wales from the Tudors to the Hanoverians. Gentry ranks were considerably more diverse in the sixteenth century than in the eighteenth. In the sixteenth century, as well as pronounced inflationary pressures, there were religious crises of conscience for some families. For example, the staunchly Roman Catholic Carne family in Glamorgan had acquired the priory and much of the land at Ewenni in the Vale of Glamorgan. Sent to Rome as Mary's ambassador to the Holy See, Sir Edward Carne did not return after Elizabeth I's accession in the knowledge that to do so would jeopardize his estates. In the following century a greater crisis confronted the gentry as the Civil War and the Commonwealth saw some families lose their estates and others emerge and prosper as government by committees and sequestration of land threatened traditional structures.

During the early eighteenth century more significant changes occurred among this landed élite. From Tudor times there were gradations among gentry families in all the Welsh counties. The Stradlings of St Donat's in Glamorgan or the Wynns of Gwydir in Caernarfonshire were leaders in the society of their respective counties by virtue of their extensive acreages, high income, luxurious lifestyle in castle or manor house and occupation of high office. There had always been lesser gentry, those whose estates would, in England, have placed them firmly in the ranks of the yeomanry. In Wales, where so much of the land was suitable for pastoral farming only and incomes consequently restricted, it was family descent and esteem among peers which served to confer gentry status. The Acts of Union had tied Wales closely to England; therefore the greater gentry, leaders in their communities and linchpins in the post-Union system, were increasingly locked in to the political and social ambience of Ludlow and London, as well as the official English-language dimensions of administration and law. But they had, on the whole, retained their Welsh roots and, in many cases, their Welsh language. This picture was modified in the later seventeenth and early eighteenth centuries. There was an unprecedented rate of failure of the male line as the heads of families married increasingly late in life or, indeed, not at all. The result was that, in family after family, continuity of inheritance was fractured, and families from Scotland and England headed great Welsh estates by the end of the eighteenth century. So, for example, the vast Margam estate, one of the four wealthiest in Wales in the eighteenth century, bought by Rice Mansel after the dissolution of the monasteries, passed to a Wiltshire branch of the family, and the Golden Grove estates of the Vaughans were bought by Lord Cawdor. Modification in the age of marriage and accidents of fertility accentuated an increasing demarcation between greater and lesser gentry, the holders of the largest estates having already become a more homogeneous and anglicized group whose allegiance to things Welsh was far less in evidence than had been the case two centuries previously.

RELIGION REFORMED

A potentially anglicizing force among all sections of the population was the state Church born of the changes introduced first by Henry VIII, extended by Edward VI and reaffirmed by Elizabeth I in 1559. It was once part of the orthodoxy of Welsh historiography that the Reformation crisis of the 1530s not only coincided chronologically with the early stages of Union but also caused it. While the notion that the move to political integration resulted from the necessity to enforce a break with Rome which was deemed likely to prompt serious opposition from the Welsh is now regarded as much too simplistic, there is no denying the concern with which the Privy Council viewed Welsh reaction to Reformation changes.

Revisionist historians now question the long-held view of the Roman Catholic Church in England and Wales as riddled with abuses and in terminal decline on the eve of the Reformation. It is now argued that without Henry VIII's marital entanglements there could have been that spiritual and moral renewal which would have revitalized the old faith. Analysis of the condition of the Welsh Church on the eve of the Reformation must take account of increasing vitality in the second half of the fifteenth century. This was a period of church building and scholarly activity signalling recovery from the depredation and dislocation following the Glyndŵr revolt.

If the debilitating effects of the familiar catalogue of abuses—nepotism and pluralism, for example—may have been over-emphasized, Wales was certainly not immune from distortions of the spiritual ideal in the Roman Catholic Church across Europe. Indeed, there is a more firmly founded tradition of criticism in the different social and linguistic situation in Wales. Medieval bishops were usually English absentees, whose concern for their poverty-stricken Welsh dioceses was minimal, while the lower clergy were, with few exceptions, poor and ill-educated. Even so, whatever the prevalence of anti-clericalism, the allegiance of the Welsh to aspects of Roman Catholicism, to shrines and holy days and to the familiar church rituals associated with the central events of their secular lives, was a matter of concern to the government. In practice, the Reformation—whether the Acts of the Reformation Parliament or the dissolution of the monasteries—provoked little active opposition from clergy or laity. Crucially, the temptation afforded by the opportunity to acquire church lands was stronger than religious devotion among the Welsh gentry and tied them—irrevocably as it proved—to the Tudor state and its successive religious settlements. The staunchest Catholics leased and bought land. It was the dissolution which provided substantial additions to the estates of the earls of Worcester and the Morgans of Llantarnam, for example, devotedly Catholic families in Elizabeth's reign.

By 1550 the uneasy Henrician Reformation had been polarized by Edward VI's Protestantism. In Wales there was little overt opposition to the dissolution of the chantries, the pillaging of church goods and the substitution of communion tables for altars. Commitment to the old order among clergy and laity was insufficient to provoke any uprising. On the other hand there was little popular support for change wrought in Edward's reign, to the consternation of the more extreme Protestants. Their concern was instrumental in spurring on the publication of religious writings in the Welsh language which would allow the clergy to mediate the core theologies of Protestantism, with William Salesbury's efforts outstanding.

Before the appearance of Salesbury's New Testament in 1567 the religious crisis had accentuated, first with the violent reversion to Roman Catholicism in Mary's reign in the 1550s, then the uneasy religious compromise worked out by Elizabeth I immediately after her accession in 1558. Although there were three martyrdoms in Wales under Mary, the general reaction to her policies in a country in which Protestantism had not taken firm root was uneasy acquiescence.

The creation of the Church of England, with Elizabeth I as its supreme governor, produced a crisis of conscience for staunch adherents to Rome. There were notable Welsh exiles—Morris Clynnog, Owen Lewis and Gruffydd Robert, for example, left to train priests and write the pamphlets so crucial to their cause. Catholic propaganda held that Wales was fertile ground for support, even an uprising in the cause of the old faith. The authorities were worried. The inadequacies of the system of local administration so recently established were a cause of concern to Privy Council and Council in the Marches alike. Such fears proved groundless. Certainly, some areas of Wales were known for their loyalty to Rome. This was most evident where there was aristocratic or gentry leadership—for example in Monmouthshire under the influence of the earls of Worcester or in the Chirk area under the leadership of the Edwards family. It was not that there was any great enthusiasm for the new order among the majority. The prevalence of such Roman Catholic practices as the use of rosaries was the despair of some committed Protestant clergy. What was essential if there was to be any substantial threat to the religious authority of the Crown was Roman Catholic fervour among a majority of the gentry. They were the leaders of their local societies and they were essential to the processes of law and order, including acting against recusancy. Such fervour was rare. In its absence the Protestant Church of England slowly put down roots.

Central to its cultivation in Elizabeth I's reign were the efforts of some outstanding Welsh bishops. Their achievements were both pastoral and literary. The effective dissemination of Protestant theology and observance depended upon the existence of the Scriptures in the Welsh language, but translating the Bible required rare scholarship in Latin, Hebrew and Greek as well as some solution to the commercial problems of production. Part of the solution came in an Act of Parliament of 1563 which authorized the translation of the Bible into Welsh by the bishops of the four Welsh dioceses and of Hereford. In 1567 there appeared Welsh versions of the New Testament and the Book of Common Prayer, but their effectiveness was limited because of Salesbury's unorthodox orthography. Then, in 1588, came the translation of the complete Bible, the work of Vicar, later Bishop, William Morgan. It is difficult to exaggerate the erudition and the linguistic mastery which made this translation the most influential literary

achievement in Welsh history. Apart from its spiritual and theological significance for countless generations, an essential tool for
Protestant congregations to learn from as it was read each Sunday,
it provided a crucial written reference point of beauty and purity
for the Welsh language.

The translation of the Bible into Welsh was only the most notable
of many publications by clergy and humanists in the wake of the
Elizabethan settlement. Roman Catholic counter-reformers did
their best to provide an essential supply of priests and instructional
literature. In 1568 two Welshmen, Morgan Phillips, once precentor
of St David's, and Owen Lewis of Anglesey were instrumental in
establishing a seminary in Douai to train priests. Morris Clynnog's
attempt to provide literary instruction for the laity was particularly
noteworthy, but the overall missionary effort was less successful.
There were relatively few priests; those who came operated in
conditions of extreme danger and agonizing punishment if they
were caught. One estimate, necessarily to be treated with caution,
puts the number of recusants at eight hundred at the time of
Elizabeth's death, compared with the 200,000 or so conformists.
Few recusants were from gentry families.

Protestant reformers were not sanguine about the quality of lay
conformity among the gentry or the other social orders. They tried
to combat it not only by provision of a Welsh version of the Bible
but also by an appeal to history and tradition which helped counter
Roman Catholic denunciations. Bishop Richard Davies, in his
preface to the New Testament of 1567, argued that the Protestant
Church was the true Church, untrammelled by the accretions of
later centuries, established within thirty years of Christ's death by
Joseph of Arimathea.

Allegiance to the new Church continued to be sufficiently muted
to exasperate the committed. Reforming Elizabethan bishops like
Davies and Robinson criticized the laity for their apathy. According
to the bishops, there continued to be a prevalence of Catholic
practices such as the elevation of the host and devotion to former
shrines. Underlying weaknesses, particularly the poverty of the
Welsh dioceses, were now accentuated by lay impropriation,
though, paradoxically, it was the latter which gave the landed laity
that stake in the new order which made any reversion to the old
unlikely. Extreme Puritanism, though little in evidence in Wales,
encompassed both concern at the lack of penetration of Calvinist

teaching and a questioning of the hierarchies of Anglican church government, with John Penry eventually coming to believe that the state did not have the authority to determine the religion of its citizens. Yet the translation of the Bible and other religious literature into Welsh is indication enough of the dedication and achievements of the reformers.

THE LANGUAGE IN CONTEXT

Secular literature in Welsh was less secure after the notable bardic achievements of the later fifteenth and early sixteenth centuries. Poets had occupied an honoured place in the courts of medieval Welsh rulers in return for eulogizing their patrons for their nobility, courage and chivalry. Wealthier gentry families in Tudor times continued the tradition. Itinerant poets performed their time-honoured function of praising the noble ancestry of their patrons, so bolstering the esteem and family pride characteristic of the Welsh gentry, whether of Welsh, Norman or English origin. Whatever their economic resources—and the Welsh gentry as a group were substantially poorer than their English counterparts—they laid great store by that lineage which conferred gentility. The bards, honoured recounters of the deeds of forebears, were central to family status, but they also emphasized the responsibility of their patrons to act towards tenants in a manner commensurate with high status. In aspiring to this mark of gentility, the Welsh gentry of the Tudor and early Stuart period were integrated into their local communities in a manner similar to that of their ancestors.

The second half of the sixteenth century saw economic and cultural influences leading to a steady decline in the practice of patronage and the bardic craft. Inflationary pressures made both patronage and lengthy bardic apprenticeships less likely. The advent of the printing press threatened oral tradition and the social, political and religious contexts made bardic eulogies and vaticinatory poetry increasingly less relevant. The household bard became increasingly anachronistic, creative springs stagnated and traditional themes seemed old-fashioned in the scholarly ambience of the Renaissance. Eventually the greater gentry's concern was to be far less with any Welsh ancestry than with their standing among their English compeers.

We have seen that religious change prompted treatises from
Roman Catholics and Protestants alike, and theological writings
continued to be prominent in a vigorous and expanding output of
prose in the Welsh language. Renaissance influences spurred
scholars across Europe to ensure that the non-classical, vernacular
languages were appropriate vehicles for the transmission of ideas.
Scholars in Wales, so many of them clerics, inevitably saw the
intellectual battleground as religious, and this, together with the
central need for mission, decreed that Welsh was such a language.
The first priority of Welsh religious scholars of the sixteenth
century, Salesbury, Bishop Richard Davies or Gruffydd Robert, for
example, was not linguistic; but publication in the Welsh language,
especially the Bible, was an essential tool of mission to the Welsh.
Indirectly, the existence of the Bible in Welsh proved essential to the
preservation of the language.

Other developments in the sixteenth century augured ill for the
future of the Welsh language. The Act of Union of 1536 had
stipulated that the language of administration and justice in Wales
should be English. Although this could not mean courts of justice
always being conducted in English in what was still largely a
monoglot Welsh society, it did ensure that the landed classes, who
held the important offices, had every incentive to work through the
medium of English. Their increasing contacts with the Welsh
'capital' at Ludlow and with the social and political centre in
London added to the sense of the superiority of English. The
anglicizing influence of gentry education, at grammar schools in
England, at the universities of Oxford and Cambridge and at the
Inns of Court underpinned a wider identity with the language and
mores of their English counterparts. Technology, too, played its
part as the gentry acquired the increasing number of books
available in English, an output with which Welsh was never able to
compete. During the seventeenth century, particularly after the
Civil War, intermarriage with English landed families accentuated
the divide between an increasingly anglicized gentry élite and lesser
gentry and yeomen farmers.

While the mass of the population continued to be monoglot
Welsh, the attitude of the landed classes was crucial. Their
increasing anglicization was inexorable but slow. A scholar
gentleman like Sir Edward Stradling of St Donat's in Glamorgan
could, in the sixteenth century, combine writing about his

ancestors' exploits in the English language—*The Winning of Glamorgan*—with generous patronage of Welsh bards and financial backing for the publication of Dr Siôn Dafydd Rhys's Welsh grammar in 1592. Such continuing gentry interest in family and local history, the Protestant concern to provide religious writing in the vernacular and humanists' determination to produce grammars and dictionaries, all combined to invigorate the Welsh language in the new era of the printing press.

POLITICAL PRIORITIES AND CIVIL WAR

If the role of the gentry in the religious and linguistic history of Wales in this period was influential, they dominated politics. Only some 4 per cent of the population were even involved in the electoral process as forty-shilling freeholders in the counties or burgesses in the contributory boroughs.

The faction politics of the Tudor and Stuart centuries were less influenced by the aristocracy in Wales than in England, though at various times in the sixteenth century the power bases of the earls of Leicester, Pembroke, Worcester and Essex were extensive in various parts of Wales. They each had their clientele of gentry supporters—and their powerful opponents. In such a context appointments to local offices and, especially, to a county or borough parliamentary seat, were of crucial importance.

It was for this reason, rather than for their influence in sporadically summoned London parliaments that landowners, in the last resort, became MPs. By the late sixteenth century and in the seventeenth century, Welsh parliamentary seats in borough and county were in the hands of a few of the wealthiest families. Even so, occasional bitter election battles could not be avoided, as in Anglesey in the 1550s when the Bulkeleys of Beaumaris competed with a faction led by the Owens of Bodowen and Fron-deg. Local rivalry was at the root of the frequent disputed elections in Caernarfonshire in the early seventeenth century. The Wynn family had predominated in the Elizabethan period, only to be superseded by the Griffith family. Consequent confrontations produced the usual catalogue of dubious practices—creating freeholders to vote, and bringing pressure to bear on the shrieval returning officer.

Welsh MPs, fourteen for the counties, thirteen for the boroughs,

had a vested interest in loyalty to the monarch. It was the policies of
Tudor monarchs which had bolstered and regularized their position
at the apex of administrative and judicial processes. Many subscribed to bardic views of the Tudor dynasty as rightful heirs to the
ancient British kingdom. Loyalty to the Tudors was transferred to
the early Stuarts. Tensions over the role of the prerogative courts,
for example, and religious controversy were, to some extent, echoed
in Wales, though, with the exception of a few families, Puritanism
elicited little sympathy among landowners. Their interests, religious
and political, led them to firm support for the Established Church.
It was there that they exerted influence as lay impropriators and
presenters to livings. The implications of some Puritan teaching,
potentially threatening social hierarchies, were wholly alien. At the
same time there was little enthusiasm for Charles I's perceived
Roman Catholic leanings.

The reasons for the sometimes muted support for Charles I in
Wales are therefore not difficult to understand, though they must
always take into account individual and idiosyncratic responses.
Grand theories of rising and declining gentry, or the determining
factors of all-embracing economic forces at work have long since
been undermined by a recognition of the importance of local
reaction. Various lines of opposition developed in response to the
policies of Charles I. Welshmen were less favoured in his court than
by James I. There was concern over the policies of Buckingham, in
particular, which resulted in the disaffection of Bishop John
Williams, the earl of Pembroke and Vice-Admiral Robert Mansel.
Then there was increasing resentment at forced loans and other
financial levies. Welsh counties grew increasingly reluctant to pay
Ship Money—with no county paying in full by 1639. However, the
financial policies of the Crown which caused such resentment
among merchants and the commercial élite, especially in London,
impinged little on Wales because of its underdeveloped commercial
life. In the unfolding crisis preceding the outbreak of war in 1642
there was no enthusiastic support for either side, merely a
realization among MPs and other gentry of the potential disaster of
armed conflict.

This apprehension conditioned the mood in Wales as the war
started. Control of both the border with England and the Irish Sea
were regarded as crucial by both sides, involving access to supplies,
recruits and Ireland. The king saw Wales as a potentially rich source

of support—ten regiments of foot soldiers were recruited immediately—but the country was by no means totally Royalist and patterns of allegiance were complicated. The landed families of Pembrokeshire were for the most part Parliamentary supporters, as were Philip Herbert, Philip Jones and Rowland Dawkin in neighbouring Glamorgan, and branches of the Myddeltons, the Thelwalls and the Trevors in north Wales. Puritanism had made some impact, too, in commercial areas like Wrexham. The two great aristocratic families of most influence in Wales were on different sides. The earl of Worcester, staunchly Roman Catholic, was one of the most loyal of the king's supporters. It is significant that, outside the ranks of his immediate gentry circle, Worcester's religion caused concern to many south Wales landowners. The earl of Pembroke was equally firmly for the Parliamentary cause.

While Welsh recruits fought in the early battles of the Civil War, Wales was little affected. Glamorgan and Monmouthshire provided more soldiers for the king in 1643 after the Royalists had captured the major port and trading centre of Bristol, but the Royalists were never able to take control of the whole of the border country nor of the whole of Pembrokeshire. That year also saw a successful Parliamentary campaign in north Wales, with the capture of strategic centres in the north-east, and although Royalist forces returning from Ireland regained control it was to be shortlived. In 1644 Parliamentary forces under Sir Thomas Myddelton once again dominated mid- and north-east Wales. In the same year both sides at some time claimed much of the south Wales coastal area as forces loyal to the king and to Parliament mounted offensives. By the end of 1645 the Royalist cause in Wales shared in wider reverses. The traditional stronghold of the earl of Worcester's Raglan held out, as did Aberystwyth in the west. Despite some Royalist counter-offensives, in 1646 Parliamentary pressure was inexorable. In February 1646 Parliamentary forces took Raglan Castle, while the capture of Chester in the north allowed a Parliamentary offensive across north Wales which, by March, 1647, resulted in the capitulation of the whole of Wales.

It was hardly surprising that the imposition of Parliamentary rule in a country in which administration had been so largely in the hands of Royalist landowners should generate opposition. This discontent was transformed into protest in Glamorgan in 1646 and 1647 but a major uprising in Pembrokeshire early in 1648 came not from Royalists but from supporters of Parliament, upset by arrangements made for paying off troops. The protest developed into the second Civil War and led to the major battle of the Civil War in Wales. At St Fagan's in May 1648, forces led by the leaders of the rebellion, Rice Powell and Rowland Laugharne, proved no match for soldiers of the New Model Army commanded by Horton. Less serious risings in north Wales were quickly snuffed out.

PURITAN RULE

The Puritan victors in the Civil War now had to translate military control into viable government. We have seen how the structure of local government and justice, laid down in the Acts of Union, required the co-operation of the landed gentry. Yet the great majority were Royalist. There were certainly some who had supported Parliament; some, like the Wynns in north Wales, had managed not to take sides; and a few, such as Bussy Mansel, or Sir John Pryce of Newtown, were notorious trimmers. But Parliamentary government lacked the underpinning of gentry commitment.

During the Civil War, county committees were established in areas controlled by Parliament to administer and control finances, though in the early years of the War lack of support for Parliament was such that a committee was set up only in Pembrokeshire. These county committees now formed an essential element in post-war government, but they were never wholly satisfactory nor part of a coherent Parliamentary strategy for Wales. They were only part of a network of committees, with others having more specific functions, such as the Committee for the Propagation of the Gospel and the sequestration committees, one for north and one for south Wales, established in 1649 and reorganized in 1650. The latter, charged with fining or sequestrating the lands of Royalist gentry, caused bitterness and accusations of corruption against the sequestrators.

The Welsh gentry's allegiance to the Crown now caused a profound problem of government in Wales. In some counties there was a small nucleus of Parliamentary supporters, as in Denbighshire under the leadership of Sir Thomas Myddelton. In other counties—Brecon, Radnor, Carmarthen and Cardigan—

there were insufficient Parliamentary supporters, and in the early days of the county committees gentry families with known Royalist sympathies had to be allowed to serve. After the second Civil War committees were purged and lesser gentry and army officers brought in. For the first time in a century many of the old-established families, particularly in south Wales, were excluded from control in their localities. The situation was modified again after Cromwell's acceptance of the Humble Petition and Advice, which saw the return of some previously excluded Royalist families, among the most significant being Sir Edward Mansel of Margam.

With Oliver Cromwell's death in 1658 Wales shared in the political turmoil which ensued. For a brief period, with the formation of militia commissions to try to resist the Royalists, extreme Puritans experienced a short-lived resurgence of influence. However, the final county committees established to prepare for the king's return brought the traditional governing gentry back into the system. Extreme Puritan minor gentry, supporters of Morgan Llwyd and Vavasor Powell, were marginalized.

The great majority of the Welsh clergy, like the gentry, had supported the king in the Civil War. But there were tensions within the Church, with increasing Puritan concern for the souls deprived of adequate insight into those Calvinist doctrines essential to salvation. If taken to extremes the rectification of these shortcomings involved solutions which had revolutionary social implications, as the mid-seventeenth century breakdown so graphically proved. Puritanism was, however, a complex phenomenon, with Vicar Prichard, for example, a faithful Anglican supporter of the king at the outbreak of the Civil War yet the advocate of a severely puritanical lifestyle in his verses for the people. Wales continued to challenge Puritans because of the adherence of so many to what were regarded as superstitious practices and the lack of penetration of Calvinist theology. Only in the border counties and parts of south-east Wales did Puritan congregations make headway, though John Miles established the first Baptist church in Gower.

The mission of the 1650 Propagation Commission to establish Puritanism across Wales was therefore a formidable one. The seventy-one members—many of them Englishmen—were charged with ensuring that the people of Wales received suitable preaching and teaching. In three years 278 ministers were ejected but finding sufficient adequate replacements, particularly in the less populous and accessible areas of Wales, proved impossible and the Commission had to rely on itinerant ministers of variable quality. The experiment was short-lived. The year 1654 saw a reversion to a conventional settled ministry under a Commission for the Approbation of Public Preachers. The difficulties remained. The range of teachings—Millenarianism and Quakerism, for example, had their Welsh adherents—was mysterious to most. The great majority of the gentry resented attempts to subvert their influence; the lower orders resented outlawing of traditional revelries. Attempts to puritanize the Welsh were proving ineffective.

RELIGIOUS DISSENT AND EDUCATIONAL ENDEAVOUR

With the Restoration, leading Welsh Puritans disappeared from the scene. Vavasor Powell went to prison and John Miles to America. The Clarendon Code of 1661–5 ensured that there would be no compromise; those not prepared to accept the communion and teaching of the Anglican Church were excluded from office, and theoretically barred from congregating for worship. Over a hundred Puritan clergy were quickly deprived of their livings. With the 1672 Declaration of Indulgence, 185 Dissenting congregations, the majority in south Wales, applied for licences and it is estimated that, in the 1670s, there were more than four thousand Dissenters and a thousand Roman Catholics in Wales. Dissent, solid and dedicated in its membership, sober and respectable in lifestyle, was well established in Wales by 1700, with an estimated seventy churches by 1715, mainly in south Wales and the border counties. Due to the social standing of its adherents—minor gentry, craftsmen, substantial tenant farmers—the Independents, Presbyterians and Baptists were substantially more entrenched in these areas than their numbers would imply.

Here was a major challenge to the Established Church. Traditionally confronted by poverty, lay impropriation, vast upland parishes, pluralism and absenteeism, bishops were faced with intractable financial and organizational difficulties. The spiritual inadequacies of the later seventeenth-century Church were to be accentuated in the rationalistic eighteenth. Yet the traditional view of the post-Restoration Church as beset by torpor has long been modified. Bishops like Bull of St David's and Humphreys of Bangor were distinguished, and their efforts were complemented by the sterling efforts of many lower clergy who, despite poverty and pluralism, were indefatigable in their mission. The Methodist revival of the eighteenth century was firmly rooted in the endeavours of both Anglicans and Dissenters in the preceding century.

Both Dissenting and some Anglican clergy preached a spiritual and moral message—of salvation by grace and the necessity for eschewing the depravities of drink, foul language and desecration of the Sabbath. While Anglican clergy were restricted to their parishes, itinerant Dissenters like William Jones of· Cilmaenllwyd took regions as their parish. The preaching effort was supported by the written word. In the second half of the seventeenth century there was considerable expansion in publication of Welsh books — over five hundred titles in the seventy years after the Restoration, usually of a devotional and moral kind. In the same period over 40,000 copies of the Bible in Welsh were printed, many distributed free by the Welsh Trust and the Society for Promoting Christian Knowledge.

This literary activity was interwoven with efforts to educate the mass of the population. It was under the aegis of the Welsh Trust and the SPCK that there came the first attempt at bringing mass literacy to the Welsh. Education in Elizabeth's reign, despite some charitable endeavours, was largely restricted to those who could afford to pay the fees, or at least the incidental expenses, of the twenty-seven or so grammar schools. Only the sons of gentry families had resources to attend the universities of Oxford and Cambridge or the Inns of Court. Puritan efforts in the interregnum resulted in the establishment of sixty schools but they were a forced growth and the great majority disappeared even before the Restoration. Yet in Wales, more than in England, the religious motive of the salvation of souls by means of individual knowledge of the Bible led to an emphasis on basic literacy. Two vicars, ejected from their livings after the Restoration, set themselves to opening schools and providing devotional literature. In 1674 Stephen Hughes and Thomas Gouge established the Welsh Trust. In the short term their achievements were impressive—nearly a hundred schools opened in the first year, perhaps as many as three hundred in total. Eight thousand copies of a new edition of the Welsh Bible were distributed, together with much other pious literature. But the experiment was short-lived, with much of its dynamism disappearing when Gouge died in 1681. There was little support from the Welsh gentry; nor was there any marked demand from the ordinary people for whom the schools were intended. There was no appetite for English-language reading and writing in the schools, but there was opposition from philanthropists, especially outside Wales, to any element of instruction in Welsh. The Trust was also a victim of rivalries within the Established Church, both Gouge and Hughes having been ejected from their livings. And the 1680s saw a renewed period of religious intolerance, so that co-operation between leading Nonconformists and Anglicans in aspects of the Trust's work became impossible.

If the achievements of the Welsh Trust were limited, its activity is indication enough of a motivation and cast of mind resulting in two educational movements which came to fruition in the eighteenth century. There were souls to be saved and a gospel of usefulness to be inculcated. The Trust left a small legacy of teachers and school sites on which the Society for Promoting Christian Knowledge could capitalize. The Society counted Neath landowner and industrialist, Sir Humphrey Mackworth, among its founders in 1699, and the patronage of other Welsh gentry, notably Sir John Philipps of Picton Castle, Pembrokeshire, was crucial in providing funds and literature. Reading and writing based on this devotional literature once more provided the staple diet, though there was some emphasis, too, on arithmetic and craft education. By 1737, ninety-six SPCK schools were in operation in Wales, owing their greater success than those of the Welsh Trust partly to the use of the Welsh language as the medium of instruction, at least in north Wales. Even so, the efforts of philanthropists to provide mass education were fraught with financial problems. The Society could not afford the teacher training, school building or resources on the scale required. More in tune with the economic and social characteristics of Wales were the more modest itinerant schools associated with Griffith Jones which concentrated on basic, Welsh-language literacy and, in the eighteenth century, constituted one of the few distinctively Welsh contributions to educational practice.

There was some attempt to provide higher education for Nonconformist clergy excluded from the universities by post-Restoration legislation. The Nonconformist academies provided the only form of higher education available in Wales, originally for ministers, and despite perennial shortages of finance and books, interdenominational wrangles and theological dispute, the best teachers were impressively learned. Equally notable was the range of subjects—the classics and Hebrew, science, mathematics, logic, even medicine.

POST-RESTORATION POLITICS

Despite their Royalist allegiance most of the traditional landed families in Wales, their ranks infiltrated by some who had profited from the uncertainties of the interregnum, emerged once more to dominate political and social life. There were modifications to the pattern of gentry hegemony. In the later seventeenth century, still more evident in the eighteenth, membership of Parliament was concentrated in fewer hands than had been the case in Tudor times. A narrowing oligarchy of families such as the Bulkeleys of Beaumaris, the Morgans of Tredegar and the Vaughans of Llwydiarth were pre-eminent for decades in both counties and boroughs, their domination guaranteed far less by direct bribery than by great wealth, influence and patronage.

Bribery did play a part in Welsh politics in the years after the Restoration—Crown bribery. Sequestration and fines had taken toll of the resources of most of the gentry who were returned to the Cavalier Parliament after 1661, and Crown ministers—Clarendon and Danby—were prepared to pay for support. Although the 'country' party had some backing in Wales, it was not surprising that most Welsh MPs were adherents of the Crown party. This drew increasing numbers of Welsh members into the orbit of English factions and reinforced the identity of interest with English gentry mores. But the intricate Welsh rivalries of the Civil War did not disappear as moderate anti-Catholic gentry opposed the increasing influence of the Catholic earl of Worcester in south-east Wales, particularly after he became president of the revived Council in the Marches from 1672.

Religion continued to influence political affiliation as the possibility of the Roman Catholic James Stuart's accession to his brother Charles II's throne became stronger. Three Exclusion Parliaments after 1679 saw a majority of Welsh members at first favour exclusion; later, there was more substantial support for the court. When James did become king in 1685 there was no marked opposition in Wales. In his only Parliament the Court party had substantial success in both north and south Wales, and Wales was one of the few areas which continued to provide some backing for James after the appearance of a male heir. This was due partly to the allegiance of some staunch Roman Catholic families such as the duke of Beaufort, the Carnes of Ewenni and the Barlows of Slebech rather than the traditional loyalty to the monarchy. Even this lukewarm endorsement was to be undermined by James's increasing intransigence, and the great majority of Welsh MPs and other gentry endorsed the accession of William and Mary.

There remained a residual Welsh Jacobitism but it had no solid base. MPs from the Welsh constituencies became closely involved in the Whig and Tory faction politics of the London Parliament and their subsidiary 'connections'. Some three-quarters of Welsh members were probably broadly Tory in sympathy, loyal to High Church Anglicanism and with some Stuart sympathies. But that could no longer be translated into a serious threat to the political order in Wales, as the Welsh reaction to the 1715 and 1745 rebellions demonstrated. The 1715 rebellion saw much Jacobite sentiment from the likes of the Wynns, Kemeyses, Pryses, Philippses and Beauforts but no practical move of any significance. By this time Whig influence was spreading in Wales and Tories were assimilating increasingly into the mainstream of London government activity. There was one constant: the gentry continued to dominate politics and administration in Wales at all levels. One longstanding tier of government, the Council in the Marches, finally disappeared in 1688 but the machinery of local government and justice established under the Tudors allowed great landowners the maximum degree of local influence—even more extensive in the eighteenth century than had been the case previously. The demise of the Council in the Marches signalled the end to the pretensions of Ludlow to be a focal point of Welsh high society, which now gravitated towards the London and Bath seasons. Ludlow's centrality had depended on the Council's, and that had been substantially limited after its initial demise in the Commonwealth, since its restoration in Charles II's reign saw it stripped of its administrative functions.

By the early eighteenth century, gentry domination of Welsh

society was more secure than ever. Their ranks had thinned; they had become a narrower élite who identified in education, taste, lifestyle and language with their English compeers. In literature, architecture, furniture, dress and leisure interests, fashion was dictated in England, especially in London. This process was accentuated in the early decades of the eighteenth century as heads of gentry families had fewer children and married later or not at all. In Glamorgan, for example, at various times during the eighteenth century three heiresses married into the aristocracy. The male line failed in leading families in the county—the Kemeyses, Stradlings and Mansels, for example. Major estates passed to English or Scottish families. With the amalgamation of estates the greater gentry were able to exercise unparalleled power at a time when central government interference was at its weakest. A concomitant of the emergence of such an oligarchy in the later seventeenth and the early eighteenth centuries was the widening of the gulf between this group and the less affluent gentry, as well as the lower orders. Distinctions of wealth were inevitably translated into differences in lifestyle and culture.

CONTINUITY AND CHANGE—WALES IN 1700

Whatever the modifications, the essential structure of society in Wales remained in 1700 as it had developed out of the decades of shift and flux following the demise of Owain Glyndŵr in the early fifteenth century and the consolidation of Tudor legislation. Greater gentry families such as the Morgans of Tredegar had vast estates yielding commensurate incomes—£4,000 per annum in the late seventeenth century. The ranks of yeomen had been swelled by lesser gentry families who had failed to withstand the economic pressures consequent on dramatic inflation and population increase in the sixteenth century and the constant hazards of bad harvests, family misfortune, animal disease, and pressure from those with greater resources who sought to enclose, engross or purchase their land. Tenants, with varying sizes of holdings and differing degrees of insecurity, continued to farm beef and dairy cattle and, especially, sheep. Farmers in the upland areas of Wales concentrated inevitably on pastoral farming, while those in the more fertile lowland parts cultivated their crops of wheat, barley and oats as well as breeding cattle. Their approach to cattle-breeding and crop cultivation had changed little. Contemporaries commented on the conservatism of Welsh tenant farmers; even in the eighteenth century experiments in drainage, crop rotation, animal breeding and soil enrichment penetrated relatively slowly.

Industrial activity increased substantially over the period, though on a small scale compared with what was to come in the late eighteenth century. From 1562 to 1624 the Welsh woollen industry was dominated by a Shrewsbury Drapers' Company monopoly in marketing Welsh cloth, a control which in practice lasted until well into the following century. The products of this staple industry, located mainly in the counties of Merioneth, Montgomery and Denbigh, were not only sold locally in fairs and markets but also exported from Bristol and London in increasing amounts. But carding, spinning and weaving remained firmly rooted in the home.

There was expansion, too, in the Welsh metal industries. Glamorgan was a major producer of iron, with forges and furnaces across the county. Its iron ordnance was of high quality and extensively traded—legally and illegally. Although the industry was small-scale, there was already anxiety over the deforestation resulting from charcoal requirements, though it remained the essential fuel until the mid-eighteenth century. Civil war disrupted production, but soon after the Restoration and the ending of the Crown's monopoly over mineral rights, greater capitalization and partnerships combined to expand production.

Before coal became the handmaiden to iron from the mid-eighteenth century its production and consumption were limited. Used as domestic fuel, sporadically in the early sixteenth century, more generally, especially in towns, in the seventeenth, the technology of production was primitive. Shallow pits, constantly subject to flooding and collapse, and coal being cut by pick and shovel kept production down. But from a very restricted base there was a fourteen-fold increase in production between 1540 and 1640, concentrated in the coalfields of south- and north-east Wales, some channelled into exports from such ports as Swansea, Neath and Chester to Ireland, the west of England and France. As with the iron industry, gentry landowners were closely involved, Sir Humphrey Mackworth being the most enterprising of entrepreneurs in the second half of the seventeenth century. Mackworth's activities also included lead mining, another metal industry which major gentry families like the Pryces of Gogerddan and the Wynns of Gwydir exploited in Cardiganshire and Flintshire. The ubiquitous Sir Humphrey also developed an important copper smelter in Neath, processing ores shipped in from Cornwall and Cardiganshire.

Mackworth's multifarious activities serve as a reminder that, until the eighteenth century, industrial development was largely a matter for individuals. Mackworth's achievements in Neath were impressive indeed—spanning copper, coal, lead and their concomitant transport infrastructures. But he was essentially a landed gentleman, an individual entrepreneur, and his resources were stretched too far. The new industrial order of the later eighteenth century was based on outside capital and consortia, leasing land from the gentry.

Industrial and agricultural trade expanded significantly during the period—in Elizabeth's reign, for example, coal exports from Swansea nearly doubled to three thousand tons. But the essential rhythms of economic life remained essentially undisturbed. Welsh towns, of a few thousand population, were closely integrated with their rural hinterland. The administrative and judicial functions associated with Carmarthen and Caernarfon, for example, ensured their importance; but the main function of the towns was as market centres, both for the surplus produce and livestock of the local areas and also the goods produced by the saddlers, glovers and clothiers of the town guilds. Main trading arteries changed little. While drovers took Welsh cattle along time-honoured routes to the Midlands or London, the state of the roads remained an enormous hindrance to trade, even by packhorse. Eighteenth-century travellers commented on the mud and boulder obstacles to easy travel by horse or stagecoach on unmade or unrepaired surfaces. It was the mid-eighteenth century before the first turnpikes came to Wales and heralded a new approach. So, the most efficient means of carriage of goods was still the small boats which plied their coastal and continental trade. They did so legally, sometimes. Elizabeth's reign had seen the institution of a system of customs control, regulated through the head ports of Chester, Milford and Cardiff, which was intended to ensure that the Crown derived its maximum revenue from tonnage and poundage. In practice, illegal trade, centred on the innumerable small ports around the Welsh coast, continued. In the seventeenth century, Turkish pirate boats

constantly harassed shipping in the seas around Wales and,
although piracy was gradually brought under control, smuggling of
tea, coffee and wines, for example, was widespread in the eighteenth
century.

By 1700 there were modifications, too, to linguistic and cultural
patterns in Wales. As in other parts of Europe—Norway or
Bohemia, for example—a gulf had opened up between the language
of the lower orders and that of the social élite. Since the patronage
and financial support of the gentry remained crucial to scholarly
and artistic activity, such a social and linguistic divide boded ill for
the future development of the language, literature and native
culture of the Welsh. We have seen that the prose tradition of the
sixteenth century was more secure than the poetic. The concern of
the humanists to ensure that Welsh was a fit vehicle for Renaissance
ideas meshed with gentry interest in scholarship, collection of
manuscripts and publication of works of history and grammar, the
most important of the latter being that of Dr John Davies of
Mallwyd in 1621.

Gentry interest in the Welsh language was steadily diluted as a
result of a variety of anglicizing forces. By the end of our period
some thirty or forty very wealthy families had an economic,
administrative and social influence out of all proportion to their
numbers, and were virtually set to rule Wales in the eighteenth
century. In education, lifestyle and social habit they grew away from
their Welsh roots. Yet, for the vast majority of the inhabitants of
Wales, Welsh remained the language of discourse. Welsh was the
language of religion, and the printing press made possible
production of books and pamphlets on an unprecedented scale,
usually for educational and religious purposes. Between 1660 and
1730 publishers produced over five hundred titles.

Inclination, education and resources channelled the energies of
some gentlemen in literary and antiquarian directions. More were
interested in deer-hunting, hawking, horse-riding, tennis and
gambling, as well as the social round. The lower orders had neither
resources nor time for such activities. Their lives continued to be
dominated by the necessity to grow sufficient crops or sell their
labour so that their families might survive in the face of constant
threats of poor harvests, or disease afflicting their animals or
themselves. In the little time which remained from eking out a
living, the husbandman and labourer could gamble at dice or cards

and drink at alehouses, much to the discomfiture of the authorities. They might play a dangerous version of football or, in Pembrokeshire, *cnapan*, and could gamble on the outcome of cock fights and wrestling matches. Dancing round the maypole, wakes, music-making with pipes and fiddles on fair days and saints' days provided other occasional escapes from the unsure and precarious work-dominated round. These recreations, with their threats to good order and puritan morality, defeated all attempts by the Council in the Marches to limit the number of alehouses and the more systematic attempts in the interregnum to stamp out what were regarded as immoral practices. That some activities took place in the churchyard and broke the Sabbath made them even less acceptable to Dissenters and many Anglicans, but it was not until the full moral force of Methodism was levelled against them in the eighteenth century that the hold of many popular pastimes was loosened.

So the essential features of life in Wales in 1700 remained much as they had been 150 years previously. The proprietors of the great landed estates were yet more dominant in the economic, political and social life of Wales. In economic terms this domination was reinforced as the Crown surrendered its right to the profits from any minerals other than gold and silver discovered on private land, so encouraging exploitation of iron, copper and other minerals. The way was being prepared for that expansion of industrial activity which would lead eventually to phenomenal wealth for some families. For the mass of the population, tenant farmers and landless labourers, enjoying varying degrees of security and stability, life was still dominated by the rhythms of the seasons and the vagaries of the climate as they impinged on a predominantly agricultural economy. The upheavals of Reformation, Civil War and interregnum permanently affected the religious experience of the Welsh as, gradually, Anglicanism, then Dissent took root. Associated with religious mission was a basic educational programme which was to come to fruition in the first half of the eighteenth century. The battle for the souls of the people depended substantially on the products of the printing press. The expansion of publishing was as significant a change as any in the period, and its association with the devotional life of the Welsh people ensured the continued virility of the Welsh language.

BIBLIOGRAPHY: SUGGESTIONS FOR FURTHER READING

John Davies, *A History of Wales* (London, 1993).

A. H. Dodd, *Studies in Stuart Wales* (second edn.; Cardiff, 1971).

E. D. Evans, *A History of Wales 1660–1815* (Cardiff, 1976).

Geraint H. Jenkins, *The Foundations of Modern Wales. Wales 1642–1780* (Oxford and Cardiff, 1987).

Philip Jenkins, *A History of Modern Wales 1536–1990* (London, 1992).

Gareth Elwyn Jones, *Modern Wales. A Concise History* (second edn.; Cambridge, 1995).

Hugh Thomas, *A History of Wales 1485–1660* (Cardiff, 1972).

David Williams, *A History of Modern Wales* (second edn.; London, 1977).

Glanmor Williams, *Recovery, Reorientation and Reformation Wales c. 1415–1642* (Oxford and Cardiff, 1987).

Gwyn A. Williams, *When Was Wales?* (London, 1985).

CHAPTER 2

THE DECLINE OF PROFESSIONAL POETRY

CERI W. LEWIS

One of the most striking features of modern Welsh literature is the sad decline that becomes increasingly evident from about the middle of the sixteenth century onwards in the standard of verse composed by the professional poets on the so-called 'strict metres'. This highly distinctive type of syllabic verse, characterized by the intricate system of consonantal alliteration and internal rhyme known as *cynghanedd* in Welsh, had manifestly lost much of its vitality and creative impulse by this period; the style and language of the bards had unquestionably become insipid and lacklustre and, with a few notable exceptions, their traditional verses, especially when set against the compositions of the great chiefs-of-song (*penceirddiaid*) who sang during the fifteenth and early sixteenth centuries, or when compared with the works of those enlightened scholars and littérateurs who had been deeply imbued with the stirring ideals of the Renaissance and the New Learning, seemed dull, stereotyped, and uninspiringly monotonous. Their work frequently displays an element of artificiality, a loss of sensitivity to the niceties of language, a falling-off in the use of meaningful imagery, errors in technical details relating to *cynghanedd* and metre, a decline of rhythmical balance, and an increasing occurrence of tedious 'filling-in words or phrases' (*geiriau llanw*), words which add very little, if anything at all, to the general sense of the poem and are used merely to satisfy the demands of the particular metre being employed. Nor are these indications of artistic decline confined to the works of just a few members of the bardic establishment; they occur in the compositions of many bards drawn from all the major historic regions of Wales. Tradition, especially one as uncommonly rich and resilient as that represented by the Welsh bardic order, died hard, and some gifted poets, such as Wiliam Llŷn, (1534/5–80), Simwnt Fychan (*c.* 1530–1606), or Siôn Tudur (*c.* 1522–1602), for example, succeeded in rising above the general level of artistic mediocrity. But such talented bards as these were disappointingly few in number, and only rarely does one encounter in the works of the majority of the poets who sang during the late sixteenth and early seventeenth centuries some vestigial traces of the exquisite artistry and sure sense of style that so clearly characterize the compositions of the great master-poets (or chiefs-of-song) who wrote verses on the strict metres between *c.* 1430–40 and *c.* 1530–40, when poetry of this genre undeniably reached its highest peak of artistic refinement and elegance. The deep conviction that all was far from well with the bardic establishment and with the works that many of its members produced during the late sixteenth and early seventeenth centuries may partly account for the intense contemporary concern for manuscripts and manuscript-transcription, and may explain the eager desire to record and preserve for posterity the works of the great *penceirddiaid* of the past before they were lost for ever.

Not only had the *awdl* and *cywydd* manifestly lost their long-established pre-eminence and artistic refinement by the mid-sixteenth century, but the very principle that lay at the root of the canonical twenty-four strict metres was being seriously challenged at that time by a fundamentally different method of scansion, represented by verse composed in the so-called 'free metres'. Now, whereas poetry composed in the strict metres carefully adhered to a prescribed number of syllables in each line, which varied according to the particular metre being employed, the metrical pattern of free verse was basically determined by the number of accentual beats it contained. This type of verse had probably flourished for centuries among those whom that intensely patriotic Renaissance scholar and Catholic exile, Gruffydd Robert (pre-1532–post-1598), appropriately called 'the unskilled folk' (*y bobl annhechnennig*), the ordinary, untutored people who could not readily appreciate all the refinements of the stylized and highly ornate poetry in the strict metres, which was mainly addressed to the nobility or gentry. However, although free-metre verse probably flourished in a much earlier period, it had hardly ever attained sufficient status to be preserved in manuscripts. But now that it was being accorded appreciably greater esteem and recognition, it became increasingly popular with a more elitist public, including some important gentry families and, more especially, those fairly substantial social groups that existed just beneath the rank of the latter. There were two

broad classes of free-metre verse, as will be made clear in the
following two chapters. One, inherited from the medieval period,
consisted of long-established Welsh metres devoid of *cynghanedd*,
though often containing intermittent touches of the latter. The
other arose from the adoption into Welsh verse of metres of
English origin, which were then in vogue and sung to popular,
catchy tunes. Some of the gentry may have begun to request from
the itinerant poets whom they were wont to patronize verse that was
at once lighter and more easily comprehensible than poetry
composed in the strict metres in the centuries-old conventional
bardic style, for the language of the free-metre poetry was simpler
and more debased, and the expression generally slacker and more
diffuse, than in the aristocratic *cynghanedd* poetry. Moreover,
because the free-metre poems often struck a decidedly more critical
and irreverent note, they inevitably appealed to a wider and less
elitist public. These free-metre compositions, on a wide variety of
themes, were sufficiently valued and appreciated to be copied into
contemporary manuscripts. For example, NLW MS 13070B
(Llanover MS B 9) contains a substantial collection, compiled and
copied by the Glamorgan bard and professional scribe, Llywelyn
Siôn (1540–1615?), of *cwndidau*, the free-metre carols, written
without regular *cynghanedd*, that were so popular with minstrels in
both Glamorgan and Gwent during this period. Some poets, deeply
disturbed by the threat that this new tendency constituted to their
status and livelihood, complained bitterly in their strict-metre
verses about the unprecedented demand that had arisen in their day
for these airs and carols. In a poem he addressed to William
Midleton, the bard Edwart ap Raff (*fl.* 1557–1606) of Bachymbyd,
Denbighshire, maintained that for every one who might request a
composition on the *cywydd* measure, there were two who demanded
a free-metre song, while others preferred a rather silly carol:

> O chais un iachus wyneb
> Gywydd o newydd i neb,
> Dyri a fyn dau eraill,
> A charol lletffol i'r lleill.

His complaint was clearly echoed by Rhisiart Phylip (d. 1641) of
Ardudwy, who declared that whereas formerly a holy *englyn*, or a
cywydd declaimed to the accompaniment of stringed instruments,
were generally popular, both had been felled in his day by one

decisive blow—it was the free-metre *dyrïau* that were now in favour:

> Da oedd englyn gwyn mewn genau—iachus
> A chywydd gan dannau;
> Darfod ar ddyrnod mae'r ddau—
> Da'r awr hon yw'r dyrïau.

But there were others among the bardic fraternity who were not averse to singing in the new metres. This tendency can be found in the works of established bards like Siôn Tudur, of Wicwair, St Asaph, Flintshire; Meurug Dafydd (*fl. c.* 1560–*c.* 1593), who came from the district of Llanisien (Llanishen), near Cardiff; Llywelyn Siôn, who was born at Llangewydd in Laleston, near Bridgend; Edward Dafydd (*c.* 1600–78?) of Margam; gentlemen-poets such as Tomas Llywelyn (*fl.* 1580–1610) of Y Rhigos, Glamorgan; and cleric-poets and humanists like Archdeacon Edmwnd Prys (1543/4–1623), who was a native of Llanrwst, Denbighshire. Tomas ab Ieuan ap Rhys (*c.* 1520–*c.* 1560) of Tythegston, Glamorgan, even used the *cwndid* measures to sing eulogies and elegies for some of his patrons among the gentry families of the county.

The increased popularity of the free metres, which naturally diminished the acceptability of the traditional *cynghanedd* poetry, and the artistic decadence that so obviously characterized much of the latter, both reflected, in their various ways, the major crisis that confronted the bardic order during this period. No attempt to analyse the nature and causes of that crisis should ignore either the deeply ingrained conservatism of the bards themselves or the senility of the tradition they represented. That tradition, as Sir Philip Sidney (1554–86) emphasized in his celebrated *An Apologie for Poetrie*, which first appeared posthumously in 1595, when it was also published under the alternative title *The Defence of Poesie*, was 'not more notable in soon beginning than in long continuing', and had reached a most venerable age long before the middle of the sixteenth century. No literary movement, tradition, or style, however strong and resilient, can be expected to continue indefinitely. Even the strongest of literary movements or traditions will begin to weaken, decay, and ultimately come to an end when the special social conditions that had once created and fostered it no longer prevail. No new development of major significance had occurred since the fourteenth century in the conventions of Welsh strict-metre panegyric verse, except that the sixteenth-century bards, largely in response to the great demand by the *nouveaux riches* for pedigree-making in the Tudor period, tended to incorporate more genealogical and heraldic data in their poems of praise (*cywyddau mawl*). This strongly suggests that all the thematic and artistic possibilities of this literary genre had by then been discovered and exhaustively exploited. Within the bardic establishment, precedent and prescription had long maintained a rarely challenged authority. Severely restricted to a few major themes, of which praise was by far the most important, and strictly enjoined by the bardic Grammar to handle them along rather narrow, clearly defined lines, the Poets of the Nobility had been consistently reluctant to pioneer any new literary movement or to experiment with any new literary forms. This stagnant conservatism is reflected even in the metrical patterns of their compositions, for although there were twenty-four acknowledged measures in their metrical repertoire, most poets showed a marked predilection for only a limited number of these. It would undoubtedly have been far better if the professional poets had been more prepared to experiment with new literary forms and metres, as suggested by Gruffydd Robert, who, in his Welsh Grammar, *Dosparth Byrr ar y rhann gyntaf i ramadeg Cymraeg*, had hinted vaguely at 'such metres as the Italians use' (*[y] fath fessurau y mae'r eidaluyr yn i arfer*). He had advocated not only a sensible relaxing of the rigid metrical rules of the bards, but also the adoption of the free metres for the composition of epic poetry. His well-intentioned exhortations, however, failed to evoke a constructive response from the bardic fraternity, for the period produced no new literary form of major importance. In that respect Wales presented a striking contrast to Elizabethan England, where the sonnet enjoyed a vogue second only to that of the drama, the crowning glory of English literature during that period, and where poets such as Edmund Spenser (?1552–99) and Sir Philip Sidney were prepared to experiment with new literary forms.

None were more deeply conscious of the shortcomings of the professional bardic fraternity and of the strict-metre verses that its members composed during this period than the sixteenth- and early seventeenth-century Welsh humanists. Their general attitude to the poets was by no means unfavourable or antagonistic, for many of them regarded the professional bards as the genuine heirs of the learned classes that had been founded by Samothes, who, according to the pseudo-Berosus, as interpreted by the celebrated English antiquary, John Bale, was the son of Japhet (and therefore the grandson of Noah) and founder of the Celtic colonies in western Europe after the Flood. It was claimed that Samothes had established a long and distinguished line of kings which included Druys (or Druiyus) and Bardus, who, it was believed, had founded the erudite order of druids and bards. An alternative myth, derived from Geoffrey of Monmouth's *Historia Regum Britanniae* (*c.* 1136), was also very popular in some intellectual circles; this regarded the Welsh bards as the learned heirs of the Greek sages who had been brought to Britain *c.* 1170 BC by Brutus, the reputed great-grandson of Aeneas of Troy, and his successors. It is hardly surprising, therefore, that many of the Welsh humanists, including William Salesbury (*c.* 1520–84?), Gruffydd Robert, Edmwnd Prys, Siôn Dafydd Rhys (1534–*c.*1619) of Brecon, and John Davies (*c.* 1567–1644) of Mallwyd, held the poets of their own day and of the two or three generations that preceded them in the highest esteem. This did not prevent them, however, from severely castigating the poets for the weaknesses that they clearly perceived in their works, and the humanist scholars, who passionately longed to see the indigenous Welsh culture enriched with classical learning and the Welsh language made a fitting medium for a wide range of new scholarship, made a number of concrete proposals with a view to arresting the gradual decline of Welsh poetic art.

In the first place, they strongly urged the bards to refrain from unduly flattering their patrons for material gain and from issuing false pedigrees, and they urged upon them the necessity to give expression in their compositions to the unadorned truth, however unpalatable this might prove at times. Siôn Dafydd Rhys referred scornfully to the convention whereby poets praised unreservedly the martial prowess of their patrons, eulogizing them for conquering thousands in battle and for razing castles to the ground, while the patrons themselves were 'in their beds sleeping without a care, without any thought or intention of the kind'! So profoundly disturbed were the Welsh humanists by the unashamed mendacity they clearly perceived in many of the eulogies the professional poets addressed to their patrons that they sometimes believed the Welsh muse had emanated from the Devil rather than from the Holy Ghost, a view that had been powerfully expressed about a century and a half earlier by Siôn Cent (*c.* 1400–30/45), who in the satirical poem he addressed to the mendacious muse (*Cywydd Dychan i'r Awen Gelwyddog*) roundly condemned the Platonic foundation of praise and its extremes of falsehood as derived not from Christ but 'from the oven of hellish nature' (*o ffwrn natur uffernawl*). The poets' mendacity was also severely castigated in the sixteenth century by Siôn Tudur, one of the last of the Poets of the Nobility (or Gentry). He composed a famous *cywydd* 'to denounce the bards' in which he strongly berated the poets for heaping indiscriminate praise on their patrons:

> Gwae ni'r beirdd gan air y byd!
> Gwae ail fodd y gelfyddyd!
> Swydd y bardd sydd heb urddas,
> Oedd enwog gynt heb ddwyn cas. . . .

> Ninnau'r beirdd a wnawn, rai bas,
> O'r arddwyr wŷr o urddas,
> A rhoi achau rhy wychion,
> A mawl i Siac mal i Siôn.

> [Shamed, the world says, we poets!
> And shamed in like manner the state of our craft!
> The role of the bard is without dignity,
> It was once renowned, not detested. . . .

> We poets, base things, make
> Of the ploughmen men of rank,
> Giving too fine a lineage,
> And praise for Jack no less than John.]

English commentators were equally disturbed by similar practices in their country: as Sir Thomas Smith observed in 1565, 'gentlemen . . . be made good cheape in England'. Criticism of the Welsh bards' frequent mendacity is also implicit in the celebrated open letter, 'To the Poets and Learned Men of Wales' which Dr Siôn Dafydd Rhys of Brecon (also known as John Davies to many of his contemporaries) wrote in 1597 as a rejoinder to the attack made three years earlier on the poets by Maurice Kyffin (*c.* 1555–98) in the introduction of his *Deffynniad Ffydd Eglwys Loegr* (1595), a translation of Bishop John Jewel's classic defence of the faith of the Anglican Church, *Apologia Ecclesiae Anglicanae*, which was published in 1562. This conspicuous failing could effectively be remedied, in the opinion of the humanists, if the poets concentrated to a far greater degree on the composition of divine poetry and regularly sang the praise of God based on the contents of the Holy Scriptures.

Secondly, the poets should seriously endeavour to make up for the alleged lack of substance in their work by acquiring from printed sources a knowledge of the liberal arts and sciences, which they could then profitably take as the theme of their compositions. The poets were severely criticized by the humanists for their manifest lack of learning, by which was meant book-learning, preferably in the classical languages, similar to that imparted in grammar schools and universities, not the extensive repertoire of mythological lore, ancient tradition, and narrative and historical material that constituted such a vital part of the instruction given to pupils in the bardic schools. 'If you will not become worse than animals,' wrote William Salesbury in his introduction to *Oll Synnwyr pen Kembero ygyd* (The Whole Sense of a Welshman's Head), published in 1547, '(which were not born to such understanding as is man's), seek learning in your tongue.' Maurice Kyffin was equally unequivocal: 'What is needful to the Welsh tongue is learning and godliness, not letters to set forth learning.' In their view, the translation of the Bible into Welsh was an important and highly effective means of bringing learning into the language, and Edmwnd Prys, Maurice Kyffin, and Siôn Tudur were all unstinting in their praise of that notable achievement. Both Edmwnd Prys and Siôn Dafydd Rhys specified the disciplines on which the poets should compose their verses, a task in which they were to be assisted, as the latter was at pains to emphasize in his open letter, by the relevant academic authority in each discipline. As Siôn Dafydd Rhys proposed to the poets:

> All the materials of the world and all arts and learning can be contained in and under the art of poetry, by taking and accepting (as you have heard) the useful things of that art not from the poet himself— as a poet and musician—but from whomsoever is expert and exact and precise in the art in which and from which those useful things are found.

Although neither Edmwnd Prys nor Siôn Dafydd Rhys made any attempt to exclude eulogy, which had constituted the major theme of Welsh bardic verse throughout the centuries, the main emphasis, with the significant exception of divine poetry, was on the composition of historical and scientific verse.

The third proposal made by the humanists was that the professional poets should skilfully employ the classical art of rhetoric and thereby effectively arrest the artistic decadence that was becoming increasingly evident in the strict-metre verse composed during this period. This is not to be interpreted as meaning that the poets were habitually averse to employing figurative language in their compositions, but rather that their general mode of expression was deemed to be routinely uniform and tiresomely monotonous. In a treatise he wrote on rhetoric, William Salesbury claimed that a young man called 'Pwl' had stated to him that the poets:

> use for the most part to make their songs, that is their *cywyddau*, their *awdlau* and their *englynion*, of the same material, the same fancy (*dyfal*), the same aspect and so completely alike in imagination as if they issued from the same heart or as if they had been made according to the same pattern or cast in the same mould.

Undoubtedly, there was considerable basis for this criticism. The humanists throughout western Europe placed great emphasis on the importance of acquiring an opulence and an abundance, not only of vocabulary but also of figures of speech and turns of phrase. Not surprisingly, therefore, many English books on the art of rhetoric were published in the sixteenth century. In 1577, for example, Henry Peacham published an interesting volume under the title *The Garden of Eloquence conteyning the Figures of Grammer and Rhetorick, from whence maye bee gathered all manner of Flowers, Coulors, Ornaments, Exornations, Formes and Fashions of speech, very profitable for all those that be studious of Eloquence, and that reade most Eloquent Poets and Orators, and also helpeth much for the better understanding of the holy Scriptures*. In his work, *The Arte of English Poesie*, published in 1589, George Puttenham declared it to be his firm intention to make 'of a rude rhymer, a learned and courtly poet', and to teach the essential elements of rhetoric to 'ladies and young gentlewomen, or idle courtiers, desirous to become skilful in their own mother tongue, and for their private recreation to make now and then ditties of pleasure'.

In a broadly similar vein, the Welsh humanists also tried to provide the professional poets of their own country with some practical assistance in this particular respect. For example, in 1552 William Salesbury produced an adaptation, with Welsh examples, of the Latin work, *Tabulae de Schematibus et Tropis*, by Petrus Mosellanus (*c.* 1493–1524), and a number of the Welsh terms he coined are still in circulation. This Welsh adaptation, which sadly remains in manuscript, was dedicated by Salesbury to his friend, the professional poet Gruffudd Hiraethog (d. 1564), 'and others of his art'. Salesbury's devoted labour did not pass unnoticed among the contemporary or near-contemporary bardic fraternity, for Simwnt Fychan, whose home—significantly, in view of the outstanding contribution the region made to Welsh Renaissance culture—was in Llanfair Dyffryn Clwyd, Denbighshire, included *c.* 1570 a copy of the adaptation at the end of his *Pum Llyfr Cerddwriaeth* (Five Books of the Art of Poesy), a work in which he brought together and classified some of the elements of the instruction given by the master-poets to their pupils in the bardic schools. Two other professional bards, Wiliam Cynwal (d. 1587/8), who was a native of Ysbyty Ifan, Denbighshire, and Robert ab Ifan (*fl.* 1572–1603) of Brynsiencyn, Anglesey, also had texts of a similar nature in their possession. Although, as we have seen, Salesbury's work was never published, it was used by Henri Perri (1560/1–1617), a native of Maes-glas, Flintshire, who spent the greater part of his life in various ecclesiastical benefices in Anglesey, as the basis for his own treatise, *Eglvryn Phraethineb. sebh, Dosparth ar Retoreg, vn o'r saith gelbhydhyd, yn dyscu lhuniaith ymadrodh, a'i pherthynassau*, which appeared in 1595 and included material the author had taken from the most recent edition of Henry Peacham's volume as well as many examples from medieval Welsh poetry. The fulsome praise heaped by Perri in the introduction to his work on the skilful employment of rhetoric is thoroughly typical of the Renaissance scholars, who regarded rhetoric as the art *par excellence*. Some time later, another manual on this subject was produced by the Denbighshire gentleman-poet, Tomos Prys (*c.* 1564–1634), the son of Elis Prys of Plas Iolyn, while the Caernarfonshire gentleman Siôn ap Hywel attempted to make a translation of the pseudo-Aristotelian treatise, *Rhetorica ad Herennium*. Neither manual was published, however, and only a fragment of the latter has survived.

The fourth recommendation made by the humanists was that the bards should renounce unreservedly the secretiveness for which their order had been so long renowned and explain the mysteries of their esoteric craft to all who genuinely wished to understand and master them. In the pseudo-antique Statute of Gruffudd ap Cynan, promulgated at the first Caerwys Eisteddfod in 1523, the poets were strictly enjoined to keep their professional art a closely guarded secret, for they naturally hoped that they could thereby preserve their special status in society and effectively protect their livelihood. This attitude contrasted sharply with the Renaissance ideal of the cultured gentleman and courtier who had mastered various artistic skills that had formerly been practised only by professionals. Gruffydd Robert complained bitterly in his Welsh Grammar that the poets 'keep their art secret, without revealing it unto any, save to some disciple who shall swear that he will not teach it to any other, or to an occasional gentleman who will promise on his honour to keep it secret', and therefore, he maintained, 'some man else must assume knowledge [of it] and set it forth, if it be desired to spread it over the face of the country and to impart it to all who should so desire'. And it is difficult to miss the note of disapprobation in William Salesbury's oft-quoted rhetorical question: 'To what purpose do ye suffer your books to moulder in corners, and to breed worms in chests, and conceal them lest anyone save your own selves should see them?' But it was Siôn Dafydd Rhys who penned the harshest criticism of the poets' stubborn reticence and inveterate secretiveness:

> And the Poets of their part (that they might even be worse than the worst), if perchance some sort of them should have any skill or curious art wherein others of their fellows should be lacking, all this they would keep as a mystery from other poets, yea, from all men; to the end that thou mightest say (as it were) that this man or this, and that man or that, had such art and skill in Welsh and poesy as no man had the like save only they. And when those Poets died then all that beauty went into the earth, where was never talk of it thereafter.

As the poets were generally so reluctant, for obvious reasons, to respond to their urgent exhortations, a number of the Welsh humanists wrote and published works that discussed the traditional poetic craft, paying special attention to the canonical twenty-four strict metres and the intricate system of *cynghanedd*. Although they were able to consult copies of the *dwned* or bardic Grammar, the earliest surviving copy of which is associated with the name of Einion Offeiriad (*fl.* 1330), they unfortunately misinterpreted at times parts of its contents, a failing that must be attributed to the fact that they lacked expert guidance and were therefore compelled to depend on their own resources when interpreting the highly technical details associated with various aspects of the bardic craft. Gruffydd Robert's *Gramadeg Cymraeg*, the final parts of which were probably composed some time after 1584, was written with a view to giving some instruction to young humanists who aspired to compose Welsh verse. One interesting feature of his work, as has already been noted, is his readiness to admit Italian metres, as well as the Welsh free or accentual metres, into the works of the bards. In his substantial work, *Cambrobrytannicae Cymraecaeve Linguae Institutiones et Rudimenta* (1592), comprising 328 pages, Dr Siôn Dafydd Rhys included *inter alia* a grammar of the Welsh language and an extensive discussion of the poetic art. He wrote this work in Latin in order to reveal the glory of the Welsh language and the details of Welsh prosody 'to the sight of all Europe in a language which is common to all'. Considerably less detailed was the manual by William Midleton (*fl.* 1550–*c.* 1600), *Bardhoniaeth, neu brydydhiaeth, y llyfr kyntaf* (1593/4), which was intended for the cultured gentleman, courtier, or clergyman, rather than for the scholar or poet, and was written, as he himself emphasized, with a view to imparting a knowledge of the bardic craft to his fellow-countrymen, an achievement that would undoubtedly have won the approbation of all Welsh humanists. Broadly similar in aim and scope were the short manuals written by Roger Morris (*fl.* 1580–1607), the copyist from Coedytalwrn, Llanfair Dyffryn Clwyd, and by the gentleman-poet-soldier Tomos Prys, but neither of these works was ever published.

The various grammars, treatises, and short manuals produced by the humanists, the criticisms made by them of the modes and criteria of the poets, as well as their earnest exhortations for change, all clearly testify in their various ways to the major crisis that confronted the Welsh bardic order in the late sixteenth and early seventeenth centuries. Of all the criticisms levelled at the professional poets, the most interesting and incisive were those made by Edmwnd Prys, who, anxious to see the poets respond constructively to the new humanist ideals, engaged in an extraordinarily long poetic controversy (*ymryson farddol*), lasting from 1580 to 1587/8 and comprising fifty-four *cywyddau* and approximately 5,500 lines of verse, with Wiliam Cynwal, one of the most prolific practitioners of the centuries-old bardic craft and a resolute defender of the old order. This is unquestionably the most significant bardic controversy in the whole history of Welsh literature, for it effectively highlights the clash between the old bardic learning, with its centuries of rich tradition, and the new learning and ideals of the Renaissance. Prys's main purpose throughout this marathon controversy was to demonstrate to his adversary and to the latter's fellow professional poets that the modes and standards of the bardic establishment were thoroughly outdated and inadequate, and that they had been shown to be so by the new Renaissance culture and by the advent of the printed book. A graduate of St John's College, Cambridge, and reputedly a master of eight languages, including Hebrew, Prys had made a commendably detailed study of the Classics, the Bible, and the Early Fathers, as well as the indigenous literary culture of Wales. It is little wonder, therefore, that he proved throughout the controversy to be a powerful and eloquent advocate of the New Learning. He argued with conviction that literature should be mainly religious and moral in purpose, a view held naturally and genuinely by one who was archdeacon of Merioneth; and he further maintained that it should be learned and printed. The word 'learning', on which the humanists placed such great emphasis, recurs frequently throughout the long controversy. Cynwal was strongly urged by Prys 'to sing of learning in your tongue'. The old Welsh learning, he asserted, was inadequate, because true learning demanded a knowledge of other languages:

> Nid iawn feistr nod awen faith
> Ond athro mewn dieithriaith.
>
> [Mere poet can ne'er our master be;
> The skilled in tongues—our master he.]

Like Siôn Cent about a century and a half before him, he regarded the praise heaped by the bards on unworthy patrons as nothing but flattering hyperbole, which was motivated by an unprincipled desire for material gain. Cynwal was accused of singing 'clear praise for high profit' (*croyw foliant er cryf elwa*). Sir Idris Bell's free translation into English rhyming verse effectively conveys once again the gist of Prys's charge on this particular count:

> To versify with flattering tongue
> Men's pedigrees, is that not wrong? . . .
> To mean and strengthless men to give
> Such praise as warriors might receive,

> Breeding and noble bounty see,
> With endless hospitality,
> In one within whose mansion's bound
> Neither bed nor board is found,
> Merit and honour to ascribe,
> Fond hope, to the worthless for a bribe,
> And boldly claim, by the same rule,
> Wisdom for the veriest fool.

Cynwal, it was alleged, was unable to differentiate between falsehood and truth:

> Ni wyddost, er a neddir
> O bwyllo gwawd, beth yw gwir.
>
> [Falsehood or truth, whate'er you stitch
> Of praise, you know not which is which.]

He deliberately included falsehoods in his compositions:

> Ac ar gân gwir yw gennyd
> Er na bai wir yn y byd.
>
> [And what the world knows for untrue,
> If set in song, is true to you.]

One glaring example of this was the way Cynwal distorted pedigrees in his poems and shamelessly declared a man to be of noble or gentlemanly lineage even if he was manifestly of quite lowly status: 'with flattering tone' (*gwenieithus dôn*) he had made 'two hundred into gentlemen'. Prys castigated his adversary and the latter's fellow-bards for stubbornly adhering to baseless papal myths and superstitions, and he strongly urged them to adopt the godly Christian muse, make a determined effort to become men of learning at the universities, forsake the intricate system of *cynghanedd*, should that be deemed desirable, and publish their remodelled verse in printed books. He stated unequivocally that though Cynwal may have succeeded in acquiring a mastery of the craft of words and indisputable skill in the structure of the *cywydd* measure, it was of little profit to him if the poetry he composed was devoid of true substance. 'It is folly, a distasteful exercise', declared Prys in an oft-quoted couplet, 'for a magnificent carpenter to measure the wind':

> Ffoledd, drwy anoff helynt,
> I saer gwych fesur y gwynt.

Wiliam Cynwal's response throughout the marathon controversy was surprisingly weak and defensive. He could do little more than declare that his adversary was not really a poet, but an ordained cleric, who had no right to interfere in another man's profession. 'You have no degree in poetry' (*Ni raddiwyd . . . dy brydyddiaeth*), he maintained; in other words, Prys had received no formal instruction or training from a recognized bardic teacher, nor had he graduated as a poet, and only a person who had done so had the right to practise the bardic craft. The acquisition of a bardic degree was a matter of fundamental importance to Cynwal and his *confrères*, as well as to many of the gentry whom they visited during their itineraries and to whom they addressed their eulogies and elegies, their 'poems of request' (*cerddi gofyn*), their verses of gratitude, their pedigrees, and heraldic devices. Because it was customary for the patron to reward the poet, he was understandably anxious that it was only a highly trained and fully qualified craftsman-bard who visited him on these special occasions, not an unskilled rhymester who had never undergone a rigorous course of training and secured the proper qualifications. The qualified bard, for his part, was equally anxious to ensure that no unskilled hucksters or inferior poetasters regularly visited the homes of the gentry, for they would unceremoniously deprive him of his livelihood. And it was in order to safeguard their status that the professional poets insisted on keeping a knowledge of their intricate craft and esoteric lore a secret among themselves. On the whole, therefore, the poets did not have a very high regard for the printing press, and they were generally averse to seeing their compositions in print. It is hardly surprising, therefore, as the professional poets were accustomed to keeping their learning a closely guarded secret, that Cynwal should curtly tell his adversary, 'Your poetic education falls short' (*Byr d'addysg ar brydyddiaeth*). He kept reiterating that he, as a graduate in the art, had acquired the traditional bardic learning in its entirety, and he taunted Prys for the sad inadequacy of his knowledge of the bardic craft.

Cynwal's standpoint throughout represented the attitude taken by most of the professional poets; the bardic fraternity did not, on the whole, respond very favourably or constructively to the concerted campaign for reform conducted by the Welsh humanists. The poets, by and large, stubbornly refused to abandon eulogy or elegy as the main themes of their compositions; they did not devote

themselves to composing long historical, theological, or scientific
poems; they paid only scant regard to the new rhetorical modes;
and they were naturally disturbed—if not, indeed, considerably
alarmed—by the attempt to give far greater scope and prominence
to amateurs. There were, however, some notable exceptions. William
Salesbury's friend, Gruffudd Hiraethog, one of the major
cywyddwyr of the sixteenth century, expressed his admiration for
humanists and, true to their ideals, prepared a short manuscript-
book, 'Lloegr drigiant ddifyrrwch Brytanaidd Gymro', in which he
included for the pleasure and edification of Welsh gentry
voluntarily living in exile in England parts of the traditional bardic
lore. Unfortunately, however, this was never published. Some of
Gruffudd Hiraethog's pupils, who graduated at the second Caerwys
Eisteddfod in 1567, manifested interests that were, to some extent,
similar to those exhibited by their bardic master; those poets
included Siôn Tudur (especially), Simwnt Fychan, and Wiliam
Llŷn, acknowledged as the most accomplished elegist in the whole
history of Welsh verse. The translation of the Latin poet Martial's
epigram on the happy life by Simwnt Fychan, 'at the request and
with the explanation' of the nobleman Simwnt Thelwall, is also an
indication, albeit a very small one, that there was some convergence
between the old bardic tradition and the New Learning. In a later
period, a very small number of bards received some grammar
school education. Two notable examples are Siôn Phylip
(1543?–1620), a pupil of Wiliam Llŷn and author of a grammar (or
manual) of Welsh metrics, of which at least two copies have been
preserved (in NLW Peniarth MS 89 and Mostyn MS 144), and Huw
Machno (*fl.* 1585–1637), who was praised by Siôn Phylip, to whom,
apparently, he had been a pupil, for his knowledge and his
command of the traditional bardic vocabulary.

Equally unsuccessful, on the whole, was the attempt made by the
humanists to create a thriving new school of amateur poets,
'singing on their own food'. It cannot be denied, nevertheless, that a
few gentlemen and clerics, some of whom had been educated at the
universities, manifested an increasingly lively interest in the
composition of verse on the strict metres. Some tried to introduce
new themes into their work. Two interesting examples are the
Anglesey clergyman 'Sir' Huw Roberts (or 'Huw Roberts Llên', *fl.*
c. 1555–1619), whose work includes a *cywydd* on the Gunpowder
Plot of 1605, and Tomos Prys of Plas Iolyn. The latter, who lived an

unusually exciting and colourful life, displayed in his work, often with an element of carefree ease, some indifference to the bardic conventions and introduced a strong flavour of adventure and camaraderie into his verse. The new themes on which he sang sprang from the highly venturesome society in which he lived and from his own stirring experiences as a soldier, sailor and pirate. In a poem on the *cywydd* measure, which is ingeniously interspersed with English nautical phrases, he painted a memorably vivid and amusing picture of his experiences when he sailed his own ship on a privateering expedition against the Spaniards. The fact that he was not a professional bard, but a gentleman of independent means, enabled him to compose verses to please himself, not any hidebound patron on whom he was economically dependent. This independence unquestionably invested his work with a verve and freshness rarely found in the poetry composed by the professional poets during this period, which, as has already been noted, is overwhelmingly devoted to eulogy and elegy.

A significant exception to the inordinate concentration on these two themes—and the elegy was really only a variant form of the praise-poem—was the increasing interest shown, partly no doubt in response to the pressure exerted by the Welsh humanists, in divine (or religious) poetry. Sometime between 1584 and 1594, Gruffydd Robert had succeeded in publishing in Milan a small collection of verse written on both religious and secular themes, and about 1595 William Midleton also published, possibly in Oxford, a collection of his own compositions on distinctly religious themes. Unfortunately, only a fragment of this collection is now extant. But Midleton's most important work was his complete setting of the Psalms in the strict metres; this work was completed in the West Indies in 1595/6 and was published posthumously in 1603 by the stationer Thomas Salisbury under the title *Psalmae y Brenhinol Brophwyd Dafydh*. Although it cannot be denied that Midleton displays some virtuosity in the manner in which he employed the traditional measures, his work can hardly be compared from a purely literary standpoint with the version of the Psalms prepared by Edmwnd Prys. Nevertheless, the work reflects the emphasis placed by the humanists on the composition of divine poetry, and it is unquestionably a valuable literary contribution to the humanist ideal of a cultured gentleman.

A particularly interesting feature of the work of the amateur poets was the increasing use made by them of the free metres, which, as we have seen, the professional poets had usually, though not invariably, firmly eschewed. Some extroverted travellers or intrepid buccaneers were prepared to compose verses about their adventures. One such poem, composed in the *awdl-gywydd* measure by Lieutenant Wiliam Peilyn in 1570, is a 'Conversation between a Man and a Pelican'. A note in the manuscript where the poem occurs informs us that it is the 'History of a company of Welshmen, who went, in the time of Queen Elizabeth, by her command, to the West Indies to take vengeance on and to despoil the Spaniards'. The story related in the poem is at once stirring and dramatic. In sharp contrast are the delightful love-lyrics composed by Richard Hughes (d. 1618) of Cefn Llanfair, Caernarfonshire. These lyrics, though circumscribed in their metrical patterns, demonstrate nevertheless by their supple style and lively language the way in which Welsh poetry could have developed during this period if the poets in general had not adhered so rigidly to writing in the strict metres or in the carol form. The main emphasis, however, was once again on religious verses, especially on composing versions of the Psalms on the free metres. The outstanding achievement in this field was Edmwnd Prys's complete metrical Psalter in Welsh, published as an appendix to the Welsh Book of Common Prayer in 1621.

Although it is possible, therefore, as the evidence presented above amply confirms, to discern a few interesting and innovative tendencies, the Welsh professional poets failed, by and large, to accommodate Renaissance learning, themes and measures within their compositions. It is hardly surprising, therefore, that some Renaissance scholars, such as Siôn Dafydd Rhys, were firmly convinced that it was the bards' stubborn obscurantism which, above all else, was responsible for the ultimate disintegration of their organization 'until in the end there was left neither art among them, nor a man skilled in art that was worthy of mention; and until, by long following of this evil practice, the Bards did draw and hale themselves clean out of all desert and dignity'. In the opinion of Sir Thomas Parry, the leading authority on the history of Welsh literature, the failure of the professional bards to respond to the winds of sixteenth-century change was 'the great disaster of our literature in the seventeenth and eighteenth centuries'. Much can be said to justify this view. But in fairness to the poets it must be emphasized that it was by no means easy for them to adjust to the proposals advanced by their critics. The suggestion that far greater scope should be given to amateurs naturally caused them considerable apprehension, for they saw it as a very serious threat to their professional status and livelihood. No poet would risk composing verses on themes related to the New Learning without being certain in advance of receiving payment from his patrons, who had regularly rewarded him in the past for the eulogies and 'pedigree poems' that had been addressed to them. It is extremely doubtful whether there existed in Wales at this time a sufficiently large audience of patrons prepared to reward the bards in the time-honoured manner for poems composed on themes advocated by the humanists. The gentry did not include among their number anyone who was endowed with the flair and vision of Sir Philip Sidney, a vital consideration which must not be overlooked. Therefore, even if the poets had genuinely tried to adjust to the views of their critics, it is extremely doubtful whether they would have achieved any lasting, significant success. Nor should it be forgotten that the new kind of bardic instruction which this adjustment demanded would have been prohibitively expensive and time-consuming, when serious complaints were already being made in the contemporary poetry about the dire effects of inflation and the constantly dwindling numbers of generous, committed patrons. Furthermore, the new-style poetry favoured by the humanists would have had to be published in books, not disseminated by means of manuscripts, or by declamation in the mansions of the gentry, and it is extremely doubtful, bearing in mind the comparatively poor economic state of the country at this time, whether there were enough enlightened patrons in Wales, or whether it contained a sufficiently large and adequately literate book-buying public, to support this new type of verse.

In fairness to the bards, therefore, it must be emphasized that most of those who belonged to the comparatively small Welsh middle class were either entirely incapable or else resolutely unwilling to take over the duties of literary patronage from the rapidly defecting nobility. Nor should it be forgotten that the whole social and economic milieu of sixteenth- and seventeenth-century Wales, an economically backward country which had no university of its own nor any other national institution of any real significance and whose only capital, in effect, was London, to which it was a somewhat remote and relatively unimportant province, was singularly unconducive to the successful adoption of the type of literary and cultural programme envisaged by the humanists. Renaissance culture and the patronage on which it heavily depended were deeply rooted in a milieu that was unmistakably courtly, aristocratic, and urban, whereas Welsh society in the sixteenth and seventeenth centuries was predominantly agricultural, pastoral and kin-based, and was unable, as a result, to create a sufficient number of literate patrons interested in books and reading to transform the humanist ideal into concrete reality. Nor was there an independent Welsh state to support a thriving indigenous humanist culture. As the centre of political gravity lay predominantly in London, the gentry were increasingly drawn into the orbit and ambience of English politics, losing much of their distinctive Welsh identity and even, in many cases, the national language itself. This process was already quite advanced by the second half of the seventeenth century. From the very outset, there was probably too wide a gulf between the humanist ideals of learning and culture as embodied in that many-faceted and highly cultivated man, *il cortegiano*, and the traditional strengths and virtues of the idealized leaders of Welsh society so triumphantly proclaimed for centuries by the professional poets in their strict-metre compositions for any meaningful and lasting reconciliation to have been effected between them. Indeed, it has been suggested that the humanists, rather than arresting the steep decline of professional poetry in their day, as they genuinely attempted to do, may have unwittingly accelerated by means of their criticisms, however constructive and well intentioned those were, that process of artistic degeneration and, as a natural corollary, may have involuntarily precipitated the eventual extinction of the Welsh bardic order.

This introvertedly conservative professional organization, which manifestly contained within itself the seeds of its own ultimate disintegration and demise, was further grievously weakened by a combination of distinctly hostile forces that impinged upon it from without. One of the most powerful of these was unquestionably the inflation of the late sixteenth and early seventeenth centuries, one of the most rapid and distressingly severe experienced in either England or Wales before the twentieth century. Its causes have been attributed to a variety of factors: the rise in population in Wales, from an estimated 278,000 in 1536 to an estimated 405,000 in 1630, resulting inevitably in a substantial increase in demand, especially for food, and a general upward movement in land values; the serious dearth caused by a succession of bad harvests; the influx of Spanish silver from the New World; the marked expansion of credit facilities; the debasement of the coinage in the 1540s and the increase in the volume of money in circulation without a corresponding increase, at least for some time, in the volume of goods produced; heavy government expenditure on warfare in the 1540s and 1590s; and the changes brought about by the Reformation, which led to the melting of a considerable amount of silver plate and the cessation of investment in various non-productive enterprises, such as church-building, chantries, or post-funerary masses.

Whatever weight is to be attached to each of these contributory factors, there can be no doubt regarding their overall effect, for economic historians who are specialists in this period are agreed that there was an acutely severe long-term rise in prices from approximately the second decade of the sixteenth century to the outbreak of the Civil Wars (1642–8). After a prolonged period of fairly stable prices during the fifteenth century, inflation began in about 1510, when the domestic price index is tentatively fixed at 103. By 1540, however, the price index had risen to 158, and during the century that followed it increased fourfold, we are authoritatively informed. This upward movement, however, was by no means a gradual one. There were two periods which witnessed an unprecedentedly sharp increase in the domestic price level, the first during the 1540s and 1550s, the second during the 1590s, an increase caused in each case by an unfortunate combination of bad harvests and heavy government expenditure on wars. Even when the immediate financial crisis had passed and prices began gradually to fall a little, they never went down to their former, pre-inflationary level, and their upward movement soon recommenced, albeit at a less disturbing rate. By the 1630s, regarded by many economic historians as a period of exceptionally acute difficulty in this particular respect, the domestic price index had soared to unprecedentedly high levels, reaching 707 in 1638.

This sharp increase in prices affected many commodities, though by no means evenly. So, for example, cattle prices more than quadrupled from an index of 152 in 1540 to 622 in 1639 (a rise of 410 per cent), while sheep prices trebled from 190 in 1540 to 577 in

1639 (a rise of 303 per cent). The price of grain, a staple commodity for all, rich and poor alike, rose from 154 in 1540 to 569 in 1639 (a rise of 370 per cent). Not surprisingly, perhaps, there were also marked differences in the upward movement of prices between one major region and another.

That wages notably failed to keep pace with inflation inevitably exacerbated the distress caused by this economic phenomenon. Although the index level of an agricultural labourer's wages had increased almost threefold between the accession of Henry VIII and the decade 1630–9, rising from 101 to 287, the level of prices during the same period had rocketed from 114 to 609. This means that the purchasing power of the ordinary labourer had fallen sharply from 84 to 47, a reduction of almost 50 per cent.

The dire effects of inflation were felt by all individuals, whatever their social status. But none suffered more acutely from its stresses than those who were not closely attached, as far as their day-to-day livelihood was concerned, to the soil and were unable to produce their own food and raise livestock. The professional bards obviously belonged to this category, and the sharp general increase in prices must therefore have caused them considerable economic distress. Naturally, when the poets continued to receive the comforting shelter and to enjoy the sumptuous board to which there are so many glowing references in the encomiums addressed to their patrons by the great medieval master-poets, they were, to some extent, cushioned against some of the direst excesses of the inflationary spiral. But when, as was frequently the case, their remuneration was in coin, the sharp rise in prices must have been felt keenly by the bards, for it is extremely unlikely that the accustomed payments kept pace with inflation. The rewards, therefore, generally fell far below what was required to support the professional poets and their dependants, and probably had a decidedly constrictive effect on the activities of the bardic schools and on bardic apprenticeship, which lasted for at least nine years if young novitiates seriously aspired to pass through the successive grades of 'temporary apprentice without a degree' (*disgybl ysbas heb radd*), 'apprentice appropriate for instruction' (*disgybl disgyblaidd*), and 'apprentice of the master craft' (*disgybl pen-cerddaidd*), before finally becoming a master-poet or chief-of-song (*pencerdd*). This, in turn, had a markedly deleterious effect on bardic itineraries, which had been an essential feature of the bardic guild for a very long period. It is clear that by the seventeenth century the circle of bardic activity was appreciably smaller; the long-established custom of roaming Wales from end to end had ceased, and there was an unmistakable tendency for a poet to maintain a connection with a single family. Bardic itineraries were becoming more and more restricted in Glamorgan, for example, from one year to another, and there was no longer any hope of bards receiving gifts or payment in the homes of those smaller local squires where Dafydd Benwyn had invariably been given a warm welcome in the second half of the sixteenth century. The ravages of the Civil Wars and the wanton burning of homes such as Mathafarn (in Montgomeryshire), or Caer-gai and Ynysymaen-gwyn (in Merioneth), whose family-owners had for long been commendably generous patrons of the bards, only served to exacerbate what was already an extremely serious situation.

Inflation also seriously eroded in many cases the income of the gentry, and it is significant that there are frequent criticisms in the *cynghanedd* poetry composed during this period of niggardly, grudging and indifferent patrons—animadversions that are frequently heard in England, Scotland, and Ireland also.

> But, ah, Maecenas is yclad in clay
> And great Augustus long ago is dead,

wrote Edmund Spenser as he dejectedly pondered the great sea-change that had come over literary patronage in England in his day. In a broadly similar vein, Morys Benwyn, who lived during the early Stuart period, drew a sharp and telling contrast in a poem he addressed to the Vaughan family of Corsygedol (in Merioneth) between their magnanimous generosity and the uncaring attitude of many less dedicated and more tight-fisted gentry, and he declared despondently:

> Oer yw'r sâl ar yr oes hon,
> Oes heb urddas i'r beirddion.
> Cenais o ddeutu Conwy,
> Cwyn mawr, nid gwiw canu mwy. . . .
> Caead fydd i brydydd brau
> Y newyddion neuaddau.
>
> [Chill is the reward in this age,
> An age which offers no status to the poets.

I sang around Conwy,
Great lament, it avails not to sing any more. . . .
Closed to a gentle bard will be
The new halls.]

Some poets specifically associated the disturbing dearth of committed patrons with the Edwardian Conquest of 1282 and looked back nostalgically to the period when Wales was ruled by its own independent princes, who, it was averred, had never shirked the duty of generous literary patronage.

Although there was much variation from region to region, or even from one gentry family to another, there can be very little doubt that, in general, committed patrons were becoming increasingly difficult to find throughout the late sixteenth and early seventeenth centuries. The upper classes, the traditional patrons of the *cynghanedd* poetry, were being enticed by a wide range of material attractions—better houses, more sumptuous attire, and more luxurious furnishings and household goods—often to the detriment of the support they were able to give to the professional poets. Even contemporary developments in domestic architecture proved to be inimical to the continuance of some long-established bardic practices. For example, it had long been the custom for *awdlau* and *cywyddau* to be ceremoniously declaimed at the high-table, before the family, in the hall of the mansion, but during the sixteenth century the first-floor hall and hall-house became obsolete. This change, it must be emphasized, was a gradual one, but it gained momentum after the middle of the century. The poets themselves were firmly convinced that the glorious days of noble patronage were virtually at an end. Although the effects of the Acts of Union of 1536 and 1543 could not have been as grievously dramatic or cataclysmic as has sometimes been supposed, it can hardly be doubted that many of the Welsh gentry gradually became more and more anglicized, losing their native speech, their interest in the life and culture of Wales, and even, in some cases, their sense of nationality as well. But this was not a sudden development, nor was it the direct result of government policy as reflected in the 'language clauses' of the Acts of Union, nor of a conscious decision by the gentry themselves, motivated, as some have erroneously maintained, by powerful anti-Welsh sentiments. A number of the gentry, it must be emphasized, kept up their knowledge of the ancient British tongue, even arranging for their sons to be sent to

Welsh families to learn it. Long after the Acts of Union, prominent gentry families held members of the bardic establishment in high esteem. The Mostyn and Wynn families both had their own household bards, while Lady Lewis of Y Fan, in Glamorgan, engaged three tutors to teach her children Welsh, Latin and French. Moreover, some of the most rapacious and oppressive of the gentry and some of the wealthiest of the recently arisen commercial families were generous patrons of Welsh letters in the late sixteenth and early seventeenth centuries. Although Sir John Wynn of Gwydir, Sir Edward Stradling of St Donat's, and George Owen of Henllys all wrote in English, they were, without exception, liberal patrons of the bards, and it was Stradling's characteristic and widely acclaimed munificence that made possible the publication in 1592 of Dr Siôn Dafydd Rhys's grammar of the Welsh language, mentioned above. Again, much of the huge expense of publishing a crop of important prose works which appeared in the 1630s was once thought to have been wholly borne by two wealthy merchants of Welsh origin, Thomas Myddelton and Rowland Heylin, a Montgomeryshire man who later became sheriff of London. Those prose works included the first cheap Welsh Bible, *Y Beibl Bach* (1630); Robert Llwyd's *Llwybr Hyffordd yn cyfarwyddo'r anghyfarwydd i'r nefoedd* (1630), a translation of Dent's *Plain Pathway to Heaven*; Rowland Vaughan's *Yr Ymarfer o Dduwioldeb* (1629), which was a translation of Lewis Bayly's *The Practice of Piety*; John Davies's *Llyfr y Resolusion* (1632); and *Car-wr y Cymru* (1630 and 1631) by Oliver Thomas. The publication of these works, which are an important contribution to the Welsh prose tradition, shows conclusively that literary patronage had not completely died out, even if Myddleton and Heylin were not responsible for the appearance of all of them.

Nevertheless, there was an unmistakable tendency for the Welsh gentry, owing to their frequent contacts in many cases with their English counterparts, to lose their knowledge of the Welsh language and their ability to speak it. For some considerable time before the 1530s, many of the Welsh gentry had acquired a firm grasp of English and they fully realized that there were many advantages in doing so. A detailed analysis of Sir John Wynn's correspondence shows that when members of the Welsh gentry class married English wives, the latter, notwithstanding their husband's express desire that they should learn Welsh, generally introduced English speech into their households, a tendency that was to be repeated over and over again in the years that followed. It was far more serious when a Welsh house ended in its heiress marrying an Englishman, for it became thereby rapidly and thoroughly anglicized. Nor should it be forgotten that some of the gentry lived for the greater part of the year outside the Principality. The English language had acquired enhanced status and esteem in Tudor England, becoming solidly entrenched as the language of the court, government, judicature, literature and refined aristocratic society. One of the most powerful of the social influences operating in Tudor England and Wales was the so-called 'cult of gentryhood' and this, with its heavy emphasis on certain prescribed social manners and graces, was an overwhelmingly English cult. Towards the middle of the sixteenth century, William Jones of Newport, in Monmouthshire, declared it to be his desire that his children be 'browghte up accordyng to the maneres and condicionez of the norture of Inglonde', and made arrangements in his will for them to reside and to be educated in Bristol until they came of age. There were many members of the upper strata of native Welsh society who sincerely believed that it was imperative to leave the Principality and live across the border in order to become fully assimilated to English life and manners and dissociate themselves completely from what they considered to be the restrictive environment of Welsh manners and speech. In 1587, David Baker (the Venerable Augustine Baker, 1575–1641), the Benedictine scholar and mystic, was sent at the tender age of twelve from his home town of Abergavenny to Christ's Hospital in order to acquire 'perfection in the English tongue and the right pronunciation of it', and in 1590, when he was still only fourteen, he proceeded to Broadgates Hall (now Pembroke College), Oxford. The closer contacts that were increasingly being created between English and Welsh, the value placed, for perfectly obvious reasons, on the ability to read and speak English, and the tendency for many Welshmen, anxious to secure their personal advancement, to go to England or into towns in Wales where English was widely spoken all contributed substantially to a wider knowledge of English among the gentry and a corresponding weakening in their command of Welsh.

The influence exerted by the educational institutions that were open to ambitious young Welshmen tended in the same direction. Sir John Wynn's great-grandfather, the founder of his house, had gone to school at Caernarfon, 'where he learnt the English tongue, to read and write and understand Latin, a matter of great moment in those days'. True to the tradition established by his great-grandfather, Sir John arranged for his own sons to be educated at Eton, Westminster, Bedford, or St Albans. Shrewsbury school proved to be a powerful magnet to the scions of Welsh gentry families during this period. On the other hand, bardic schools, where the master-poets had taught the closely guarded secrets of their esoteric craft and had instructed young and aspiring novitiates in various matters relating to the Welsh language, were steadily decreasing in number, although Gruffudd Hiraethog still had a number of able pupils towards the middle of the sixteenth century. These institutions, as well as the monastic schools that vanished with the Dissolution, were replaced by a number of Tudor foundations (or refoundations), some of which were financed out of the endowments of the monasteries or collegiate churches. Schools were created at Abergavenny, Bangor, Brecon, Carmarthen, Cowbridge, Rhuthun (Ruthin), and other places. In all, about two dozen endowed grammar schools sprang up in Wales in the century following the Acts of Union. The education imparted in these institutions had no connection of any real significance with the indigenous culture of Wales and was completely alien to the bardic traditions. The senior pupils were expected to converse in Latin and Greek, while the junior boys were permitted to speak English; but Welsh was strictly prohibited. Furthermore, in 1571 Queen Elizabeth, in response to a petition by Dr Hugh Price of Brecon, the treasurer of St David's, granted a charter for the establishment of Jesus College, Oxford, which, for various reasons, rapidly came to be regarded as a college for the Principality. The final upshot was, therefore, that the sons of the leading gentry families were educated in the great English public schools or at the Inns of Court, Lincoln's Inn being very popular; those of the lesser gentry received their education in the newly created grammar schools of Wales; and some, including a substantial number of clergy, proceeded to Jesus College, Oxford. Beyond doubt, these institutions were all heavily anglicized, because one of the principal aims of Tudor education was to teach the manners of towns and courts, and a thorough knowledge of English was deemed to be a *sine qua non* for any man of culture. All the educational facilities that existed for ambitious young Welshmen, therefore, were decidedly inimical to the native

language and to the indigenous culture of which it was unquestionably its most vital constituent element. Nor should it be
forgotten that the traditional patrons of the bards were becoming
increasingly interested in English books of various kinds and were,
as a corollary, far less prepared than they had been in the past to
give their support to the authors of the strict-metre poetry.

Although the process of cultural reorientation was a slow and
gradual one, many of the Welsh gentry came to regard the Welsh
language and culture as something inherently inferior and began to
look disdainfully on the bards. The picture drawn by the latter may
at times have been an excessively sombre one, for bards were still
being patronized in various parts of Wales, albeit to a significantly
reduced extent, during the late sixteenth and early seventeenth
centuries, and bardic instruction persisted during that period,
though admittedly on a less secure basis. Some gentry families
genuinely welcomed bards to their homes to entertain them in the
traditional manner and to present them with admiring poetic
attestations of their recently acquired social status. John Salusbury,
the descendant of many generations of generous patrons, is a case
in point. Having adroitly re-established his family's honour, status,
and prestige following the dark cloud it had been under as a result
of the Babington Plot, he invited during the Christmas activities in
1595 seven bards, four harpists and two crowthers to Lleweni to
celebrate the remarkable change in his fortunes. Even new families,
who could boast of no tradition of literary patronage, were anxious
to secure from the bards a formal public attestation of their social
status. In Gwent and Glamorgan, two regions where the decline of
the bardic order was undoubtedly proceeding apace, we find that
the extraordinarily productive Dafydd Benwyn, although his
successors were not warmly welcomed by some of the local minor
squires, as we have seen, was still being supported during the second
half of the sixteenth century by a wide circle of patrons, many of
whom belonged to the 'first generation'. Nor were Gwent and
Glamorgan unique in this respect. The great number of poems
composed in other parts of Wales during the first half of the
seventeenth century—over a century, it must be emphasized after
the Acts of Union of 1536 and 1543—shows beyond any doubt that
there were some gentry who still valued the encomiums addressed
to them by the bards. The remarkable Phylip family of Ardudwy
succeeded in producing four poets between approximately 1560 and

1677: Siôn Phylip (d. 1620), who, in addition to composing a large number of verses on the *englyn* measure, was the author of 195 *awdlau* and *cywyddau*; his brother, Rhisiart (d. 1641); Siôn's son, Gruffudd (d. 1666); and another son, Phylip Siôn Phylip (d. *c.* 1677). Their activities and their output provide conclusive proof that there was still considerable vitality in the bardic life of some parts of Wales in the early seventeenth century. As well as being the author of some enchanting love poems, Siôn Phylip addressed eulogies to the gentry of Anglesey, Arfon, Llŷn, Merioneth, and the Vale of Clwyd. Significantly, he also participated, in the traditional manner, in various bardic contentions, especially with such doughty champions of the bardic craft as Siôn Tudur and Edmwnd Prys, an undeniably clear indication of the vigour that still persisted in the bardic life of that part of Wales. Another example of a family interest in the composition of strict-metre verse is provided by the career of Siôn Cain (*c.* 1575–*c.* 1650), the son of Rhys Cain (d. 1614), poet and herald, of Oswestry. The last of the herald bards to travel through north Wales, Siôn was the author of many genealogical poems, mainly in the period from 1607 to 1648, and he addressed compositions to the gentry of Maelor, Montgomeryshire, and the Vale of Clwyd, as well as a few to families located in Arfon and Merioneth.

A large number of relatively insignificant poets, including Siams Emlyn, Siams Dwn, Rhisiart Cynwal, Gruffudd Hafren, Huw Machno, Watcyn Clywedog, and others, continued to compose poems of praise to the gentry down to the middle of the seventeenth century. Indeed, this practice persisted until much later. John Davies (Siôn Dafydd Las/Laes), who died in 1694, was regarded as the family bard of Nannau in Merioneth, although he composed verses for other gentry families in north-east Wales, being one of the last to receive such patronage. Owen Gruffudd (*c.* 1643–1730), who was born in the parish of Llanystumdwy, Caernarfonshire, composed a large number of *cywyddau* to the gentry of Llŷn, Eifionydd, the borders of Merioneth, and other areas. He won considerable renown in his day as a poet and was a recognized genealogist. However, he was a weaver by trade and cannot therefore legitimately be regarded as one of the few surviving professional bards. To him, as to so many other men who practised the bardic craft during the seventeenth century, the composition of poetry was a pleasantly diverting cultural hobby, not an essential means of earning a living. Furthermore, as already noted, the long-established practice of going on bardic itineraries throughout the whole of Wales had come to an end by this period, and some of the poets mentioned above showed an unmistakable tendency to become connected with a single family, as Siôn Phylip and his son, Gruffudd, did with Corsygedol, or Rhisiart Phylip and Siôn Dafydd Laes with Nannau.

The picture, therefore, was not one of unrelieved gloom, as the frequent complaints made by the bards tend to convey. Nevertheless, there can be no doubt that, in general, those complaints provide us with a fair and accurate portrayal of contemporary trends. And the bards' bitter diatribes against those anglicized gentry, the 'feebly learned, straightmouthed, unkindly manikins', who, slavishly affecting English modes and manners, had lost all interest in the indigenous culture of Wales and who were no longer prepared to shoulder the responsibility of literary patronage, are frequently echoed in the works of the sixteenth-century humanists. Gruffydd Robert, unflinchingly patriotic and earnestly solicitous of the fortunes of the ancient British tongue even during his exile after 1559 in Rome and, later still, in Milan, dismissed them with mordant contempt:

> You will find some men that, so soon as they see the river Severn, or the belfries of Shrewsbury, and hear an Englishman but once say 'Good morrow', they shall begin to put their Welsh out of mind, and to speak it in most corrupt fashion. Their Welsh will be of an English cut, and their English (God knows) too much after the Welsh fashion. And this cometh either of very foolishness or of a saucy pride and vanity. For he is never seen for a kindly, virtuous man that will deny whether it be his father, or his mother, or his country, or his tongue.

It was the peculiarly enunciated speech of these emigrant Welshmen, as well as their inordinate delight in their reputed descent from the ancient Trojans, that the English of the Tudor and Jacobean periods found so highly amusing. One writer of doggerel could not resist the temptation to tease these Welsh visitors or immigrants:

> Pye Got, they bee all Shentlemen
> Was descended from Shoves none lyne, [i.e., Jove's own line]
> Parte humane and parte divine . . .

And from Ffenus, that fayre Goddesse,
And twenty other shentle poddies,
Hector stoute and comely Paris,
Arthur, Prutus, King of Ffayres.

Clearly, the anglicization of the gentry, which took some
generations to complete, was ultimately bound to have a grievously
adverse effect on their attitude to the language of the poets and to
the highly distinctive cultural milieu which the work of the latter
created; it effectively undermined the connection that had long
existed between the indigenous literary culture and those who, by
their patronage, had provided it with its indispensable economic
basis.

The serious plight in which the professional poets found
themselves from *c.* 1550 onwards was further exacerbated by the
dissolution of the monasteries and mendicant orders and the
suppression of the chantries and guilds. It has been calculated that,
in all, the regular orders had about fifty houses in Wales on the eve
of the Reformation. As the compositions they addressed during the
medieval period to some of the heads of these monastic foundations amply confirm, the bards during their itineraries had been
generously patronized there. In particular, the Cistercian order of
White Monks, which had houses, for example, at Tintern,
Whitland, Cwm-hir, Strata Florida, Strata Marcella, Cymer, Llantarnam, Aberconwy, Valle Crucis, Neath, Margam, Basingwerk and
Dore, to name only the most important, became markedly Welsh in
sentiment and were staunch patrons of Welsh letters and learning.
Undoubtedly, the suppression of the monasteries and friaries added
appreciably to the severe economic plight in which the professional
poets found themselves.

It is easy to understand, therefore, why so many members of the
bardic establishment were absolutely convinced that the old society
and traditional values were rapidly disintegrating. As Simwnt
Fychan dejectedly observed:

Mae'n darfod y glod, y glêr—ni cherir
    Na chwarae na haelder,
    Na gwyliau, pan eu gweler,
    Nac aberth rad nowddgad Nêr.

[Praise is at an end, the poets are not loved
    Nor entertainment, nor generosity,

Nor festival days when they come,
Nor the free sacrifice of the Lord who gives aid in battle.]

In the poem he composed to show 'that the world detested poets', the same bard asserted that rejecting praise poetry was tantamount to rejecting the Holy Spirit, for the Welsh muse, it was claimed, was of divine origin. Siôn Mawddwy (*fl. c.* 1575–1613) complained bitterly about those among his compatriots who had become 'lost Englishmen', while Edwart ap Raff (*fl.* 1557–1606) of Bachymbyd, Denbighshire, ruefully declared in his elegy to Siôn Tudur in 1602 that the world he saw around him was decidedly anglicized:

Seisnig arbennig yw'r byd.

Edwart unreservedly castigated the gentry both for their miserliness and for being so heavily anglicized:

Y freugerdd lwys, frigwyrdd, lân,
Felys, aeth heb flas weithian;
Ni fynnant foliant, filoedd;
Ni ad tra chwant. Ond trwch oedd?

[Sweet, pure, newly-minted, beautiful, flowing verse has now lost its savour; thousands reject praise; excessive cupidity will not allow it. Was it not unfortunate?]

This was precisely how the situation appeared to that cultured poet-gentleman, Robert ab Ifan (*fl. c.* 1572–1603) of Brynsiencyn, Anglesey. In 1587, he made a copy for himself of a bardic grammar, and he also compiled a history of the bardic order in which he complained bitterly about the marked disrespect shown to the bardic profession in his own day. He asserted that even common thieves received greater respect than did the contemporary poets; the thief was always assured of the company of leading citizens because he had a groat to spend, while the professional poet was, alas, compelled to wander aimlessly devoid of congenial fellowship, for every one deliberately eschewed his company lest, should they become the object of his praise and commendation, they would be expected to recompense him. There were many, Robert ab Ifan further averred, to whom a vain and wasteful life was infinitely preferable to listening to instrumental music or tales narrated by an expert storyteller, or a *cywydd* or an *awdl* or a refined *englyn* or mention of the Holy Scripture. Forty years later, Rhisiart Phylip, in

a *cywydd* he addressed in 1627 to the erudite Dr John Davies of
Mallwyd, greeted the Welsh language thus (to quote Sir Idris Bell's
free translation in rhyming verse):

> Chill now thou art, in sorry plight,
> Resourceless tongue, whom all men slight.
> Alack! thy children, idle grown,
> Their English lisp in whispered tone,
> Denying thee—O shameful deed!—
> Abandoned in thy sorest need.
> With length of years thy strength decayed,
> All succour spent, call God to aid.
> Come, tell me now, dear tongue of mine—
> Thy judgement still is rich and fine—
> Lives there a man who will avow,
> Of all thy kin, he knows thee now?

The situation appeared no more hopeful to Edward Morris
(1607–89) of Perthillwydion, Cerrigydrudion, Denbighshire, for
some time later he wrote (to quote once again Bell's translation):

> Britain's bright tongue today despised
> Lies unrewarded and unprized;
> Men pass it by with scornful brow,
> And none will bring it succour now.
> The tongue of Wales is rent and torn,
> And on the *cywydd* men pour scorn;
> Dispraised—but oh, what deeds it did!
> Or lurks it in safe covert hid?

This was not a sudden, totally unforeseen development. About a
century earlier, Wiliam Llŷn, who has appropriately been described
as 'the supreme elegist in the whole history of Welsh poetry',
sorrowed not only for the passing of bosom friends, but also
experienced profound grief as he intuitively foresaw in the elegy he
wrote on the death of his friend, the poet Siôn Brwynog (1510–62),
a native of Llanfflewin, Anglesey, that the venerable tradition of
classical Welsh bardic poetry was moving slowly and not entirely
unmajestically to its sad, ineluctable end:

> Dydd brawd ar gerdd dafod aeth.
>
> [Judgement Day has come to the art of poetry.]

The advent of that day was unquestionably hastened by the new

intellectual currents of the age, which, in conjunction with the
political, social and economic forces that were at work in this
period, proved to be distinctly inimical to the continuance of the
Welsh poetic tradition. That resplendent tradition had been
indissolubly linked with the time-honoured Taliesinic ideal of
heroic panegyric, an ideal which had as its philosophic basis the
medieval conception of the world according to which every person
had a permanent, pre-ordained position in society. The concept of
the 'Great Chain of Being' powerfully buttressed belief in a
permanent, unchanging structure of society, which most of its
members, whatever their precise status, deferentially accepted.
Although, as Huizinga rightly emphasized in his celebrated study,
The Waning of the Middle Ages, 'the transition from the spirit of
the declining Middle Ages to humanism was far less simple than we
are inclined to imagine', it is nevertheless true that the restlessly
inquiring spirit of the humanist scholars directly challenged and
eventually undermined the medieval conception of an ordered
universe arranged in an essentially fixed system of hierarchies, a
conception that expressed the infinite plenitude of God's wondrous
creation, its enduring stability, and its ultimate unity and strength.

   This world-view, however, commanded less respect in the
sixteenth century, when public morality was low and the desire to
acquire landed estates and monetary wealth, in order to gratify
one's social ambitions, was great. 'Everywhere', one distinguished
historian of this period has observed, 'private interests predominated over public: everv one "gaped" for gain.' Money was power
and some contemporary English poets unreservedly extolled its
manifold virtues:

> Money, the minion, the spring of all joy;
> Money, the medicine that heals each annoy;
> Money, the jewel that man keeps in store;
> Money, the idol that women adore!

Land hunger among the upper classes became inappeasable, and in
the struggle to acquire more landed estates many powerful men were
not averse to adopting distinctly harsher and more callously grasping
attitudes. As Professor Lawrence Stone has observed, 'The behaviour
of the propertied classes, like that of the poor, was characterized by
the ferocity, childishness and lack of self-control of the Homeric age.'
The century from the Act of Union of 1536 to the outbreak of the

Civil Wars witnessed substantial changes in the balance of land distribution, resulting in a vast reallocation of wealth and income to the general advantage of the upper classes. These were also the classes best able to exploit for their own ends the dire misfortunes experienced by weaker men during a period of unprecedentedly severe inflation. Vast changes in the distribution of wealth result in new classes coming to the forefront of society, and those classes, in turn, are instrumental in creating a new social environment. Money is expended on new interests and new material things, new fashions replace the old, and the whole attitude of society is radically transformed. Such a change occurred in Elizabethan England and Wales.

The works of the poets provide us with some valuable insights into the new spirit of the age. Major strict-metre bards like Simwnt Fychan and Siôn Tudur vehemently castigated contemporary pride and avarice, dishonest land transactions, unprincipled oppression of defenceless tenants, unscrupulous litigation and extensive official corruption. Nor is it only in the works of some of the leading *cynghanedd* poets that we encounter these harsh criticisms. The authors of the free-metre religious poems, the *cwndidau*, which were evidently so popular in Glamorgan and Gwent, had little love for what they saw in their society. They frequently depict, especially in the verses they composed on 'the state of the world', a hard, uncaringly acquisitive society, in which men were insatiable in their desire for land, wealth, possessions, luxuries, large houses, and sumptuous raiment. According to Ieuan ap Rhys, cupidity had become life's major force or incentive, and just as Judas had callously betrayed Christ 'for thirty pieces of silver' (*er deg ar hugain gwabar*), so in the poet's own day many persons in authority were quite prepared to be at any man's behest if the financial reward was sufficiently alluring; even the common people, he claimed, 'took pains to labour with the bad against the good for some trifling amount of gain':

> a'r cyffredin, blin yw'r hoen, hwy gymran' boen a labar
> gyda'r drwg yn erbyn iach, er gronyn bach o wabar.

It was little wonder, declared some of the *cwndidwyr*, that they were so frequently and grievously afflicted by bad harvests, spiralling prices, and serious food shortages, for they 'are portents for us,' warned Harri Brydydd Bach, 'that our sins are grievous . . . it is our sins which are the cause':

dyna argoelion i ni'n awr, ein bod ni'n fawr yn pechu . . .
ein pechodau ni a'u pair.

True charity had vanished from the world, complained Tomas
Llywelyn, and had been replaced by avarice, pride, hypocrisy, and
unscrupulous self-advancement. When a society experienced these
unpardonable vices, it was the poor and the paupers who invariably
endured the greatest suffering, wrote the free-metre poets. Men no
longer paid any attention to the piteous state of the pauper or to his
desperate pleas, 'conscience went to the hedge; a penniless, needy
and starving pauper received no welcome but was sent away bare-
backed'. Complaints such as these were not confined to Welsh
strict- and free-metre verse. Many contemporary English writers
dejectedly observed that begging was of little avail, for private
charity had virtually ceased since the dissolution of the
monasteries. 'A poor man,' wrote Robert Greene (1560?–1592), the
English pamphleteer, dramatist, and novelist, 'shall as soon break
his neck as his fast at a rich man's door.' It was a cruel world to
those whom the relentless pressure of rapid economic and social
change had reduced to helpless indigence.

Clearly, the whole intellectual and social ethos of the sixteenth
and seventeenth centuries, with their unbridled emphasis on
individualism, private enterprise and personal aggrandizement,
often to the detriment of the common weal, was as alien and as
hostile to the classical Welsh poetic tradition as it was to Dante's *La
Divina Commedia*. It is little wonder, therefore, that the members of
the bardic establishment increasingly lost confidence in their craft.
In that respect their compositions present a strikingly depressing
contrast to the brilliant sunburst of *cynghanedd* poetry composed
by the exceptionally talented master-poets who sang during the
fifteenth and early sixteenth centuries, for that substantial body of
verse, composed for a social class so supremely confident of its
position and reflecting a *Weltanschauung* so unquestioningly
accepted, regularly exudes an air of stately grandeur and a tone of
unalloyed assurance that strike the reader as forcibly as does its
pregnant and aphoristic economy of style, its verbal felicity, its
command of deeply meaningful imagery, and its superb technical
accomplishment in details relating to metre and *cynghanedd*. The
members of the bardic establishment, it is true, still had a
profession of sorts to pursue, although, for the reasons adduced, it

was becoming increasingly difficult for them to do so; they were still required, from time to time, to trace—or ingeniously fabricate!—pedigrees, or to address panegyric verses to a steadily decreasing circle of gentry, who might feel inclined, such was the force of habit and custom, to patronize, albeit in a markedly attenuated manner, the indigenous bardic tradition. But their work, as the bards themselves undoubtedly came to realize, had lost its *raison d'être* in the new intellectual and social environment of Elizabethan and Jacobean Wales, and it is therefore not surprising that, with a few notable exceptions, it gradually degenerated into a somewhat mediocre corpus of *vers de circonstance*, devoid of any significance wider than the particular events it routinely commemorated.

The level to which the classical tradition of Welsh poetry had sunk in Glamorgan before the end of the sixteenth century is strikingly illustrated in the colourful account that Sir John Stradling (1563–1637) wrote of the lawsuit fought over the sand-blown burrows of Merthyr Mawr, near Bridgend. In his account the author informs us that the Glamorgan bard, Meurug Dafydd, whom the defendant had brought to the court 'to trye pettigrees', had on one occasion visited Beaupré (Y Bewpyr), when he was 'resorting a brode to gentlemens howses in the loytringe time betweene Christmas and Candlemas to singe songes and receave rewardes'. During his visit he presented 'the good ould squier', William Basset, 'with a cowydh, odle [i.e., awdl] or englyn . . . containinge partelie the praises of the gentleman, and partelie the pettygrees and matches of his auncesters'. Although William Basset generously rewarded the poet with a noble (6*s.* 8*d.*), he could not disguise his great contempt for the poem that had been presented to him, for he proceeded, after making absolutely sure that there was no other copy of the work extant, to 'put it sure enough into the fier'. Unfortunately, no hint is given of the way the poet himself reacted to this embarrassingly overt demonstration of disdain for his work. However, we can now tell, with the advantage of hindsight, that the flames which consume Meurug Dafydd's composition in Sir John Stradling's description symbolically engulf the whole distinctive, time-honoured tradition of poetic panegyric that many generations of highly accomplished professional bards had fashioned and devotedly fostered.

That bona fide members of the bardic establishment were becoming increasingly confused during this period with the unskilled minstrels and hucksters who roamed the country in such large numbers only served to add to the scorn that was poured on them from so many quarters. Part of the problem may well have been that the number of professional poets far exceeded the committed patrons who were prepared to support them in the traditional manner. The position was no different in England. 'The multitude of writers of our age,' wrote Thomas Evans in 1615, 'hath begotten a scarcitie of patrons.' It was, perhaps, inevitable in a period when local authorities, as well as the central government in London, were seriously worried about the swelling population of paupers and vagabonds who regularly tramped the highways and byways, creating an intractable problem for town and parish officials and constituting, in the opinion of the latter, a grave menace to public order and, in some circumstances, a serious threat to public health, that a determined effort should have been made to introduce a more stringent discipline into the professional guild of bards, and to make a clear distinction between the genuine, highly trained poets and the 'vagrant and idle persons naming themselves minstrels, rhymers and bards'. It is significant that among those included in the definition of the term 'vagabond' in England were players of interludes and minstrels 'not belonging to any baron of the realm'. The position was essentially the same in Ireland. So, for example, when a special commission was granted in 1571 to Gerald, earl of Kildare, and Piers fitz James, of Ballysonnon, they were, among other things, 'to punish *by death*, or otherwise as directed, *harpers, rhymers, bards, idlemen, vagabonds*, and such horseboys as have not their master's bill to show whose men they are'. There was also the fear experienced by the ruling authorities that wandering bards or minstrels could frequently compose poems with a strong political connotation and that such compositions, during a period of economic hardship, could very easily lead to widespread social unrest. The official minute, 'Bards.—All their poetries tending to the furtherance of vice and the hurt of the English', adequately summarizes the attitude taken by the government to the Irish poets. It is hardly surprising that the King's Commissioners in Limerick ordained in 1549 that

> No rhymer [poeta] nor other person whatsoever shall make verses [carmina] or any other thing else called auran to any one after God on earth except the King, under penalty of the forfeiture of all his goods.

The state authorities viewed the Welsh bards and minstrels with equal suspicion.

This general background provides the key to understanding the main purpose of the two famous eisteddfodau held in Caerwys, Flintshire, in the sixteenth century, the first in 1523, the second, under a commission granted by Queen Elizabeth I herself, in 1567. These were not eisteddfodau in the modern sense, but rather bardic assemblies that were convened to define the rules governing the crafts of the poet and the musician, and to scrutinize carefully the qualifications of those who claimed to be members of the professional guild. Both assemblies were probably held under the patronage of the influential Mostyn family of Flintshire, the heads of which were Rhisiart ap Hywel ab Ieuan Fychan in 1523, and William Mostyn in 1567. As the Roll (or Proclamation) of the first of these two eisteddfodau states, it met on

> the second day of the month of July in the fifteenth year of the crowning of Henry VIII before Rhisiart ap Hywel ab Ieuan Fychan Esquier with the collaboration of Sir Wiliam Gruffudd and Sir Roger Salusbury and with the personal counsel of Gruffydd ab Ieuan ap Llywelyn Fychan and Tudur Aled, a chaired poet, and many gentlemen and wise men besides in order to bring order and government to the craftsmen in poetic art and their craftsmanship according to the words of the Statute of Gruffudd ap Cynan, Prince of Gwynedd, namely to certify and confirm master craftsmen and those who were previously awarded a degree and to award [a degree] to whomsoever deserved it and to give space [of time] to others to learn and meditate as deeply as conscience allows and by the Statute of Prince Gruffudd ap Cynan.

Although this pseudo-antique Statute that is associated with the first Caerwys bardic assembly stipulated that an eisteddfod should be held every three years, the second, as already stated, did not take place until 1567. The terms of the commission of the bardic assembly that was convened in that year proclaimed unambiguously that the unlicensed rhymesters and paltry poetasters had increased into an 'intolerable multitude within the principality of north Wales' and that by their 'shameless disorders' they had become a vexatious nuisance to the gentry. Clearly, the main purpose of the two eisteddfodau held in Caerwys in the sixteenth century was to protect the professional poet, whose status in society was being seriously undermined by the infiltration of inferior and manifestly less skilled practitioners. Underlying both assemblies, and especially the one held in 1567, there was a very important political and administrative criterion, as well as a formal test of professional skill: under the enlightened leadership of the Mostyn family, which may have had a house in Caerwys, near the town square, and supported by the gentry and literati who had an intimate knowledge of the ancient Welsh bardic tradition, the genuine members of the bardic establishment made a resolute effort to uproot the 'weeds', that is, to prevent any unlicensed rhymester or vagrant or idle person, who falsely claimed that he was a qualified poet or minstrel, from wandering the countryside and becoming a pestiferous nuisance to the gentry. As Gruffudd ab Ieuan ap Llywelyn Fychan (c. 1485–1553), the gentleman-poet from Lleweni Fechan (or Llannerch), near St Asaph, Flintshire, and one of the five commissioners at the Caerwys Eisteddfod of 1523, unequivocally enjoined:

> Nac aed mwngler i glera.
>
> [Let no bungler go on bardic itinerary.]

Only bona fide poets who had undergone a course of rigorous training and had graduated in the bardic 'schools' had the right, it was deemed, to go on itineraries to the houses of the gentry and receive payment for their strict-metre compositions. The rigid imposition of this rule and the introduction thereby of some semblance of order and discipline into the activities of the accredited craftsmen in poetic art would not only safeguard the professional status of the latter, but also ameliorate, it was felt, the grave and potentially dangerous social problem created by the ever-increasing floating population of rogues, paupers, 'sturdy beggars' and vagabonds, who were regarded by the central government and by the local authorities in Tudor England and Wales as the 'caterpillars of the commonwealth'. But very little of any real importance was settled.

A request was made in 1594 for a commission to hold 'at a convenient place' another eisteddfod similar to those that had been held at Caerwys. The petition was sent to the Council in Ludlow and was signed by a number of well-meaning and influential gentlemen, such as Tomos Prys of Plas Iolyn and Sir John Wynn of Gwydir. Not surprisingly, in view of the contemporary developments, the aims of the petition were basically the same as those that

lay at the roots of the two eisteddfodau that had been held at
Caerwys earlier in the century, namely, to protect the professional
status and privileges of the genuine bardic craftsmen and to get rid
of sturdy beggars and idle vagabonds. But nothing resulted from
this well-intentioned petition. By that date the bardic order, unable
to adapt itself to a changed society and a new intellectual ethos, was
in steep decline and the need to safeguard the interests and
privileges of its members, which had been considered to be one of
such great importance earlier in the century, was rapidly
diminishing. Swept along by a powerful concatenation of forces
that were as decidedly inimical in their effects as they were widely
diverse in origin, the professional poets did their best to ply their
trade from day to day, clinging desperately to those patrons who
were still willing to give them some support, however attenuated
that might have been in a period of unprecedentedly severe inflation
which savagely eroded the incomes of the gentry as well as the
incomes of those of much lower status in the social hierarchy, and
eagerly accepting the largesse of those among the aspiring *nouveaux
riches* who were not averse to paying for eulogies and pedigrees if
they could thereby add to their newly acquired material gains a
poetic attestation of their social respectability. As Edward Dafydd
(*c.* 1600–78?), a native of Margam and the last of the professional
bards of any note in Glamorgan, so despairingly declared in one of
the elegiac *englynion* he sang in 1655 on the death that year of
Watcyn Powel, the gentleman-bard and genealogist of Pen-y-fai in
Tir Iarll, the world in which the poets of his day lived and moved
was a singularly uncongenial one:

> Nid yw'r byd hwn gyda'r beirdd.
>
> [This world is not with the poets.]

That anguished *cri de cœur* is frequently echoed during this period
in the works of many bards drawn from all the major historic
regions of Wales. The complaints began in the first half of the
sixteenth century, increased appreciably in volume as the century
wore on, and continued unabated throughout the century that
followed. Nor can these frequently expressed grievances be
construed as a case of special pleading by the professional poets, for
the serious plight in which they found themselves was noted by less
partial contemporary observers. As the anonymous author of *The*

Three Antiquities of Bryttaen, preserved in NLW Llanstephan MS 144, in the hand of John Jones (*c.* 1583–5 – d. 1657/8) of Gellilyfdy, so despairingly declared, though probably not without an element of exaggeration:

> And at this time all the greate knowledge of the Bards, there credyt and worth is altogether decayed and worne out, soe that at this time they are extinguish[ed] amongest us./ And the *Prydyddion* [poets] at this time likewise are of noe estimatione for divers reasones.

Between approximately 1550 and 1650, therefore, the Welsh bardic order, the professional organization which, more than any other group, had given expression and continuity to Welsh national identity, was moving gradually to its close. However, even during this period of marked decline there were still some rare flashes of the artistic elegance that had characterized the works of the great master-poets who sang during the fifteenth and early sixteenth centuries. But the bardic order was unable to survive the serious ravages of the Civil Wars and the political upheavals that followed, and by the latter half of the seventeenth century it had become defunct as a professional and social institution. With the passing of the last of the professional poets there came to an end a resplendent, centuries-old tradition, one of the most resilient and abundantly productive in the whole of western Europe.

BIBLIOGRAPHY

J.W.H. Atkins, *English Literary Criticism: the Renaissance* (reprint; New York and London, 1968).

W. Ambrose Bebb, *Cyfnod y Tuduriaid* (Wrecsam, 1939).

Idem, *Machlud yr Oesoedd Canol* (Swansea, 1951).

H.I. Bell, *The Development of Welsh Poetry* (Oxford, 1936), chapters V–VI.

Idem, *The Nature of Poetry as conceived by the Welsh Bards* (Oxford, 1955).

S.T. Bindoff, *Tudor England* (Harmondsworth, 1950).

J.B. Black, *The Reign of Elizabeth, 1558–1603* (Oxford, 1936).

D.J. Bowen, 'Graddedigion Eisteddfod Caerwys, 1523 a 1567/8', *Llên Cymru*, 2 (1952–3), 129–34.

Idem, 'Gruffudd Hiraethog ac Argyfwng Cerdd Dafod', ibid., 2 (1952–3), 147–60.

Idem, 'Ail Eisteddfod Caerwys a Chais 1594', ibid., 3 (1954–5), 139–61.

Idem, *Gruffudd Hiraethog a'i Oes* (Caerdydd, 1958).

Idem, 'Agweddau ar Ganu'r Unfed Ganrif ar Bymtheg', *Transactions of the Honourable Society of Cymmrodorion (=Trans. Cymm.)* (1969), 284–335.

Idem, 'Cywyddau Gruffudd Hiraethog i Dri o Awduron y Dadeni', ibid. (1974–5), 103–31.

Idem, 'Y Cywyddwyr a'r Dirywiad', *Bulletin of the Board of Celtic Studies* (=*BBCS*), 29 (1980–2), 453–96.

Idem, 'Canrif Olaf y Cywyddwyr', *Llên Cymru*, 14 (1981–4), 3–51.

F.P. Braudel and F. Spooner, 'Prices in Europe from 1450 to 1750', *Cambridge Economic History of Europe*, 4 (Cambridge, 1967), 378–486.

Y.S. Brenner, 'The Inflation of Prices in Early Sixteenth-Century England', *Economic History Review*, ii, 14 (1961), 225–39 and 'The Inflation of Prices in England, 1551–1650', ibid., 15 (1962), 266–84.

E.H. Phelps Brown and S.V. Hopkins, 'Wage-rates and prices', *Economica*, 24 (1957), 289–306 and 'Builders' Wage-rates, Prices and Population: some further Evidence', ibid., 26 (1959), 18–38.

F. Caspari, *Humanism and the Social Order in Tudor England* (Chicago, 1954).

C.E. Challis, 'The Debasement of the Coinage, 1542–1551', *Economic History Review*, 20 (1967), 441–66.

R. Alun Charles, 'Teulu Mostyn fel Noddwyr y Beirdd', *Llên Cymru*, 9 (1966–7), 74–110.

Idem, 'Noddwyr y Beirdd yn Sir y Fflint', ibid., 12 (1972–3), 3–44.

Ceri Davies (ed.), *Rhagymadroddion a Chyflwyniadau Lladin 1551–1632* (Caerdydd, 1980).

Idem, *Latin Writers of the Renaissance* (Cardiff, 1981).

Idem, *Welsh Literature and the Classical Tradition* (Cardiff, 1995).

Dyfrig Davies, 'Siôn Mawddwy', *Llên Cymru*, 8 (1964–5), 214–30.

Glenys Davies, 'Noddwyr y Beirdd yn Sir Feirionnydd: Caer-gai a Glan-llyn', *Cylchgrawn Cymdeithas Hanes a Chofnodion Sir Feirionnydd*, 7, 72–93.

Eadem, *Noddwyr y Beirdd ym Meirion* (Dolgellau, 1974).

J.H. Davies, 'The Roll of the Caerwys Eisteddfod of 1523', *Transactions of the Liverpool Welsh National Society* (1904–5/1908–9), 87–102.

Eirian E. Edwards, 'Cartrefi Noddwyr y Beirdd yn Siroedd Morgannwg a Mynwy', *Llên Cymru*, 13 (1974–81), 184–206.

Euros Jones Evans, 'Noddwyr y Beirdd yn Sir Benfro', *Trans. Cymm.* (1972–3), 123–69.

J.D. Gould, 'The Price Revolution Reconsidered', *Economic History Review*, 17 (1964), 249–66.

R. Geraint Gruffydd, 'Wales and the Renaissance', in A. J. Roderick (ed.), *Wales through the Ages. Volume II: Modern Wales* (Llandybïe, 1960), 45–63.

Idem, 'The Renaissance and Welsh Literature', in Glanmor Williams and Robert Owen Jones (eds.), *The Celts and the Renaissance* (Cardiff, 1990), 17–39.

Vernon Hall, *Renaissance Literary Criticism* (New York, 1945).

Gerallt Harries, 'Ail Eisteddfod Caerwys', *Llên Cymru*, 3 (1954–5), 24–31.

A. Lloyd Hughes, 'Rhai o Noddwyr y Beirdd yn Sir Feirionnydd', ibid., 10 (1968–9), 137–205; 12 (1972–3), 120.

G.H. Hughes, *Rhagymadroddion 1547–1659* (Caerdydd, 1951).
Idem, '"Ffasiynau'r Dadeni"', *Ysgrifau Beirniadol* (=*YB*), 5 (Dinbych, 1970), 62–70.
J. Huizinga, *The Waning of the Middle Ages* (Pelican edn.; London, 1955).
Branwen Jarvis, 'Llythyr Siôn Dafydd Rhys at y Beirdd', *Llên Cymru*, 12 (1972–3), 45–56.
Bedwyr L. Jones, 'Siôn ap Hywel ab Owain a'r *Rhetorica ad Herennium* yn Gymraeg', ibid., 6 (1960–1), 208–18.
E.D. Jones, 'Presidential Address', *Archaeologia Cambrensis*, 112 (1963), 1–12.
G.P. Jones, 'Wiliam Cynwal', *Llên Cymru*, 11 (1970–1), 176–84.
J. Gwynfor Jones, 'Addysg a Diwylliant yng Nghyfnod Syr John Wynn', *Taliesin*, 20 (Gorffennaf 1970), 87–97.
Idem, 'Diddordebau Diwylliannol Wyniaid Gwedir', *Llên Cymru*, 11 (1970–1), 95–124.
Idem, 'Awdurdod Cyfreithiol a Gweinyddol Lleol yng Ngogledd Cymru yn y Cyfnod 1540–1640 yn ôl Tystiolaeth y Beirdd', ibid., 12 (1972–3), 154–215.
Idem, 'The Welsh Poets and their Patrons, *c.* 1550–1640', *Welsh History Review* (=*WHR*), 9 (1978–9), 245–77.
Idem, 'Y Bardd a'r Uchelwr, 1540–1640: Rhai Argraffiadau', *Taliesin*, 39 (Rhagfyr 1979), 9–22.
Idem, 'Patrymau Bonheddig Uchelwrol yn Sir Ddinbych', *Denbighshire Historical Society Transactions*, 29 (1980), 37–77.
Idem, 'Reflections on Concepts of Nobility in Glamorgan *c.* 1540–1640', *Morgannwg*, 25 (1981), 11–42.
Idem, 'Hanfodion Undod Gwladwriaethol, Cyfraith a Threfn yng Nghymru Cyfnod y Tuduriaid: Tystiolaeth Beirdd yr Uchelwyr', *Llên Cymru*, 15 (1984–8), 34–105.
Idem (ed.), *Class, Community and Culture in Tudor Wales* (Cardiff, 1989).
Idem, *Wales and the Tudor State. Government, Religious Change and the Social Order 1534–1603* (Cardiff, 1989).
Idem, 'Braint, Awdurdod a Chyfrifoldeb Uchelwriaeth: Agweddau ar Waith Syr Philip Sidney (1554–1586) a Beirdd yr Uchelwyr', *Llên Cymru*, 16 (1989–91), 212–24.
Idem, *Concepts of Order and Gentility in Wales 1540–1640* (Llandysul, 1992).
Idem, 'The Gentry of East Glamorgan: Welsh Cultural Dimensions, 1540–1640', *Morgannwg*, 37 (1993), 8–39.
R. Brinley Jones, *The Old British Tongue: the Vernacular in Wales 1540–1640* (Cardiff, 1970).
Idem, '"Yr Iaith sydd yn Kychwyn ar Dramgwydd"', *YB*, 8 (Dinbych, 1974), 43–69.
R.L. Jones, 'Wiliam Cynwal', *Llên Cymru*, 11 (1970–1), 185–204.
T. Gwynn Jones, 'Bardism and Romance', *Trans. Cymm.* (1913–14), 205–310.

Ruth Kelso, *The Doctrine of the English Gentleman in the Sixteenth Century* (Urbana, 1929).

P.O. Kristeller, *Renaissance Thought* (New York, 1961).

Ceri W. Lewis, 'The Literary History of Glamorgan from 1550 to 1770', *Glamorgan County History. Volume 4: Early Modern Glamorgan*, ed. Glanmor Williams (Cardiff, 1974), 535–639 and 687–97.

Arthur O. Lovejoy, *The Great Chain of Being* (Cambridge, Mass., 1936).

W. Alun Mathias, 'Llyfr Rhetoreg William Salesbury', *Llên Cymru*, 1 (1950–1), 259–68; 2 (1952–3), 71–81.

J.A. Mazzeo, *Renaissance and Revolution: the Remaking of European Thought* (London, 1967).

R.B. Outhwaite, *Inflation in Tudor and Early-Stuart England* (London, 1969).

G. Dyfnallt Owen, *Elizabethan Wales: the Social Scene* (Cardiff, 1962).

Thomas Parry, 'Statud Gruffudd ap Cynan', *BBCS*, 5 (1929–31), 25–33.

Idem, 'Siôn Dafydd Rhys', *Y Llenor*, 9 (1930), 157–65, 234–41; 10 (1931), 35–46.

Idem, *A History of Welsh Literature*, translated from the Welsh ... by H. Idris Bell (Oxford, 1955; reprinted 1962), chapters VI–IX.

P.H. Ramsey, *Tudor Economic Problems* (London, 1965).

Idem, *The Price Revolution in Sixteenth-Century England* (London, 1971).

Brinley Rees, *Dulliau'r Canu Rhydd 1500–1650* (Caerdydd, 1952).

D. Hywel E. Roberts, 'Noddwyr y Beirdd yn Sir Aberteifi', *Llên Cymru*, 10 (1968–9), 76–109; 13 (1974–81), 291–2.

Enid P. Roberts, 'Siôn Tudur', ibid., 2 (1952–3), 82–96.

Eadem, 'The Renaissance in the Vale of Clwyd', *Flintshire Historical Society Publications*, 15 (1954–5), 52–63.

Eadem, 'Wiliam Cynwal', *Denbighshire Historical Society Transactions*, 12 (1963), 51–85.

Eadem, 'Eisteddfod Caerwys, 1567', ibid. (1967), 16, 23–61.

Eadem, 'Teulu Plas Iolyn', ibid., 13 (1964), 38–110.

P.R. Roberts, 'The "Act of Union" in Welsh History', *Trans. Cymm.* (1972–3), 49–72.

J.E. Spingarn, *A History of Literary Criticism in the Renaissance* (London, 1963).

J. Thirsk (ed.), *Agrarian History of England and Wales: IV. 1500–1640* (Cambridge, 1967).

Gwyn Thomas, *Eisteddfodau Caerwys: The Caerwys Eisteddfodau*, bilingual publication (Caerdydd/Cardiff, 1968).

Idem, 'Y Portread o Uchelwr ym Marddoniaeth Gaeth yr Ail Ganrif ar Bymtheg', *YB*, 8 (Dinbych, 1974), 110–29.

J.D.H. Thomas, *A History of Wales 1485–1660* (Cardiff, 1972).

David Williams, *A History of Modern Wales* (London, 1950).

Glanmor Williams, *Religion, Language and Nationality in Wales: Historical Essays* (Cardiff, 1979).

Idem, 'Religion and Welsh Literature in the Age of the Reformation', *Proceedings of the British Academy*, 69 (1983), 371–408.

Idem, 'Dadeni, Diwygiad a Diwylliant Cymru', in *Grym Tafodau Tân: Ysgrifau Hanesyddol ar Grefydd a Diwylliant* (Llandysul, 1984), 63–86.

Idem, *Recovery, Reorientation and Reformation: Wales c. 1415–1642* (Oxford and Cardiff, 1987). The best general history of the period. It contains an extensive and extremely valuable bibliography.

Idem, 'The Renaissance' in Glanmor Williams and Robert Owen Jones (eds.), *The Celts and the Renaissance* (Cardiff, 1990), 1–15.

G.J. Williams, *Traddodiad Llenyddol Morgannwg* (Caerdydd, 1948).

Idem, 'Llythyr Siôn Dafydd Rhys at y Beirdd', *Efrydiau Catholig*, 4 (1949), 5–11.

Idem, 'Traddodiad Llenyddol Dyffryn Clwyd a'r Cyffiniau', *Trafodion Cymdeithas Hanes Sir Ddinbych*, 1 (1952), 20–32.

Idem, 'Leland a Bale a'r Traddodiad Derwyddol', *Llên Cymru*, 4 (1956–7), 15–25.

Idem, *Agweddau ar Hanes Dysg Gymraeg*, ed. Aneirin Lewis (second edition; Cardiff, 1985), chapters II–V.

Gruffydd Aled Williams, 'Golwg ar Ymryson Edmwnd Prys a Wiliam Cynwal', *YB*, 8 (Dinbych, 1974), 70–109.

Idem, *Ymryson Edmwnd Prys a Wiliam Cynwal* (Caerdydd, 1986).

Gwyn Williams, *An Introduction to Welsh Poetry from the Beginnings to the Sixteenth Century* (London, 1953), chapters VI–VIII.

Ifor Williams, 'Cerddorion a Cherddau yn Lleweni, Nadolig 1595', *BBCS*, 8 (1935–7), 8–10.

J.E. Caerwyn Williams, *Traddodiad Llenyddol Iwerddon* (Caerdydd, 1958).

Penry Williams, *The Tudor Regime* (Oxford, 1979).

Rhiannon Williams, 'Wiliam Cynwal', *Llên Cymru*, 8 (1964–5), 197–213.

W. Ogwen Williams, 'The Survival of the Welsh Language after the Union of England and Wales: the First Phase, 1536–1642', *WHR*, 2 (1964–5), 67–93.

CHAPTER 3

EARLY FREE-METRE POETRY

CENNARD DAVIES

Although poetry in the free metres is first found in any abundance in the manuscripts of the sixteenth century, there is ample evidence to suggest that from the very earliest times there has existed in Welsh a substratum of verse which contrasts dramatically in language, subject matter and form with the mainstream classical tradition. Whereas the syllabic length of the line was the basis of the strict metres, the new poetry was based upon rhythm and accentual scansion. It was closely associated with music and dance, egalitarian in concept, popular in its appeal, and as such demanded a far greater directness of expression than its strict-metre counterpart.

Evidence of the existence of such verse stretches back to the dawn of Welsh literature. By a happy stroke of fortune, someone included a charming nursery rhyme in the text of *Y Gododdin*, the earliest extant Welsh poem. It is a lullaby, perhaps dating from the ninth century, in which the mother tells her child, Dinogad, of his father's prowess as a hunter. We meet his dogs, Giff and Gaff, and sense the excitement in his voice as he gives them their instructions. The child's clothes are described in some detail, as are the hunter's weapons, and the whole poem gives us a brief glimpse of ordinary family life rarely revealed in formal court-poetry. It has been suggested that someone jotted this lullaby on a blank page in a manuscript containing Aneirin's poem and that this interpolation was later incorporated in the text by some careless scribe. This is not untypical of the fate of free verse up to the sixteenth century as it was rarely considered worthy of inclusion in the accepted canon.

However, the confidence with which sixteenth-century poets handle the new verse forms suggests that they did not appear suddenly. Although their simple, direct language is much closer to the vernacular than that of the mainstream tradition, it rarely reflects a particular dialect. It is written, rather, in a more general register, which, despite the occasional colloquialism, could be easily understood by Welsh speakers throughout the country. This is further proof of a long tradition which gradually evolved a homogeneous style and language well suited to the needs of the itinerant performing poet who had to appeal to a variety of audiences over a wide geographical area.

There is little doubt that these poems were performed—recited or sung to the popular tunes of the day. They often begin with the word *Gwrandewch* (Listen) or *Dewch i glywed* (Come and hear) and there are sometimes references to singing:

> A lle byddo llancese
> fo fydd canu dyrïe
> ac ar ddiwedd pob dyri
> hai lwlian, hai lwli.

[And where there are girls, there will be the singing of verses and at the end of each verse, 'Hai lwlian, hai lwli'.]

As has already been suggested, scribes rarely considered this popular poetry worthy of preservation, but between the appearance of the ninth-century nursery rhyme and the explosion of free verse in the sixteenth century there is evidence, both direct and circumstantial, of the existence of poets and poetry of a lower order. Collectively these bards were known as *y glêr*. Sir John Morris-Jones attributes the authorship of the first poem in the Black Book of Carmarthen to such a poet writing at the end of the twelfth century and states, 'I don't know how old the name *clêr* is, but the type existed at all times'. One wonders whether these were the *beirdd ysbydeit* or *goveird* (poetasters) referred to in the *awdl* written sometime before 1222 by Phylip Prydydd or the *beird keith Kaeaw* (the serf poets of Caeo) so heartily chastised by Casnodyn (*fl.* 1320–40) for their *sothachieith* (worthless language). Gruffydd Robert, the Renaissance scholar, who published his Welsh Grammar in Milan in 1567, was certainly aware of this genre of poetry as he refers to *messurau rhyddion y mae'r bobl annhechnennig, yn i arfer wrth ganu, carolau a chwndidau, neu rimynnau gwylfeydd* (the free metres which the unskilled people use for singing carols, conduits or festive rhymes). The eisteddfodau held at Caerwys, in north-east Wales, in 1523 and 1567 certainly bear witness to a lower order of poets. Unlike the present-day eisteddfod, these were more akin to meetings of a craftsmen's guild where the recognized poets laid down the ground rules of their craft, admitted new poets to the various grades and orders and set strict standards of behaviour. As well as being prohibited from entering taverns, playing dice and cards or becoming involved in any form of gambling, they were specifically warned against the practices of *y glêr* whose lifestyle and behaviour seem to bear a close resemblance to those of their continental counterparts, the *clerici vagantes.*

Whether sung or spoken, the words of these performing poets had to be immediately understood and as a result they leaned heavily on the contemporary spoken form of the language. Whereas the writers of *cywyddau* often preserved archaic words and syntactic forms in their work, such conservatism was completely eschewed by the free-verse poets. Contractions such as *syma* (*sy yma*), *rhowyr* (*rhy hwyr*) and *marnaf* (*mae arnaf*) abound; vowels disappear—*fale, clenig, pradwys*—and plural endings of nouns, more often than not, are the colloquial *-e* / *-a* rather than the formal *-au*. Slang and English borrowings are not uncommon. There is, therefore, a marked contrast between the linguistic standards of the free- and strict-metre poets, but both could justly claim that their chosen medium is in keeping with their particular objectives. The many variant readings found in the manuscript copies of individual free-verse poems clearly indicate that we are not dealing with ossified texts but with performers' scripts, which can be modified in varying degrees according to the place, time and mood of the performance.

Music had a major influence on Elizabethan poetry in general and Welsh manuscripts of the period often refer to the tunes to which words were set. These frequently bore English titles such as 'The Parson of the Parishe', 'Aboute the Bancke of Elicon' or 'Adew my Pretie Pussie'. They may well have been imported from England, although it is strange to find that many of them are not listed in contemporary English sources. One possible explanation is that poets pandered to the current vogue by giving indigenous Welsh tunes English titles.

Be that as it may, there is little doubt that Welsh poetry was greatly influenced during this period by developments in England. This was to be expected, considering the profound implications of incorporating Wales into the English state with the concomitant changes in government, law, religion and language. The English court,

army, universities and schools of law, together with the increasing
opportunities in commerce, were an attraction to young Welshmen
and it was inevitable that the influence of these institutions would be
felt in all aspects of Welsh life, not least in the nation's literature. In
looking at the free verse which appeared in the sixteenth century, two
distinct strands can be discerned, the one indigenous, the other
imported. They are perhaps best exemplified in the work of two very
contrasting poets, Robin Clidro and Richard Hughes (Dic Huws).

Clidro (*fl.* 1545–80) lived in the Vale of Clwyd, the heartland of
the classical tradition. He knew many of the poets who wrote in the
strict metres, one of whom, Siôn Tudur, was bold enough to write
an elegy to him whilst he was still alive. Although he described
Robin Clidro in that poem as *Gore bardd a fydd ac a fu* (The best
poet who will be or ever was), he was obviously speaking with his
tongue in his cheek, for contemporaries, as well as poets of
subsequent generations, regarded Clidro as something of a buffoon.
In many ways this reputation was undeserved and might well have
been a defence mechanism used by those who had suffered the
barbs of his satire. It is evident from his work that Clidro was
steeped in the classical tradition and used this insider knowledge to
maximum effect in mounting his attack on the literary establishment. Whilst they wrote elegies to members of the aristocracy, he
wrote one to his cat; whilst they promoted the eulogy and
panegyric, Clidro resorted to invective. Parody was often the basis
of his humour. This was in keeping with the characteristics of the
lower order of poets; as one ancient triad states, 'Three things
typify a member of *y glêr*: mendicancy, satire and defamation.'

The main feature of Clidro's verse is its narrative. This is undoubtedly performance poetry. There is usually a humorous story to focus
the attention of the audience, with Clidro often having fun at the
expense of his own misfortune and shortcomings. His escape from
the clutches of a lawyer in Ludlow is a typical example:

> Pan agorodd o'r wiced, mi a ddechreues redeg;
> Chwi a'i gwelech fo ar f'ôl yn cerdded fal gwraig yn corddi.
> Mi a neidies gae cornel i ganol pwll barcer
> Drwy ei grwyn a'i offer i waelod uffern.
> Mi a ddienges fel bwbach drwy ei gyrn a'i gywarch
> Ar draws ei risgach a'i 'winedd a'i esgyrn.

[When he opened the gate I started to run. You could see him walking after me like a woman churning. I leapt across the corner of a field into a tanner's pond, through his vat and his implements to the depths of hell. I escaped like a scarecrow through his horns and hemp, over his bark and his claws and bones.]

One cannot help wondering, in noting the similarity in content between this type of poem and some of Dafydd ap Gwilym's picaresque adventures, to what extent the fourteenth-century poet tapped into the sub-literary tradition so graphically represented two centuries later in Robin Clidro's work.

Another feature which is usually absent from the work of the mainstream poets is the malediction, another hallmark of Clidro's poetry. In his well-known *Awdl y Gath* (Ode to a Cat) his invective is vitriolic:

> Os gŵr mewn cyfle a'i lladdodd hi ag arfe
> Ne a chŵn dichware, hen gath wych wrol,
> Y peswch a'r meigrin a chainc o glwy'r brenin,
> A'r fors a'r bildin i'w glwyfo bob eildydd;
> A'r cryd cymale, a'r gwewyr i'w fulgre,
> A gwryf ar ei geillie yn gryfa' ar y galler.

[If a man at an opportune moment killed her with weapons, or with unplayful dogs (fine, brave old cat), may coughing and migraine and a dose of scrophula, together with rupture and gall, trouble him every other day; and rheumatism and belly ache and may his balls be squeezed as hard as possible.]

Attention has been rightly drawn to the similarity of this poem to the slightly earlier diatribe against the cat that killed his pet bird by that eccentric English poet, John Skelton:

> When thou my byrde untwynde
> I wold thou haddest ben blynde!
> The leopardes sauage,
> The lyons in theyr rage,
> Myght catche the in theyr paws,
> And gnawe the in theyr iawes!
> The serpantes of Lybany
> Myght stynge the venemously!
> The dragones with their tonges
> Myght poyson thy lyver and longes!
> The mantycors of the montaynes
> Myght feed then on thy braynes.

Such vituperation, as we have already seen, seems to have been a feature of the work of the lower orders of Welsh poets and Clidro's lines closely echo sentiments expressed by Y Nant, a Glamorganshire poet of the late fifteenth century. It is also interesting to note in passing that they use the same metre, a subject to which we shall return:

> Y hesgyrn cyrinon
> ay kyrff yn ddihyrion
> ae cwaet ay rofyon
> yr cŵn yn rafe
> ac y na bo un cwmwt
> heb gael llemystwt
> a fob lleitir heb scrwt
> i'r cŵn yn fysyryt

[Their withered bones and their bodies odious, their blood and their shovelfuls [of flesh] to the dogs in ribbons; and may not one commote be without its sparrow-hawk and every thief without burial be a pig-feast for the dogs.]

The poetic convention of allowing birds and animals to speak, so often observed in the work of Dafydd ap Gwilym, is used with telling effect by Clidro in his *Cywydd to Marchan Wood*. With the wood under threat of destruction, the animals march on London where the squirrel, their chief spokesperson, addresses the Star Chamber:

> Pan roed llyfr dan ei llaw,
> A choel oedd i'w ch'wilyddiaw,
> Hi a ddyfod wrth y beili,
> 'Syr Breibiwm, trwm wyt ti'.
> Ar ei llw hi ddyfod fel hyn.
> Anrheithio holl goed Rhuthun,
> A dwyn ei thŷ a'i sgubor,
> Liw nos du, a'i chnau a'i stôr.

[When the book was put under her paw with the intention of belittling her, she told the bailiff, 'Sir Bribe 'Em, you are a wretch'. Under oath she accused him of despoiling all Rhuthun's trees, robbing her home and barn of her nuts and provisions by night.]

This poem cruelly parodies one of the favourite themes of Celtic literature, namely, the lament for past glory. In the following passage, the bathos of the description of the maid with the runny nose is obviously meant to undermine the purported serious intent of the poem:

Annwyd sy'n lladd y forwyn,
Oer ei throed, a defni o'i thrwyn.
Nid oes gar nac ysgyren
I'w chael i achub gwrach hen.
Gwir a ddyfod Angharad,
Oni cheir glo, yn iach i'n gwlad.

[Cold is killing the maid, cold of foot and her nose running. There isn't a stick or lath to be had to save an old witch. Angharad quite rightly says that unless we get coal we can say goodbye to our country.]

Despite his shortcomings as a poet, Robin Clidro can lay claim to some degree of immortality in having a metre named after him— *Mesur Clidro*. However, as we have already seen, in referring to Y Nant, this metre was in use long before Clidro's time. This raises an interesting question in relation to the development of verse in the free metres. We know that many of the poets used verse forms which were later to be included in the twenty-four strict metres, albeit with *cynghanedd* incorporated. In all probability, the metre known as *Mesur Clidro* was a form of the *rhupunt* or *cyhydedd hir*. In its non-alliterative form there are examples of it in the work of the Ustus Llwyd in the fourteenth century, in verses written by Y Nant in the mid-fifteenth and, by the end of that century, in the poetry of Dafydd Llwyd. By the sixteenth century it is being used by a group of Denbighshire poets including Sir Ellis, Sir Robert Llwyd and Owen Llwyd, as well as Clidro himself. It would be wrong, therefore, to look solely in the direction of England for a full explanation of the development of free verse. It was deeply rooted in the Welsh tradition and, in the case of Robin Clidro, depended a great deal upon that tradition for its form, subject matter and satirical edge.

Richard Hughes (Dic Huws) (d. 1618), whom we briefly met in the last chapter, is a very different kind of poet. Although born and bred on the Llŷn Peninsula, he made his way to the Court in London, where he is described as 'equerry to Queen Elizabeth' and *pedisequus*. It is interesting that a poet writing in Welsh should be in this position at one of the most important periods of creativity in the history of English literature, and it is hardly surprising that many of the fashions of contemporary English poetry are reflected in his work. In the Elizabethan court, poetry was a much desired skill, used by some as a means of drawing attention to themselves and gaining access to the monarch. Gary Walker in his *English*

Poetry of the Sixteenth Century has stated, 'It was one of the colourful rituals by which a Raleigh or an Essex displayed his desirability (along with dancing, music and general self-display) and so advanced his political fortunes.'

Love is one of the major themes of the period; not love as we understand the term today, but erotic desire, *eros*, strictly constrained by Petrarchan convention. It is characterized by a frustrating balance of powerful antitheses—the lady's desirability and her inaccessibility, the lover's infatuation and the female's indifference, accompanied by the incessant juxtaposing of hope and despair. Waller has argued that Elizabeth, the Virgin Queen, encouraged her male courtiers to relate to her in the role of Petrarchan lovers, 'always in hope, caught between desire for advancement and fear of losing their places, singleminded in their devotion to the hopeless attainment of her favour, and grateful for any token'. Be that as it may, those conventions which first appeared in the work of Wyatt and Surrey found a place in the Welsh poetry of the period through the writing of Richard Hughes.

One of the poet's most frequently used strategies is to establish a formal framework within which to operate. This might consist of a string of allusions to classical heroes or, as in this example, a catalogue of the physical attributes of the Petrarchan mistress, beginning with her eyes:

> Cynta' man o'th gorff a hoffais,
> y ddau dduon loywon lednais;
> y rhain a ddichon ag un troead
> lwyr iacháu neu ladd dy gariad.

[The first parts of your body which I fancied were the two dark, glistening, gentle eyes, which with one glance can completely kill or cure your lover.]

In an age when repartee was a much admired skill, the cold and calculating mistress is not found wanting with her response:

> Bychan iawn yw gwraidd dy gariad
> O cynhwysi fo'n fy llygad,
> Howsa' man y medra' i guddio,
> Lleia' ei sym ond rheitia' wrtho.

[The root of your love is very small if it can be contained in my eye—the easiest place to hide, the smallest part, but the most essential.]

The word *gwraidd* (root) marks the beginning of an ornately contrived sub-theme, inextricably intertwined with the dialogue between the forlorn poet and his indifferent mistress. It is based on terminology relating to that symbol of formality and order, the Elizabethan garden. The poem incorporates the rose and lily, with their metaphorical overtones, the cool fountain and the act of planting and watering. The beautiful and ordered garden acts as a mirror image of the inaccessible object of the poet's desire. It is only when the girl's feelings begin to soften a little that any concession is made to nature outside the confines of the cultivated garden. The poet then invites the maiden to join him in a hazel grove, but lest feelings get the better of them in such a romantic setting, the cerebral and sanitized nature of their relationship is underscored by the use of that most English of poetic devices, the pun:

> I'r glas lwyni cyll tan irddail,
> Lle mae'r cnau yn brigdrymu'r gwiail,
> Tyrd a hel o'r cnau gwisgïa'
> A chadw dair heb dorri'n gyfa'.

[Come to the hazel groves with their fresh leaves, where the nuts are weighing down the branches; come and collect the ripest nuts and keep a cluster of three without splitting it (or, keep your word without breaking it).]

The fully ripened nuts bring the cycle of planting, watering and growth to its natural conclusion, a maturation which consciously counterpoints the state of the poet's relationship with his mistress.

The poem ends in a conventional way, by incorporating the poet's name in the last verse:

> O gofynnir pwy a'i canodd,
> Dic a merch erioed a garodd.
> Rwy' fel Indeg yn ynfydu
> Na alla' ei henwi, ei chael na'i chelu.

[If anyone asks who wrote it; Dick and a girl he has always loved. I am, like Indeg, going out of my mind as I cannot name her, possess her or hide her.]

This concluding stanza follows a pattern which is typical of much free-metre poetry. As in the French *chanson d'aventure* and similar verse written in English, the beginnings and endings of poems rarely stray from convention. Very often they will begin *A m'fi* (and

I) or *Fel yr oeddwn* (as I was) and end, as we have seen, by revealing the poet's identity. It has been suggested that this was because of the poet's lack of artistic ability to start and conclude the poem in an original manner. It is probable, however, that conservative, rural audiences would expect performing poets to respect age-old conventions in the same way as they expected to encounter stereotyped themes and stock characters in the miracle plays and dramatic interludes of the period.

It is its cleverness, its verbal dexterity and skilful weaving of imagery, which gives this poetry its charm rather than the expression of personal feeling which we associate with later lyrical verse. Feelings are contained within conventional frameworks and constrained by tried and tested formulae. Sometimes the poet will make a general statement such as:

> Synnwyr, cryfder a duwiolder
> Ym marn dyn a ddichon lawer
> A heb allel stopio cariad—
> Dyna glwy' a laddodd fagad.

[Wisdom, strength and godliness can, in man's opinion, achieve a great deal without being able to stop love. That's an ailment which killed many.]

He then proceeds to list those biblical characters whose fall can be attributed to the love of a woman: Solomon, for all his wisdom; Samson, despite his strength; and even the pious King David. Another device used to underline the forsaken lover's predicament is that of the echo:

> Yno y gelwais inne o'r un modd
> Ar y dduwies bert a'm nychodd,
> 'A ga' i fy 'wyllys, ai na cha' i?'
> Ar gais, 'Na chai', hi atebodd.

[There I called in the same way to the fair goddess who tortured me 'Shall I have my way or shan't I?' 'Shan't', was her immediate reply.]

Richard Hughes is obviously aware of those images so often used for effect in English literature of the Elizabethan age. A good example is that of the dying swan:

> O wir drymder canu yr wy',
> Nid o nwy' na maswedd,

> Ond un modd â'r alarch gwyn
> Yn cwynfan cyn ei ddiwedd.

[I sing out of true sadness, not because of passion or wa
the white swan lamenting before it expires.]

However, after emphasizing the profound influence o
court on his verse, one is struck by the way his verse- ..uis, often
the *awdl-gywydd* and the four-stressed line so common in the
penillion telyn (stanzas sung to harp accompaniment), are as firmly
rooted in the Welsh tradition as are those of Clidro. If the tone,
style, framework and matter of Richard Hughes's poetry reflect a
strong English influence, its form is undoubtedly Welsh.

In reading the formal love poetry of this period, both in English
and Welsh, one can be forgiven for regarding the poets as poseurs.
They assume conventional attitudes rather than express genuine
feeling. This befits poetry which has as its background the
fashionable society of the court. When poetry emanates from a
pastoral, upland society, stripped of the trappings and security
provided by affluence, life becomes less certain and the primal
feelings of love and longing, joy and sadness assume far greater
importance. In the *penillion telyn*, poetry is the handmaiden of
feeling. Even when the poet is painting a seemingly mundane
picture, it is transformed by the underlying emotion, as in this
simple verse where the ecstasy of love totally transforms the soiled
canvas sails of a cargo vessel:

> Dacw long yn hwylio'n hwylus
> Heibio i'r trwyn ac at yr ynys;
> Os fy nghariad i sydd ynddi
> Hwyliau sidan glas sydd arni.

[There goes a ship sailing past the promontory towards the island. If my
love is on it, it has blue silken sails.]

Unlike the formal love poets, these folk poets use imagery to elicit
an appropriate emotional response, as in this verse where we are
expected to react to the maiden as we would to the loveliest months
of the year, to sunlight and to wheat. The *cynghanedd* of the last
line, as well as reflecting the harmony of the relationship, highlights
the play on the word *gwenithen* (ear of wheat/paragon):

> Blodau'r flwyddyn yw f'anwylyd,
> Ebrill, Mai, Mehefin hefyd;
> Llewyrch haul yn twnnu ar gysgod
> A gwenithen y genethod.

[My love is the year's flowers, April, May and June also; the flash of sunlight on shadow and the foremost amongst maidens.]

In this poetry, concrete images take on other meanings by analogy, as in this almost allegorical verse:

> O, f'anwylyd, cyfod frwynen
> Ac ymafael yn ei deupen;
> Yn ei hanner, torr hi'n union
> Fel y torraist ti fy nghalon.

[Oh, my love, take a reed and, holding it at both ends, break it exactly in two, as you broke my heart.]

This corpus of poetry, which has as yet received scant attention from literary critics, stands in stark contrast to the work of poets such as Richard Hughes. The difference between the two genres might be likened to that which exists between folk-song and the operatic aria. However, of their type, many of these verses are undoubtedly masterpieces in miniature, although they can rarely be attributed to any particular author.

The sixteenth century was a period of religious turmoil. Starting with Henry VIII's reformation and passing through the reigns of Edward, Lady Jane Grey, Mary and Elizabeth, the period is characterized by continuous change in religious emphasis. It is therefore hardly surprising that religious verse forms the bulk of the century's poetry. Sometimes it can be militantly Catholic, as in the carols of the martyr, Richard White (Richard Gwyn) (*c.* 1557–84):

> Gwrandewch ddatgan meddwl maith
> A sydd o waith pererin
> Gwn a gyrch garchar dwys
> Cyn mynd i eglwys Calfin.

[Listen to the long-considered thoughts of a pilgrim whom I know will seek a sad prison before entering Calvin's church.]

He paints a graphic picture of the consequences of breaking with the old faith:

> Y gainc oddi wrth y pren a dyr
> Ni wna hi ar fyr ond crino,

A'r aelod êl oddi wrth y corff
Ni ddaw mo'r ymborth iddo.

[The branch that breaks away from the trunk will but quickly wither, and
sustenance will not reach the limb which leaves the body.]

White is by no means a lone voice, as these lines written by a
Glamorgan poet of the period testify:

Fe fu'r ffydd hyn lawer blwyddyn
Â'r saint bob tro yn cytuno;
Fe ddaeth heb gêl, gan y cythrel,
Bedwar yn eu lle, o'i wŷr ynte,
Luther, Calvin, Beza, Zwinglin.

[For many a year this faith agreed always with the saints. Openly, the
Devil replaced them (i.e. the four Evangelists) with four of his men,
Luther, Calvin, Beza and Zwingli.]

On the other hand, Tomas Llywelyn (*fl.* 1580–1610) lays into the
Catholics with no holds barred. He is probably the first of the free-
metre poets to express a militantly Protestant viewpoint and his
long poem, which takes the form of a dream in which the church
and the tavern debate their respective merits, is one of the most
interesting of its type in the language:

Â'r idol roedd offeiriaid
Yn twyllo pobloedd ffyliaid
I gael arian o'u pyrsau
Dros ddywedyd off'rennau.

[With the idol, priests deceived foolish people in order to obtain money
from their purses for saying mass.]

Although the church and the tavern alternately extol their
respective virtues, Tomas Llywelyn cunningly allows the latter to
defend the Catholic Church, presumably on the premise that being
seen to have such friends will, undoubtedly, weaken the case!

Tomas Llywelyn's dream is a comparatively lively poem, but the
bulk of the religious verse of the period is pedestrian in the extreme,
completely lacking any poetic distinction. Much of it is didactic in
nature and it has been suggested that this poetry, written in free and
popular metres, was an attempt to make up for the lack of religious
instruction which resulted from the decline in the quality of
preaching during the late medieval period. In Thomas ab Ieuan
Madog's elegy to Siôn Thomas we read:

> Fo wnâi'n ddifeth, gerdd o bregeth,
> Yn sampol yn ni bob blwyddyn,

[Without fail, he would, every year, produce for us a sermon in verse as an example.]

There is no doubt that the versification of parts of the Scriptures was seen as a means of bringing the gospel to a largely illiterate populace. One does not have to go back very far in search of antecedents for the type of verse which was later popularized and used so effectively by Vicar Prichard of Llandovery (for whom see the following chapter). For example, the words of Christ at the Last Supper are encapsulated in this stanza:

> Dyma i chwi fy mhriod waed
> A gyll o'm traed a'm dwylo,
> Ac o'm dwyfron hyd y llawr,—
> Coffewch bob awr amdano.

[Here is my own blood running to the floor from my feet, hands and breast. Remember it every hour.]

There are also versions of the Lord's Prayer like this one by John Meurig, which begins:

> Y Tad tirion, gwrando, clyw,
> Gwir Dduw byw'r uchelder:
> Yr Hwn ydwyd yn y Nef,
> D'enw a'n llef santeiddier.

[Gentle Father, listen, hear; True living God on high, who art in Heaven; May your name be sanctified.]

The same poet has written versions of the Credo and the Ten Commandments. Here is his rendering of 'Thou shalt not kill.'

> Na ladd undyn yn dy lid,
> Na ddilyd ddim creulonedd;
> Câr, pe gelyn, yn ddi-ffael,
> O mynni gael trugaredd.

[Do not kill any man in anger or pursue cruelty. Love even your enemy unfailingly if you wish to obtain mercy.]

Some poems were based on specific texts such as Siôn Morys's *Carol from the fourth chapter of Mathew*; others retold some of the parables. One of the most popular of these was the story of

Lazarus and the rich man. In his version, the Glamorgan poet, Matho William, graphically describes the rich man's plea from hell:

Lasar, gwylch dy law'n y dŵr os wyt ti ŵr trugarog,
Gollwng ddeigryn wrth dy fys, 'dwi'n llosgi 'mysg y rhysog;
Cofia beth a wnaed ag e pan oeddit dre'n oludog,
Ni ddaw o'r nef yna neb, pe baet ti heb dy benglog.

[Lazarus, wet your hand in water, if you are a merciful man. Release a teardrop from your finger as I'm burning amongst the avaricious. Remember what was done to him when you were a rich man at home; nobody will come to you from heaven, even had you lost your skull.]

The poor man has at last reaped his just reward and the role reversal, so graphically illustrated in the parable, no doubt gave hope and succour to those who were only likely to experience poverty and deprivation in this world. Such poetry was a powerful weapon within a state intent upon creating civil order, obedience and total allegiance to the Crown. It is little wonder that we find numerous metrical versions of this parable in English as its message effectively reinforces a political philosophy whose main purpose was to establish and maintain a stable social order.

Although it has not yet been shown that many Welsh religious poems were translations or adaptations from English, translation was by no means uncommon. This is hardly surprising when one considers the amount of English religious prose that was translated into Welsh during this period (see Chapter 7). Richard White, for example, openly acknowledges that his anti-Protestant poem, quoted in part earlier, was based on material written by Robert Persons. However, it must be remembered that many of the themes of Welsh religious poetry were common throughout Western Europe in the Middle Ages. This common heritage is shared with poets writing in the strict metres and there are examples of religious songs, or *cwndidau*, which can be shown to be based on the *cywyddau* of Siôn Cent.

It must be admitted that wading through the religious poetry of the period can be an onerous task for the modern reader. It is often turgid in the extreme with the occasional striking metaphor or colourful turn of phrase shining like a beacon in the almost unmitigated gloom. It is utilitarian verse, stolidly didactic, written in an age when, for most people, life was agonizingly short with pain, hardship and poverty in constant attendance. Their main

hope was to reap their reward, like Lazarus, in the next world.
Richard White expresses it thus:

> Gwnawn ein penyd tra fôm byw,
> Ni a'i cawn yn Dduw trugarog;
> Ef a'n gelwir ni byrnhawn
> Ac yno y cawn ein cyflog.

[We shall do our penance whilst we live. We shall find him a merciful God.
He will call us of an afternoon and there we shall receive our reward.]

If much of the religious poetry of the period is lacking in artistic
merit, Archdeacon Edmwnd Prys's metrical versions of the Psalms
are certainly an exception to the rule. Like most of the free-metre
poets, Prys uses a measure which was once a part of the strict-metre
canon but which had been commandeered and made more
accessible by the lower order of poets. In his case, it was the *awdl-
gywydd.*

Hymn-singing, now so much part of the Welsh tradition, had no
place in the life of the Church at this time. The Act of Uniformity
(1549) permitted a Psalm to be sung or recited at the beginning or
end of the Church service and the task of remembering them was
facilitated when returning Marian exiles brought John Calvin's
metrical versions into the country from the Continent. Already by
1547 Sternhold had produced metrical versions in English and these
were soon to be augmented by Hopkins's equally felicitous
translations. In order to facilitate communal worship in Wales,
similar attempts were made to render the Psalms in verse form.
Poets such as Siôn Tudur (*c.* 1522–1602) and William Midleton (*c.*
1550–*c.*1600) had tried to use the classical metres to this end. Their
efforts were cumbersome, often marred by the use of meaningless
interpolations to meet the demands of the metre. As a result, these
Psalms could not be meaningfully sung, and soon poets such as
Edward Kyffin (*c.* 1558–1603) began experimenting with the free
metres. There is little doubt that these poets were influenced by the
efforts of the English translators but it was the Cambridge-
educated archdeacon of Merioneth, Edmwnd Prys (1543/4–1623),
who produced by far the best version of the Psalms, publishing
them as an appendix to the Book of Common Prayer (1621). This
was the only hymn-book available to Welsh churches until the
eighteenth century and Prys's versions of the Psalms are still sung
by both Anglican and Nonconformist congregations today.

Working directly from the Hebrew text and using mostly the simple Psalm-measure based on the *awdl-gywydd* ('this poor measure', as he called it), Prys produced verses which could be easily remembered and meaningfully sung. Perhaps it was because he was such an accomplished poet in the strict metres that he understood their limitations so well. He also had a masterful command of the Welsh language and utilized his rich vocabulary, his wide knowledge of idiom and sure grasp of syntax to embellish the simple measure which he employed.

In his foreword to the translation the archdeacon justifies his choice of metre:

> Three things decided that the blessed psalms should not be translated in one of the twenty-four metres. One is that I could not dare to constrict the holy Scripture so much, lest in keeping to the metre I lost the meaning of the Spirit and thus sin against God in order to satisfy man.
>
> Secondly, God's word is to be sung in unison in a large congregation, praising God with one voice, one mind, one heart; which they can do in this poor measure whilst only one could sing a cywydd or awdl.
>
> Thirdly, all children, servants and uneducated people will learn a verse of a carol where only a scholar could learn a cywydd or other learned song.

One brief example will give us a taste of Prys's translation. This is his rendering of the first part of Psalm 23:

> Yr Arglwydd yw fy mugail clau,
> Ni ad byth eisiau arnaf;
> Gorwedd a gaf mewn porfa fras,
> Ar lan dwfr gloywlas araf.
>
> Fe goledd f'enaid, ac a'm dwg
> 'R hyd llwybrau diddrwg cyfion;
> Er mwyn ei enw mawr di-lys,
> Fe'm tywys ar yr union.

The vocabulary is simple and direct, the syntax taut and the internal rhyme, between the last syllable of the first and penultimate lines and the middle of the second and final lines, effectively unobtrusive. The apparent simplicity of expression, the accuracy of the translation and the carefully concealed artistry bear the hallmark of a master craftsman and great scholar. Edmwnd Prys's poetry must certainly be included among the highlights of the literature of the period and it is little wonder that his versions of the Psalms are still sung and appreciated by congregations throughout Wales.

There is a certain irony in the fact that Edmwnd Prys, the archetypal Renaissance man, should have sent a *cywydd* to his fellow poet, Siôn Tudur, requesting him to write a prognostication. These were usually printed in the almanacs of the day and purported to foretell what would happen in the coming year in relation to such matters as the weather, health, war and peace and the state of the economy. The emergence of the printing press and the growth in literacy were both factors in the development of the almanac into one of the most popular forms of written literature of the day. Although the prognostication was a form known throughout Europe in the Middle Ages, it was its appearance in the almanacs that gave it a more general currency. As well as the almanac and the prognostication for the coming year, the publication would usually contain a collection of useful information for the reader such as the phases of the sun and moon, dates of fairs and the state of the tides. Predictions were deliberately vague but were purported to be based upon the movements of the planets. Like our present-day tabloid press editors, the compilers targeted the lower echelons of society. Almanacs and prognostications were certainly not deemed worthy of attention by the intelligentsia of the age except as a source of fun. Consequently, it became fashionable to parody the prognostications in particular, and it is certain that this is what Edmwnd Prys expected of Siôn Tudur. He was not to be disappointed when he read *Prognosticasiwn Dr Powel* (Dr Powel's Prognostication). The prescience of the following stanzas could hardly be challenged:

> Fo fydd y flwyddyn nesa'
> Weithie yn law, weithie'n hindda,
> Weithie'n rhew, weithie'n eira,
> Weithie'n wanwyn, weithie'n ha'.
>
> Rhai'n iach a rhai'n gleifion,
> Rhai'n dlawd, rhai'n gywaethogion,
> Rhai'n weinied, rhai'n gryfion,
> Rhai'n hael, rhai'n grinion.

[Next year will sometimes be wet, sometimes fine; sometimes with frost, sometimes snow; sometimes spring, sometimes summer. Some will be well, others sick; some poor, others rich; some weak and some strong, some generous and some mean.]

Coupled with the parodying of the traditional prognostications one often has a strong element of satire, particularly at the expense of some of the professions such as lawyers, doctors, craftsmen and merchants. Doctors, for instance, receive short shrift from Siôn Tudur:

> Dyma flwyddyn i ffisygwr
> I ysbeilio pob gwanwr
> Ac i addo yn iach ei wneuthyd
> O'r saith anaele glefyd.
>
> A chael dwybunt i ddechre
> Am werth grot o gyffurie,
> A rhoi iddo arian lawer
> A'r claf yn waeth o'r hanner.

[This is a year for physicians to plunder every weak man, promising to cure him of the seven awful diseases. Taking two pounds to start for four pennyworth of drugs and the patient twice as bad after giving him so much money.]

However, it should be said that he is equally critical of the sycophancy of his fellow poets and the vacuous nature of their eulogies:

> Dyma flwyddyn i brydyddion
> I ganu celwydd ddigon
> A thaeru ar ŵr bonheddig
> Ei fod yn gythrel ffyrnig,
> A doedyd arno ladd
> Bedwar ugain yn ymladd
> A thorri cant o gestyll
> A'u dryllio yn fil o gandryll
> Ac ynte wrth y tân
> Yn ymeuflyd â'r cwpan
> Heb wneuthur erioed niwed
> I un dyn ar a aned.

[This is a year for poets to write untruths in abundance and to insist to a gentleman that he is a fierce devil, claiming that he has killed four score in battle, destroyed a hundred castles, smashing them to smithereens. And he by the fire, grasping a cup, having never harmed a living soul.]

Just as Robin Clidro based his satire upon his audience's knowledge of the classical poetic tradition, so Siôn Tudur used the most popular form of literature of his day as the butt of his caustic brand of humour. It is possible that vague similarities between the prognostications and the long tradition of prophecies or *cerddi brud* which existed in Welsh added to the fun. Although that tradition was drawing to its close by the late-sixteenth century, there were still remnants in existence, even in free-verse form.

Ballads relating events of the day were popular during the Elizabethan Age in England. Battles, murders, executions, robberies and plots against the Crown were often the subject matter of popular verse, as were more bizarre happenings such as tales of people living for months without eating or women giving birth to strange creatures. Given the political union of England and Wales, it is little wonder that poets in both languages wrote about the same events. An anonymous Welsh poem, written by someone who claimed to be a Doctor of Music, describes the many unsuccessful plots against the queen. The melodrama often verges on the ridiculous:

> Fo ddaeth i'r Court ei neges,
> Ar odde lladd ein brenhines:
> Y tac dur ollyngodd ati;
> Angel a roes rybudd iddi.
>
> Fo'i disiarsiodd ati'n union
> Dan ben i bron at ei chalon;
> Yr oedd ei gorff i gyd yn crynu;
> Cododd ei ffroen ar i fyny.
>
> Crist a gadwodd ei grasol wyneb;
> F'aeth y peleda dur drwy'r garreg;
> Rhag maint y gwres yn myned heibio,
> Eurwallt Elsbeth oedd yn deifio.

[He came to Court with the aim of killing our queen; he released the steel tack but an angel gave her warning. He discharged it straight at her, under her breast and at her heart. His body was all ashiver; he lifted its muzzle up. God protected her gracious face; the steel pellets went through the stone; such was the heat that, as they went by, Elizabeth's golden hair was singed.]

The defeat of the Armada in 1588 was greeted by poets in both languages. However, the author of one Welsh version, Thomas Jones, vicar of Llanfair in Monmouthshire, also wrote a poem about another event of that year which was of far greater significance to Wales, namely the translation of the Bible into Welsh. Seafaring was, of course, a high-profile subject which received its stimulus from the voyages of discovery and sea battles of the age. One of the more interesting poems is *A conversation between a man and the Pelican, namely the tale of a crew of Welshmen who went in the time of Queen Elizabeth to the West Indies at her command to wreak vengeance upon, and to despoil the Spaniards.* It is written by a sailor, Lieutenant Wiliam Peilyn. The pelican offers to act as a messenger and fly back to Britain to tell friends and family how the Welshmen are faring. The bird is given instructions:

> Hed pan ddelych gynta' i dir
> I'r Cwrt â'm gwir newyddion
> At Dwysoges ddigymhares,
> Ein Brenhines gyfion.

[Fly when you first reach land to the Court with my true news to an incomparable princess, our just Queen.]

Their voyage is mapped out and the numerous battles with the Queen's enemies are listed, together with lurid descriptions of the savages they encounter on the way:

> Cenawon cythreulig, geirwon lun ffyrnig
> A'u crwyn yn baentiedig, Satan 'r un llun,
> A weir yn eu ffroenau, fel baeddod a diriau
> A'u safnau sy'n malu mwy ewyn.

[Devilish curs of fierce, rough physique, their skins painted and looking like Satan; wire in their noses like boars and rascals with their lips foaming froth.]

The poet names his brave Welsh compatriots and tells the pelican that they intend to return home via Newfoundland and Ireland. The poet states that little did their mothers think they would undertake such a voyage and then sends the pelican on its way:

> Ffarwél; bydd wych, yr eden gain,
> Os ei di i Brydain drosom,
> Annerch ein holl ffrins i gyd
> A dywed y byd sydd arnom.

[Farewell, goodbye, fair bird; if you go to Britain on our behalf, address all our friends and tell them how we are faring.]

If it was such dramatic events as these which were destined to be the main focus of attention, there were changes of a more mundane nature taking place at home. South Wales was experiencing the first effects of industrialization and in the anonymously written poem *Coed Glyn Cynon* (The Woods of the Cynon Valley), the poet attacks the English who have cut down the trees to smelt iron. This charming poem with its 'green' message strikes a modern note. Both people and animals suffer as a result of despoiling the countryside:

> O bai gŵr ar drafael dro
> ac arno ffo rhag estron,
> fe gâi gan eos lety erioed
> yn fforest coed Glyn Cynon.

[Were a man on the run, fleeing from an enemy, the nightingale would always give him harbour in the wooded forest of the Cynon Valley.]

The forest, which was once home to birds and wild animals, is now ablaze:

> Llawer bedwen glas ei chlog,
> ynghrog y byddo'r Saeson,
> sydd yn danllwyth mawr o dân
> gan wŷr yr haearn duon.

[Many a birchtree, green of cloak (May the English hang!) is now a flaming heap of fire with the blackened ironworkers.]

Even the red deer have fled the district to seek refuge in the north:

> Clywes ddoedyd, ar fy llw,
> fod haid o'r ceirw cochion
> yn oer eu lle' yn ymado â'u plwy';
> i Ddugoed Mowddwy yr aethon.

[By my oath, I heard it said that a herd of red deer, bleating sadly, left their reserve and went to Dugoed Mawddwy.]

The poet, we learn, is not a dispassionate observer of this catastrophe for he has his own very personal reason for lamenting the demise of the forest:

> Ac o daw gofyn pwy a wnaeth
> hyn o araith greulon,
> dyn a fu gynt yn cadw oed
> dan fforest Coed Glyn Cynon.

[And if one is asked who wrote this cruel dirge, it is a man who once made a tryst 'neath the trees of Glyn Cynon Forest]

If *Coed Glyn Cynon* is a poem which records social and ecological change, the fact that it was written in free metre is indicative of a significant development in the Welsh literary scene. This survey of free verse in the sixteenth and early seventeenth century has so far tried to show that the emerging poetry written in the free metres is an interesting amalgam of indigenous and imported elements. Its metrical forms display a heavy Welsh bias, but it is inevitable that it was profoundly influenced by the political, social and cultural ethos of an age which saw dramatic developments in the centralization of the state. However, despite these powerful external influences, a central factor which cannot be ignored is that this poetry coexisted with the far more prestigious strict-metre tradition and was inevitably influenced by its subject matter and style.

For example, from the point of view of content and expression, the following passage from Siôn Stradling's elegy could have come from any of the elegaic *cywyddau* of the period:

> Cryf a chefnog, dewr wrth raid, ac oen i weiniaid yma,
> a'i gampau gyda haelder, Siôn oedd un o'r gweision gwycha'.

[Strong and wealthy, obviously brave but like a lamb to the weak; his feats together with Siôn's generosity [made him] one of the greatest heroes.]

The description of the nobleman's lavish hospitality in this extract also clearly echoes the classical tradition:

> Ni wn ei fod, gŵr o Lislod,
> Fath berchen tŷ, yn holl Gymry . . .
> Can gwenith gwyn, pob rhyw enllyn,
> Pum rhyw ddiod, cwrw a bragod;
> Gwin coch a gwyn, a meddyglyn
> A'u rhoi'n ddi-gost, ac yn ddi-fost,
> I bob rhyw ddyn, heb ei w'rafun.

[I don't know that there is, man of Lislod, such a householder throughout Wales . . . white wheat flour, various sorts of relish, five varieties of drink—beer and bragget, red and white wine and mead and he gives them free, without boasting, to every man, never refusing.]

Even some of the stylistic embellishments of the *cywyddwyr* have been incorporated into the free metres. There are numerous examples of *cymeriad*—the linking of lines in a verse of *cywydd* or *awdl* by beginning each line with the same letter or word, by alliterating or rhyming the first word in each consecutive line, or by allowing the sense to extend from one line into another. *Trychiad*, the splitting of two closely related words by interposing another word or phrase, is another common feature of the traditional metres which has been adopted, as in this couplet:

> Syr Siors sydd, Harbert ddedwydd,
> uwchlaw digon o farchogion.

[Although the lines simply state that the happy Sir George Herbert is head of many knights, the syntax has been radically changed and reads literally, 'Sir George is, happy Herbert, head of many knights'.]

It is hardly surprising that the more prestigious strict-metre poetry exerted a profound influence on verse in the free metres. In some ways both groups of poets wrote under similar constraints inasmuch as they worked within strict conventions which regulated both the form and content of their poetry. Originality of expression, the exploration of personal feeling and the subjectivity we associate with later lyrical poetry is rarely found in either form, except for the *penillion telyn*. The charm of the free-metre poetry usually lies in its graceful manipulation of accepted conventions of style and imagery. What is said is less important than the manner of saying. Its *raison d'être* lies in its ability to entertain, teach and transmit accepted wisdom, sometimes in an elegant and elaborate form but often in a direct, down-to-earth manner and always in the idiom of the common folk. It is in the use of the vernacular that we detect the greatest difference between the two traditions and undoubtedly this is the most significant contribution of the free-metre poets to the development of Welsh poetry in general. In this sense, the appearance of their work in the manuscripts of the sixteenth century marks an important watershed in the development of Welsh literature.

BIBLIOGRAPHY

Cennard Davies, 'Robin Clidro a'i Ganlynwyr', unpublished MA thesis, University of Wales, 1964.
J.H. Davies, *Cymdeithas Llên Cymru* 2–6, 1900–5.
H. Meurig Evans, 'Iaith a Ieithwedd y Cerddi Rhydd Cynnar', unpublished MA thesis, University of Wales, 1937.

L.J. Hopkin-James and T. C. Evans (Hopcyn a Cadrawd), *Hen Gwndidau* (Bangor, 1910).

D. Lloyd Jenkins, *Cerddi Rhydd Cynnar* (Llandysul, n.d.).

Thomas Parry, *A History of Welsh Literature, translated from the Welsh by H. Idris Bell* (Oxford, 1955).

T.H. Parry-Williams, *Carolau Richard White* (Caerdydd, 1931).

T.H. Parry-Williams, *Canu Rhydd Cynnar* (Caerdydd, 1932).

Brinley Rees, *Dulliau'r Canu Rhydd 1500–1650* (Caerdydd, 1952).

G.J. Williams, *Traddodiad Llenyddol Morgannwg* (Caerdydd, 1948).

Gwyn Williams, *An Introduction to Welsh Poetry* (London, 1953).

CHAPTER 4

LATE FREE-METRE POETRY

NESTA LLOYD

In this context the adjective 'late' refers to free-metre poems composed between *c*. 1620 and 1700. The number of such poems written in the seventeenth century is enormous but most remain unedited and unread in the manuscript collections in the great respositories. Seventeenth-century poets labour under the double disadvantage of being considered less important than the prose writers of the same period such as Morgan Llwyd, Charles Edwards or Ellis Wynne and also to be greatly inferior to their bardic predecessors of the classical period of *cerdd dafod*. Consequently, few, apart from Huw Morys and Edward Morris, have been studied in any detail; Morgan Llwyd's poetry is now being studied in the wake of general interest in *Llwydiana*, while Rhys Prichard has attracted attention because 1994 was the three hundred and fiftieth anniversary of his death.

Except for Prichard, most of the seventeenth-century poets wrote in both strict metres and free metres. The poets were increasingly literate and many wrote their own poems in commonplace books, while by the end of the century the compilations of Thomas Jones, printed in Shrewsbury but sold all over Wales, were gaining in popularity. Ephemera like almanacs and collections of free-metre poetry were the mainstay of publishers like Jones, who sold to an increasingly literate lower order of society.

It has long been acknowledged that side by side with the twenty-four traditional metres of *cerdd dafod* there had existed less complex metres which had been used by the poets, probably on more informal occasions. Earlier, however, the poets who wrote in the less strict genres were not always the same people as the praise-poets of *cerdd dafod*: indeed the bardic Grammar strictly forbade the *penceirddiaid* from meddling with *gogangerdd*; nevertheless, there are examples, published by D.H. Evans, Twm Morys and Dafydd Johnston, of even respectable bards writing lewd poems, using metres rarely used by the *penceirddiaid*, but still employing *cynghanedd*. It has been assumed that there existed, alongside the poetry of the *penceirddiaid*, a flourishing market for less intricate and more comprehensible poetry. The suppliers of this largely unrecorded poetry were known as *y glêr*, or more disparagingly *clêr y dom* (dung flies). There is evidence that many of the *uchelwyr* were like the auditors in *Breuddwyd Rhonabwy*: they might not understand much of a poem sung in their presence but they *knew* that it was in praise of themselves and their family *because that was what they were paying for*. But once the formal part of the wedding feast or funeral was over, or at one of the church festivals, there is evidence that while the mead and bragget circulated, even the grandest poets, like Iolo Goch, would occasionally entertain their patrons with songs of a bawdy or satirical nature. By the seventeenth century any pretence at keeping a distance between the *penceirddiaid* and *y glêr* was a lost cause, and many of the best-known poets of *cerdd dafod* were proud to put their names to compositions in the free metres. The trend was established by the sixteenth century and a well-known *pencerdd* like Siôn Tudur did not always spurn the free metres.

But there was a seismic shift during the seventeenth century. Whereas previously *y glêr* might have been of a different bardic class, and a *pencerdd* like Siôn Tudur might use the free metres for an informal poem, by the second half of the seventeenth century Huw Morys could, and did, use free-metre poems in the same context as he would strict-metre poetry. The most striking example of this is the fact that he composed two free-metre poems as well as a *cywydd* to mourn Barbra Miltwn, the distinctly upper-class wife of one of his patrons. I have suggested elsewhere why Morys did this, but a fifteenth- or sixteenth-century *pencerdd* would not have insulted his patron by using any metres save the twenty-four of *cerdd dafod* for such a solemn occasion. The transition can be explained partly by the way a poet such as Huw Morys was writing for a much wider range of people than the earlier poets—many of his poems are dedicated to artisans, craftsmen, ordinary workers on farms and in trades, who would never have figured as patrons of the earlier poets. It is only to be expected, therefore, that much is written in a less complicated mode and in metres which would be known to the audience from other sources. Also, by the second half of the seventeenth century, as Brinley Rees has pointed out, the

soubriquets of several of the poets suggest that they themselves
were not solely, or even primarily, dependent on poetry for their
living; for example, a poet might be referred to as a weaver, a
gamekeeper, a sexton or a smith. Even an important poet such as
Edward Morris earned his living as a drover.

Another reason advanced for the increase in free-metre poetry is
the anglicization of the gentry and their estrangement from Welsh
country life. By the middle of the seventeenth century many of the
great families were aliens in their native land and ignorant of the
Welsh language. Their interests centred on the professions in
London, such as the law, or positions at court; allegiance to their
Welsh estates was diluted as a consequence of the marriages of
heiresses into English families and especially of English girls
marrying into the Welsh gentry class. While some of their ancestors
might have found the eulogies or elegies declaimed in their halls
tedious and difficult to understand, they understood the social
function of the bards and could look forward to some fun later in
the evening when *y glêr* produced their songs. Their anglicized
descendants did not appreciate the old means of expression, but
they would be more at ease with recognizable, often English, tunes.

What is known about these free metres and where did they
originate? This is an unresolved problem, but two sources for the
free-metre poetry of the seventeenth century can be discerned.
Some of them are obviously derived from the strict metres of *cerdd
dafod*, such as *cywydd deuair fyrion* and *awdl-gywydd*, stripped of
cynghanedd; they are therefore syllabic, and their form is
determined by counting the number of syllables in a line. Others are
connected with the metres popular in the English poetry of the
sixteenth and early seventeenth centuries and are accentual, where
the number of syllables in a line can vary so long as the number
of accents or stresses remains constant. J. Glyn Davies stated
categorically that 'All our lyric metres except four are mere copies of
English metres'. The fact that so many of the later free-metre poems
have the requisite tune specified in their title and that those tunes
have similar or identical names in English and Welsh suggests some
intimate connection between them, for example *Gadael Tir* (Leave
Land), *Y Galon Drom* (Heavy Heart), *Anodd Ymadael* (Loath to
Depart); it is far too simplistic, however, to attribute direct
borrowings from English in all cases, as the work of Phyllis Kinney
has clearly demonstrated.

The old Welsh metres, which had been embellished with *cynghanedd* by the fifteenth century, were simplified and stripped of their *cynghanedd* once they were used by the free-metre poets; but the imported English metres, however metrically intricate they already were in English, were made yet more complicated by being adorned with *cynghanedd* by the Welsh poets who adopted them. This led to poems more intricate in their metrics, rhyme schemes and *cynghanedd* than any before or since.

It is clear that in the early seventeenth century the majority of recorded poems in the free metres were in the simplified old Welsh metres, such as Richard Hughes's carol metre, the *awdl-gywydd* in its non-*cynghanedd* form, or the popular *Triban* metres of many of Rhys Prichard's poems; however, virtuoso creations such as Edmwnd Prys's 'Baled Gymraeg', complex in metre and embellished with *cynghanedd*, are at least as old as the sixteenth century, so it is dangerous to be dogmatic about precisely when the change occurred as much depended on the individual poet. The popularity of the anonymous quatrains of the *Hen benillion* in the seventeenth century must not be overlooked, and they almost invariably used the simplest rhyming couplets. Even a verbally dextrous poem such as Peter Lewis's *Cathl y Gair Mwys* (The Song of the Pun) at the end of the century uses the quatrain of rhyming couplets for its metre. By the end of the century, therefore, there was a much greater variety of metres available to the poets than previously, some of which were inordinately complicated, as Thomas Parry demonstrated in *Baledi'r Ddeunawfed Ganrif*. He argued that the phenomenon called *y canu rhydd* lasted a mere century, from *c.* 1550 to *c.* 1650, and that what followed was a variant of the *canu caeth* (strict metre) tradition, with full *cynghanedd*, but using new, accentual metres as opposed to the traditional syllabic metres.

In E.G. Millward's anthology, *Blodeugerdd Barddas o Ganu Rhydd y Ddeunawfed Ganrif*, twenty-nine different tunes are cited to which the poems could be sung; Richard Morris (1703–79) testified that he could 'sing on the viol' over sixty airs; in the manuscript which he copied in 1718 he listed a further 350 tunes known to him. Millward selected poems from the work of over fifty different poets, twenty-six of whom are represented by one poem only and a further nine by two poems. The companion volume, *Blodeugerdd Barddas o Ganu Caeth y Ddeunawfed Ganrif*, edited by Cynfael Lake, names only twenty-five different poets and, as the editor himself points out, two-thirds of the poems were written by five poets only and of the remainder, twelve had one poem each and four other poets contributed two poems each. This shows that the centre of gravity of Welsh poetry had shifted decisively by the eighteenth century from being predominantly *canu caeth* to being overwhelmingly *canu rhydd*.

Is it possible to determine when this happened more precisely than a vague 'second half of the seventeenth century'? Probably not. Much of what is said about seventeenth-century poetry is impressionistic, since most of the evidence is unedited; conclusions are tentative and liable to be disproved in the light of further research. Bearing in mind these *caveats* however, some suggestions may be made. The decisive figure was Huw Morys, but since he lived from *c*. 1622 to 1709 and wrote poetry throughout his adult life this affords little help. His younger contemporary, Edward Morris (*c*. 1633–89) was also influential, although he wrote less than Huw Morys and the proportion of his work in the free metres was also less. Thomas Parry compared the influence of Huw Morys on the development of *y canu caeth newydd* with the impact Dafydd ap Gwilym had on the development of the *cywydd* from the *traethodl*. Morys's verbal dexterity was such that he seems to have been totally bewitched by the complicated rhythms and patterns which occurred when the complexities of *cynghanedd* were added to the equally intricate metres of some of the tunes to which the words were set. Increasingly during the century the work of the poets has survived in copies written by the poets themselves, so they have priority in any editorial decisions. Unfortunately, neither of these prolific poets is well represented, since the only fairly substantial manuscript in Edward Morris's hand is Peniarth 200 (thirty-two pages) with occasional insertions in his hand in another half dozen manuscripts; there are better attested examples of Huw Morys's *llaw deilo* (mucking hand) as he himself disparagingly called it, but both poets were popular with copyists and there is no shortage of texts of their poems. Huw Morys was one of the most copied poets in the whole of Welsh literature as well as being one of the most prolific with over 550 poems attributed to him in the computer index of poems at the National Library (December 1995). Some are obviously wrong attributions, but the very number makes the preparation of reliable editions of his poems very difficult. David

Jenkins's pioneering study of his life and work in 1948, still largely unpublished, now needs updating to take account of the additional manuscript versions that have come to light since he prepared his edition.

Huw Morys wrote in different modes: he could write formal strict-metre poetry using the literary language and all the traditional embellishments such as *sangiadau*, *cymeriad*, etc. albeit liberally sprinkled with English loan-words since he was living in Llansilin, close to the English border. He was also the greatest exponent of the new, complicated free-metre poetry, based on existing tunes and with added *cynghanedd*, to produce virtuoso compositions of dizzying complexity. But he was equally adept at composing stanzas with neither adjectives nor *cynghanedd* to distract from the direct importance of the narrative. Jenkins chose the following verse, starkly rooted in verbs and nouns, to illustrate this point.

> Angylion a ganodd, bugeiliaid a'u gwelodd,
> A'r doethion a deithiodd, goleuodd ein gwlad
> Gan seren i'w sirio, rhoen offrwm yn effro—
> Aur, thus a myrr Iddo—mawr roddiad.

[Angels sang, shepherds saw them/ And the wise men journeyed, our country was illuminated/ By a star to cheer it, they gave an offering alertly/ Gold, frankincense and myrrh to Him—a great gift.]

Huw Morys was born in 1622, a younger son of Morris ap John ap John Ednyfed. The family moved to Pontymeibion, Llansilin, Denbighshire, the farm always associated with the poet's name, after 1647, when Huw was already twenty-five years old. His education is a matter of conjecture although he is reputed to have been apprenticed to a barker in Gwaliau, Overton, Flintshire. As a younger son who never married, but who lived at home with his parents and then with his elder brother's reasonably prosperous family, he had plenty of time to compose poetry and to indulge in the old tradition of *clera*—attending a patron's house on the occasion of a marriage or burial or at the great festivals of the Church, when itinerant poets were instructed to present their poems to the patrons. It is unlikely that Morys depended on his earnings as a poet, but since he would receive food and drink and gifts from his patrons on his visits, and since he had no dependents, he probably managed better than most. He revelled in visits to his patrons: the

Myddeltons of Chirk Castle and the cadet branch at Tŷ Newydd in his own parish of Llansilin; Sir William Williams, speaker of the House of Commons, married to the heiress of Glasfryn, also in Llansilin; the Mostyns of Gloddaith and the Owens of Brogyntyn—all were praised in his strict-metre poetry as patrons particularly generous to himself. Gwyn Thomas has made the telling point that 'complaints about lapsing liberality and a failing patronage are not numerous in Morys's poetry' although it was one of the most repeated themes in seventeenth-century poetry.

One of the most notable features of Huw Morys's work is that he used the free metres to fulfil the same purpose as his strict-metre poetry, that is to praise and elegize his patrons, as well as to beg for their gifts. He was not the first to do this but it is in the generation represented by him and Edward Morris that the practice becomes commonplace. The Chirk Castle accounts reveal that poets, harpers and other musicians were paid for their free-metre poems and carols just as they were paid for their more conventional poems. Another feature of Huw Morys's free-metre poetry, as already noted, is that the social status of the people whom he addressed in his poems varied more than usual. Thus, there are several poems where Morys asks an *uchelwr* for a gift on behalf of a member of a lower social class, for example a delightful poem asking Wiliam Salesbury (II) of Rug (grandson of the poet discussed below) for a viol for William Probert, an old *cerddor* (musician/poet) who had fallen on hard times because, according to Huw Morys's insinuations, he fell on his viol and shattered it when he was drunk. Probert was well known as an entertainer, successful in eisteddfodau and in English Shropshire. The description of the old man's playing is both funny and inventive:

> Er bod y cerddor pêr leferydd
> Yn medru chwilio a chwalu ei cholydd,
> Mae diffyg anadl yn ei ffroenau
> Yn dwyn y sŵn o dan ei asennau;
> Mi gyff'lyba ei fwa a'i feiol
> I lais anniddig gŵydd ar farrug, gwaedd arferol;
> Llesg iawn ydyw, llais ci'n udo,
> Llais hen olwyn neu lais morwyn ar lesmeirio.

[Even though the sweet-talking musician/ Can search out and disperse its guts (gut strings),/ The lack of air in his nostrils/ Brings the noise from under his ribs;/ I shall compare his bow and his viol/ To the peevish voice of a goose in a frost, the usual cry;/ He is very feeble, the voice of a howling dog,/ The voice of an old wheel or the voice of a maiden on the point of fainting.]

He compares the old violinist's playing to a squealing sow, a saw being sharpened, a brass pan or a caterwauling cat, images both vivid and apt. Similarily a *crwth* (viol) is asked on behalf of Ffowc Rhisiart and a plough is sought from the wardens of Corwen on behalf of Dafydd Morys, Tregeiriog and an oak from Owen Salesbury, Rug (the father of Wiliam Salesbury (II) petitioned above for a viol), on behalf of Roger Edward the cooper, to make barrels, all obviously artisans. There is much satire and fun at the expense of the giver and supplicant in these poems, and a description of the gift features in exactly the same way as it did in the traditional poems. Because the traditional begging poems had always contained these descriptive elements the transition of them into free metres was facilitated.

The fact that Morys wrote three elegies on the death of Barbra Miltwn, a formal *cywydd*, a dialogue elegy and an intensely personal threnody, both in free metres, was unusual. The *cywydd* shows Barbra Miltwn to be one of the Wynns of Melai and her lineage is traced to the princes of Powys and Owain Gwynedd; the family is connected by blood or marriage to every important family in north Wales and Barbra is described as *seren naw o siroedd* (the star of nine counties). Her breeding and status were impeccable, and although the cadet branch of the Myddelton family into which Barbra married was *nouveau riche* compared with her family, yet Morys would not have insulted the widower by presenting him with poems which showed a lack of respect or in any way diminished the status of the family. So by 1695 when Barbra died, a free-metre elegy was as acceptable as a *cywydd*. When Richard Miltwn, Barbra's widower, died in 1700 the only extant elegy to him by Huw Morys is in the same free metre and seems to be a companion poem to his *galarnad* (threnody) at Barbra's death. Miltwn had married Dorothy Thelwall after Barbra's death, but the widow is ignored in Morys's elegy on Miltwn—he states bluntly that he has lost all the ones whom he most loved:

> Collais y rhai a gerais fwya',
> Ber yw byrroes, marw heb hiroes mae'r rhai pura'.

[I have lost those whom I loved best/ Short is the brief life, the purest die without a long life.]

The shortest-lived in this context was Barbra, who died around Midsummer's Eve 1695, aged twenty-three years, and barely six months wed.

Huw Morys apparently lived and died a bachelor, but he is famous for his poems in praise of women's beauty. In these poems his technical virtuosity is revealed at its most developed, but in order to sustain the rhymes and consonantal patterns which he imposed on himself, some wordiness and superfluity of adjectives and compound words was bound to occur. But, as Thomas Parry observed, it is difficult accurately to judge the effect of this poetry when it is read silently from a book as compared with hearing it declaimed, with its accompanying tune on harp or *crwth*; for example:

> Fy nghariad i,
> Teg wyt ti,
> Gwawr ragori, lili lawen,
> Bêr winwydden;
> Fwynaidd feinwen,
> Y gangen lawen lun;
> Blodau'r wlad
> Mewn mawrhad,
> Hardd ei 'mddygiad, nofiad nwyfus,
> Bun gariadus
> Haelwen hwylus,
> Y weddus foddus fun;
> Lloer wiw ei gwedd, lliw eira gwyn,
> Yn sydyn rhois fy serch
> Ar f'enaid fain
> Sydd glir fel glain,
> Rywiog riain irfain yrfa,
> Na chawn ata'
> Ddyn ddiana'
> I'w meddu, mwyna' merch!
> Ond, blodau rhinwedd croywedd Cred,
> Er teced ydwyt ti,
> Y galon fach
> A gadwa'n iach;
> Pur glanach, gwynnach, gwenfron,
> Nid â thrymion
> Caeth ochneidion
> Dan fy nwyfron i.

[My sweetheart,/ Fair are you,/ Dawn surpassing, joyous lily,/ Sweet vine,/ Gentle slender white,/ The branch of happy form;/ The country flowers/ In honour,/ Handsome its demeanour, lively swimming,/ Lovable girl,/ Generous, white, healthy,/ The seemly, mannerly girl;/ A fine moon her appearance, the colour of white snow,/ Quickly I set my love/ On my slender spirit/ Who is as clear as a jewel,/ Delicate maiden fresh, slim race,/ O that I could have/ The faultless girl/ To possess, the finest girl!/ But, virtuous fresh-faced flowers of Christendom,/ Despite your fairness/ The little heart/ I will keep whole;/ If you were fairer, whiter, fair-breasted [one]/ Heavy, captive sighs/ Will not go/ Under my breast.]

In addition to the abundance of superlative and comparative adjectives and compound epithets, the language of this poem is full of puns and echoes from the earlier love poetry with its stereotyped similes and metaphors. The Mayday carols show the same lightness of touch and fanciful wordplay, but because they use simpler metres they are distinctly less wordy.

In stark contrast, and as testimony to Morys's range of technique, there are poems which deal with specific historical occasions. Apart from a very few such as *Ar ofyn gostegion yn amser Cromwel* (On proclaming marriage banns in Cromwell's time), which must be later than the Marriage Act of August 1653, Morys prudently hid his hatred of the Puritan cause by using the iconography popularized by vaticinatory poets since the Middle Ages; thus the Lion and the young Lions represent Charles I and his sons; the Lamb is the Church of England, the Sheep are the loyal subjects of Charles and the Shepherds are the priests; Cromwell is usually the Fox or some such predatory animal; it was not until after 1660 and the restoration of Charles II to his martyred father's throne that Morys vented his spleen on named individuals. *Drych yr Amseroedd cyn 1660* (A Mirror to the Times before 1660) was written post-1660 and contains denunciations by name of two of the leaders. Vavasor Powell is accused of arrogance:

> Un Vavasor Powel oedd eu pen bugel
> A'i hediad fel angel yn uchel tua'r ne'

[One Vavasor Powell was their chief shepherd/ and his flight was like an angel, high towards heaven.]

Morgan Llwyd, who had died in 1659, was charged with hypocrisy and the poisoning of minds:

Trwy weniaith a rhagrith caed efrau'n ei wenith
A gwenwyn ar lefrith ei lyfrau

[Because of flattery and hypocrisy tares were found in his wheat/ And
poison on the milk of his writings.]

Morgan Llwyd is accused of justifying the evil ways of his friends in
his books, an important reminder that in the eyes of many of his
contemporaries Llwyd was a traitor to his class. Perhaps the one
verse which sums up the attitude, not only of Huw Morys but of
most of the poets discussed here, is from *Ymddiddan rhwng
Protestant ac Eglwys Loeger* (A Dialogue between a Protestant and
the Church of England):

Pan oeddwn i'n fachgen mi welais fyd llawen
Nes codi o'r genfigen flin, filen fu fawr,
I ladd yr hen lywydd a dewis ffydd newydd
Ac arglwydd aflonydd yn flaenawr.

[When I was a boy I saw a happy world/ Until there arose the grievous
jealousy, great its fierceness,/ To kill the old leader and choose a new
faith/ And a new disturbing lord as leader.]

The regret for a lost world which seemed to have gone for ever with
the Civil War and the interregnum is the dominant theme of many
of the poems of the second half of the century.

Huw Morys was regarded by his contemporaries as the best poet
of his age—the only dissenter being Mathew Owen, Llangar, who
favoured Edward Morris because, as he said, *Ned a gân enaid y
gerdd* (Ned sings the soul of the song). The latter was not as prolific
as Huw Morys and he lived for thirty years fewer. Edward Morris
was born into a comfortable farming family and spent his life at
Perthillwydion, Cerrigydrudion, Denbighshire. But he had a 'day-
job' as a drover, accompanying herds of cattle from north Wales to
fairs in southern England; he died in Essex in November 1689. He
combined this seasonal droving work with the traditional bardic
round of *clera* and visited a number of the most important centres
of patronage in north Wales, many of them the same houses as
those favoured by Huw Morys also. His favourite house was
Gloddaith, the home of Sir Thomas Mostyn, closely followed by
Bodysgallen, where Robert Wynn held court just as the *uchelwyr* of
old had done. Edward Morris's mastery of *cerdd dafod* was

remarkable—he revelled in its complexities far more than Huw Morys did. Huw Morys's strict-metre work was largely restricted to such relatively simple metres as *cywyddau, englynion* and a few *awdlau*. On the other hand, of Edward Morris's four *awdlau* two use all the twenty-four metres of Dafydd ab Edmwnd's classification; a third (unfinished) has twenty metres but was intended to contain twenty-four according to the title; the fourth has fourteen metres including three 'new' combinations of two metres. He uses the traditional flourishes of *cymeriad* (starting every line either with the same letter or even the same word) and *cyrch-gymeriad* (starting a new 'verse' with some of the last word(s) of the previous 'verse') to bind together different metres and knit the composition into one cohesive whole; he also used the *sangiad* (parenthesis) most effectively. The technical wizardry and mastery of *cerdd dafod* shown by such feats is crowned, however, by his *cywydd 'wyneb a gwrthwyneb'*, a *tour de force* only very occasionally attempted by a few virtuosi in earlier centuries and referred to by Thomas Parry as the greatest test of skill of the old poets. Morris's verbal dexterity was in no way less than Huw Morys's, yet his use of the free metres is far more restricted and he did not experiment with new metres in the way that Huw Morys did. A rough calculation shows that Edward Morris used fewer than twenty free metres; of named metres in English and Welsh, eight are used only once each, and of the rest the *tri thrawiad* (three beats metre) accounts for thirty-three poems, three times more than the next popular measure, *Anodd Ymadael* (Loath to Depart). Huw Morys also used the *tri thrawiad* far more than any other metre, but he did use about fifty other named tunes as well as several which are merely designated *rhydd* in the computer index of poems. It must be remembered, however, that Huw Morys wrote far more poems than Edward Morris, and lived for twenty years after the younger poet's death.

The subjects of Edward Morris's free verse are very similar to those of Huw Morys: love poetry, religious and moralistic carols, begging poems, eulogies and elegies and a few cautious poems dealing with contemporary events. Gwenllian Jones has suggested that he may have been careful in expressing political opinions because he spent so much time around London where it would not have been prudent to criticize Cromwell's regime, much as he hated the Lord Protector and his henchmen. The relief and sincerity of his welcome to Charles II in May 1660 is obvious, for it is not just a political restoration in which the poet rejoices, but the restoration of the whole natural order of the universe, which had been disturbed with the execution of Charles I. The heavens, angels, sun, moon and stars, the earth with all its different terrains, animals and vegetations and the great oceans, filled with myriad creatures, all are called on to praise God for his mercy in restoring Charles to his father's throne.

> Fe dynnodd Duw'r awran bob un i'w le'i hunan
> A'r gonest, pureiddlan yn gyfan o'i gur;
> Charles oedd ben arnom yn hyn a gollasom,
> Charles eilwaith a gawsom drwy gysur.

[God has now pulled each one into his own place/ And the honest, clean and pure totally out of his pain;/ Charles was our head in what we lost,/ Charles secondly we have had through comfort.]

God's approbation was revealed by the largely peaceful and bloodless way the Restoration was accomplished.

Morris's Christmas and other carols are very similar to Huw Morys's, telling the story of man's redemption from the Fall in Eden to Calvary, not limiting the story to the Nativity. His strong religious sense is emphasized by the fact that he wrote more religious poems and carols than any other type, and did so especially for the Church festivals. His staunch Anglicanism is obvious throughout and his hatred of the Quakers, as they were contemptuously known, is evident in many poems. The latter were scorned by many Welsh Anglicans (Ellis Wynne is another good example), as much for their refusal to acknowledge the social *mores* as for their religious beliefs. They grated on Morris's moderation and sense of humour. He not only revelled in the hospitality of his patrons but also indulged in the more earthy pursuits of less-exalted poets. There are carols describing the welcome afforded to the poet, with an abundance of ale and bragget being a notable feature. Although the broaching of barrels was a pastime much enjoyed and generosity the virtue most prized, drunkenness was not countenanced—the point of the drinking was the companionship engendered. At such times, as in the strict-metre tradition, carousing gave rise to humourous and funny songs and Morris was not averse to producing such poems to entertain a merry audience. One such, aimed at both men and women, was *Hanes Gwragedd Llundain* (The Story of the London Wives). This was a well-known motif, where women lamented the shortcomings of their husbands. In Morris's version, six wives lay claim to having the worst husband and most cause of complaint in marriage. Humour is its keynote, not moralizing, for in the end and despite everything, the wives conclude that married love is the truest.

Two of the most charming of Morris's poems are those where he sends Summer as a messenger to his lady love and Winter to the kinsmen of Wiliam ap Thomas in Dolwyddelan. These are fine examples of the same motif employed for quite different purposes. *Carol yn gyrru'r Haf at ei gariad* is a dialogue between the Lover and Summer in which Summer, personified very much in the Dafydd ap Gwilym mode of a young, generous nobleman scattering flowers and nature's bounty, agrees to take a message to the Lady and the virtues of summer as a season for lovers is extolled:

> Y Cymro llawn pleser, prysura at ei mwynder,
>   Cyn darfod fy nghwarter, fy llawnder a'm lles;
> Mi fydda'n ufuddol, o'th du di'n wastadol,
>   I'w denu hi i'r faenol, aur fynwes.

[You Welshman full of pleasure, hurry to her gentleness/ Before my quarter ends, my fullness and my benefit;/ I shall be obedient, constantly on your side,/ To entice her, golden hearted, to the dale.]

The Winter poem shows that although the cold, storms and short days and long nights of winter are recognized, it is also the season when man's thoughts turn to his kinsmen, especially at the time of Christ's Nativity, and Winter acknowledges Wiliam ap Thomas's love of his country. The poem was considered by Gwenllian Jones to reflect Edward Morris's thoughts on his many winter sojourns in southern England, when he would have much preferred to have been at home with his family:

> Lle mager y Cymro y chwennych ef dario,
>   Fe gâr y fan honno er llwyddo'n yr lled;
> Pe câi o fyd diball, can gwell mewn gwlad arall,
>   Ni feder ef ddeall mo'i ddäed.

[Wherever a Welshman is reared that is where he wishes to tarry,/ He loves that place despite succeeding elsewhere;/ If he had a world without stint, a hundred times better in another country,/ He cannot understand that it is better.]

The preponderance of the *tri thrawiad* metre over all others is particularly obvious in the work of both Huw Morys and Edward Morris, except that the former experimented with a greater variety of metres. This is true of the work of most of the free-metre poets of the second half of the seventeenth century, to the detriment of poetry, as J. Glyn Davies claimed many years ago: 'There is a lot of bad work in the Tri Thrawiad metre, which is too long for what it usually has to say.' The popularity of the *canu caeth newydd* was more an eighteenth-century phenomenon, as Parry intimated and Millward's anthology amply testifies. In the second half of the seventeenth century Huw Morys was a *rara avis* and few had the expertise to follow him, but his example became more accessible in the following century.

The *tri thrawiad* did not find favour with the most published poet of pre-nineteenth century Wales, Rhys Prichard (*c.* 1579–1644) *yr Hen Ficer* (the Old Vicar). About fifty editions of his work appeared between 1659 and 1820 with several large compendia appearing later in the nineteenth century. There were four separate editions in 1770 alone and another three in 1771, but in the present century not one edition of the complete works has appeared nor is this likely to happen ever again. Fashions in poetry change, and interminable sequences of quatrains, rhyming aabb with a steady iambic rhythm, seem dull in the extreme, while the theology and moral ideas do not accord with our times. But the very features that deter the modern reader were the ones that made the work attractive to earlier generations, many of whom were illiterate, or barely literate. The short lines and verses, the monotonously regular rhythm and the obvious rhymes all made the verses immediately accessible and memorable. In one verse the Vicar explains why he chose to write his verses:

> Abergofi pur bregethiad,
> Dyfal gofio ofer ganiad
> A wnaeth im droi hyn o wersau
> I chwi'r Cymry yn ganiadau.

[The complete forgetting of pure preaching,/ the diligent remembering of frivolous verse/ made me turn these lessons/ into verses for you Welsh (people).]

He maintained, probably correctly, that the verses were very easy to remember:

[Marginal handwritten notes:]

y Ficer

Hanes / Cyhoeddi / ei waith

Ei waith = pam / yn boblogaidd / yn ei oes, pam / ddim cynaint / hedaiu.

Ni cheisiais ddim cywreinwaith
Ond mesur esmwyth, perffaith,
Hawdd i'w ddysgu ar fyr dro
Gan bawb a'i clywo deirgwaith.

[I did not attempt any work of art,/ only a smooth, perfect metre,/ easy
to learn in a short time/ by everyone who might hear it thrice.]

Many of these quatrains fall into the trap of too-easy
versification—the rhymes are usually the obvious ones and he was
quite blatant in recycling his own work, with the same lines
appearing in different poems. Favourite characters from the Bible
and well-known heroes of antiquity are used several times to
illustrate moral points. Alexander the Great was a great stimulus to
his imagination and appears several times as a warning to sinners:

> Alexander a goncwerodd
> Yr holl fyd, y ffordd y cerddodd;
> Ond y ddiod, yn dra 'sgeler,
> A goncwerodd Alexander.

[Alexander conquered/ the whole world whichever way he traversed;/ but
drink, very infamously,/ conquered Alexander.]

In another poem differing only in the third line, it was death that
conquered him, *Angau, gwedi'r concwest 'sgeler/ A goncwerodd
Alexander*. In yet another poem, Alexander is used twice as an
example, once as a drunkard destroyed by wine, *Gwin orchfygodd
Alexander*, but later he is lauded as a plain eater. Other characters
appearing frequently are Daniel, David, Dives, Zacchaeus, Rachel,
etc. but these portrayals are not always consistent.

Rhys Prichard was born about 1579, the eldest son of a
reasonably prosperous family in Llandovery. He matriculated at
Jesus College in 1597, then the most Protestant as well as the most
Welsh of the Oxford colleges. The strict religious regimen of Jesus
impressed itself deeply on the young man, becoming a feature of his
own life and a standard which he forever urged on others, especially
his only son, Samuel. He graduated in 1602 and in September came
to Llandingad in Llandovery, a living which he held until his death
in 1644. It is as the vicar of Llandovery that he is always known,
although he later attained higher office culminating in the
chancellorship of St David's cathedral in 1626. But it is with the

ordinary people of his town and parish that his poems deal, and it was for their spiritual welfare that he composed his hundreds of easily remembered verses.

Most of the poems were written between about 1615 and 1635. The Sami poems, written to his son while at school and later at Oxford, can be dated to 1615–25. One of these refers to him as being *Plentyn bach o ddeng mlwydd oedran* (a small child ten years old) and that would be about 1615. There is also *Cyngor Episcob i bob enaid oddi vewn y Episcobeth* (A Bishop's counsel to every soul within his diocese), bound with a Catechism intended for a child about to be confirmed and printed in 1617, the only poem to appear in print during the Vicar's lifetime. It is possible that both were written to prepare Samuel for his confirmation in his early teens. I have shown elsewhere that some of the poems used the 1629 translation by Rowland Vaughan of Lewis Bayly's *The Practice of Piety* (*Yr Ymarfer o Dduwioldeb*), and are therefore post-1629. The famous poem extolling the virtues of the 1630 edition of *Y Beibl Bach* (the Little Bible) needs no comment and clearly dates that particular poem. Otherwise, the poems are undated and are, indeed, timeless.

The Vicar ministered to a flourishing population in the town of Llandovery, a rapidly growing droving centre. The lush pastures of the upper Tywi Valley provided an ideal gathering place for herds driven from west Wales to England, but the trade brought problems as well as profit in its wake. The seasonal influx of drovers and their camp-followers into a small rural town affected its social stability: while it brought prosperity to innkeepers, smiths and farriers, and later supported the first Welsh bank, it also brought less desirable elements, in the form of hordes of unruly, rootless men, intent on easing a hard and callous life with whatever entertainment and comfort the town could offer. As in the frontier towns of the American West, taverns, alehouses and brothels (*stywdeiau*) sprang up in Llandovery to service this transient population, and the Vicar chastised the populace in much the same way as the hellfire preachers of the Westerns were to do later; he begged them to repent of their sins before the wrath of God descended to destroy the town in his famous poem, *Mene tecel, tre' Llanddyfri*. These words, from the story of Belshazzar's feast in the Book of Daniel, when the Babylonian king and his concubines were desecrating the holy vessels rifled from the temple in Jerusalem, make it quite clear which sins the Vicar had in mind. Other words in the poem reinforce this—*brynti, anwiredd, sorod, meddwdod, puteindra* (filth, dishonesty, dregs, drunkenness, prostitution)—and the town is explicitly compared to Sodom and Gomorrah, the most notoriously dissolute towns in the Bible.

These people would almost certainly be illiterate. The Bible was translated into Welsh in 1588 and revised in 1620 by learned Renaissance scholars. These Bibles had been read in every church in Wales for a generation as had the translation of the Book of Common Prayer. Edmwnd Prys's Psalter might have been used in many parish churches also, but all these tomes had one enormous drawback as far as the Vicar of Llandovery was concerned—the language in which they were written was standard literary Welsh, predominantly the dialect of north Wales that was the accepted language of the poets and prose-writers. The translators had striven to clothe God's Word in the most elevated language possible and, since most of them were from the north, the Welsh of Holy Writ was probably unintelligible to the people of Llandovery. Rhys Prichard was nothing if not a populist; he was a persuasive preacher, and it is reputed that crowds came to listen to him at Llanedi, where he is supposed to have had a portable pulpit in the churchyard, and at St David's, where the nave of the cathedral was said to be too small to contain them. He realized that the noble cadences of the Bible and the Book of Common Prayer, the standard service of the Anglican Church, were way beyond the comprehension of his listeners even though they were in their own language. He therefore set out to adapt the Bible for their needs. His poems tell stories, from the Garden of Eden through the Old Testament to the Nativity, and the main stories of the life of Christ, culminating in the Crucifixion and Resurrection. But he does not stop there since he also versifies some of the most complex theological concepts ever to have engaged the human mind. This he does with consummate competence and confidence in poem after poem, uniting the simple story and the theology as in his most popular work, the Christmas poem, *Awn i Fethlem* (Let us go to Bethlehem). The first forty-four lines tell the story of the Nativity as related in the Gospels of Mathew and Luke, with all the well-loved elements included—the full *ostri* (hostelry), the stable, the star, the shepherds, the Magi with their gifts of gold, frankincense and myrrh, and the choir of angels. But the remainder of the poem,

[handwritten marginal notes:] Anllythrennedd a diffyg dealltwriaeth ar Gymraeg "Churfiol yr bês" —Ficer yn sylwi ar hyn

Beibl yn ei gredd:

lines 45–104, confronts squarelý the doctrine of the Incarnation and sets forth in simple language the paradoxes of God made Man, the Creator becoming one of His own creatures, and the Father/Son being suckled by the daughter/mother:

> Awn i weld y ferch yn Fam
> A'r Fam yn Ferch ddi-nwyf, ddi-nam:
> Y ferch yn magu 'Thad o'i rwymyn
> A'r Tad yn sugno bronne'r plentyn.

[Let us go to see the daughter as mother/ and the mother a daughter, faultless:/ the daughter nursing her father in his swaddling-clothes/ and the Father suckling the child's breasts.]

Prichard's grasp of Protestant teaching was deep: he did not shy away from difficult doctrines and he was uncompromising in his dismissal of what he regarded as Roman Catholic dogma.

But the Bible was not the Vicar's only source of inspiration. As already mentioned, he paraphrased several passages from *Yr Ymarfer o Dduwioldeb*, Rowland Vaughan's translation in 1629 of Lewis Bayly's *Practice of Piety*, a devotional book addressed mainly to heads of households who were expected to interpret the devotions and to institute the observances of holy living advocated in it in their own families. Like the *Ymarfer*, Prichard wrote poems and exhortations covering every conceivable action from getting up in the morning to retiring at night; from breast-feeding babies to putting affairs in order before dying; from preparing for a journey to prayers whilst engaged in any number of occupations.

The Vicar's language has been a stumbling block to many people who have discussed his verses. His first editor, Stephen Hughes, complained that the language contained too many English words as well as too many southern dialect forms. He went as far as to employ a Caernarfonshire man, Henry Maurice, to gloss the text for the benefit of 'our dear neighbours in Gwynedd' so they 'can participate more fully of the beneficial knowledge which is to be had in this booklet'; and Maurice glossed and reformed (*diwygio*) to his heart's content. The 1681 edition restored some of the dialect endings, but even so, the language quite clearly is not that of the Vicar Prichard—it is a sanitized and standardized version of his dialect that appears in all the printed editions. Manuscript sources for some of the poems, which predate the printed versions by over twenty years, are a far more reliable guide to the language of the

Vicar Prichard. As he himself stated, his concern was to make his verses memorable and to this end he used the language of the people for whom he was writing—dialect, corrupt vocabulary, English borrowings and all. His verses were an *aide-mémoire* for his listeners to take away with them from his sermons, so that they would remember the Bible stories and the doctrines necessary for salvation. The close link between the Vicar's poems and his preaching is revealed in the manuscript of sermon notes in his own hand in Jesus College Oxford MS 145, and in the sermon published in 1802, where several phrases echo phrases found in the poems.

Rhys Prichard died at the turn of the year 1644/5; how he, a faithful adherent of Church and state, would have reacted to the execution of Charles, king by divine right, is not difficult to imagine. Fortunately, he was not called upon to witness such atrocities.

Plenty of other poets did, however, and they expressed their outrage in their poems, although many were sufficiently circumspect to muffle their most strident criticisms until after the Restoration when it became customary to castigate Cromwell and all his works. Most of the Welsh poets supported the king's cause as (on the whole) did their paymasters, the gentry. But the outstanding literary personality of the Civil War period was firmly on the Puritan side and although his fame rests on his prose-writing rather than on his poems in English and Welsh, these cannot be totally overlooked. He was Morgan Llwyd (1619–59), the son (or grandson) of Huw Llwyd, Cynfal, Ardudwy. The latter was also a poet, who 'sang on his own food' (*canu ar ei fwyd ei hun*), as well as being a soldier of fortune in the Low Countries in the last decades of the sixteenth century. He returned to Cynfal to the life of a Welsh *uchelwr*, and was a generous patron to other poets as well as a practitioner in his own right, in both strict and free metres. It seems that Morgan Llwyd did not inherit Huw Llwyd's skill as a *cynganeddwr*, however, as his few experiments in that field are singularly inept.

Over fifty poems, in English and Welsh, overwhelmingly in a simple ballard metre, are attributed to Llwyd and many are in his own handwriting. These can all be classified as 'religious', since even poems with titles like 'The English Triumph over Scottish Traitors' are essentially of a religious nature; for Llwyd every aspect of life was permeated with religion. M. Wynn Thomas, in his monograph on Llwyd in the *Writers of Wales* series, maintains that despite Llwyd's mastery of the English language, his poetry in Welsh:

> is significantly richer in its social connotations, its personal reverberations and its literary quality,

because:

> Llwyd's sensibility had been decisively formed by a specifically Welsh culture, so that it is only when he uses the vernacular that the fine nexus of his powers of mind and feeling is fully evident.

The autobiographical poem *Hanes rhyw Gymro* was analysed by Hugh Bevan, who showed that the biographical details take on a universal quality, so that the towns visited by Llwyd become symbols of transience in an age of change, but then lead on to the picture of the nature of God as fixed and immutable:

> Duw a'm carodd, Duw a'm cofiodd,
> Ceisiodd, cafodd, cadwodd, cododd;
> Haul fy mywyd drwy farwolaeth,
> Ffynnon f'ysbryd, swm fy hiraeth.

[God loved me, God remembered me,/ He sought, got, kept, raised [me];/ The sun of my life through death,/ The fountain of my spirit, the sum of my longing.]

Nevertheless, with a few notable exceptions such as this poem and *Caniadau: Ar ôl tôn psalm 113*, it is unlikely that Llwyd's reputation would be as high as it is today had he written only poetry.

The breakdown in the social fabric and the disorientation which is revealed in some of these poems no doubt hastened the end of the old system of patronage, although it had proceeded apace even before the turbulence of the Civil War, as the second chapter in this volume makes clear. The most interesting poems of this period, however, are not the work of the dwindling ranks of professional bards but of the gentry themselves. These poets, essentially amateurs, used free metres as they wished and some interesting experiments are found in their work. The poems of a great number of these gentry poets are preserved in the manuscripts, but here a few will be referred to as representative of a large and popular group.

They are Rowland Vaughan, Caer-gai, Llanuwchllyn (1587?–1666), already referred to as the translator of Lewis Bayly's *Practice of Piety*; his elegist, John Gruffydd, Llanddyfnan (*c.* 1611–69); Wiliam Salesbury '*Hen Hosananu Gleision*' (1580–1660); and Wiliam Phylip, Hendrefechan, Llanaber (?1579/80–1670). All four lived through the turbulent years of the Civil War, the Commonwealth and Protectorate and all survived to see Charles II restored to his martyred father's throne, although Salesbury died almost immediately after the Restoration. All four were ardent Royalists and all suffered to a greater or lesser degree because of their allegiance to the king. Vaughan saw his home, Caer-gai, burnt to the ground by vengeful Roundheads in 1645, and Wiliam Phylip's most famous poem is his poignant farewell to his home, Hendrefechan, although the date of that event is not known. Vaughan fought at the king's side at Naseby in 1645. Salesbury entertained Charles I for four days in September 1646 in Denbigh Castle, which he had restored at his own expense; the old cavalier told his sovereign a few home truths during that stay and made such an impression on Charles that before his execution the king sent him a gold-embroidered cap as a keepsake. Wiliam Phylip wrote a long *cywydd* on the death of Charles, and Vaughan translated Charles's *Eikon Basilike* within a year of the execution, an obvious work of *pietas*.

All four wrote free-metre poetry—but Salesbury was the only one not to write in the strict metres as well. The other three used the *cerdd dafod* metres for elegies and begging poems, but for their religious and more overtly political poems they used free metres. Salesbury was influenced by the Vicar Prichard and, as I have argued elsewhere, acquired a manuscript (or manuscripts) of the Vicar's poems before 1637, which he copied twice, with very great care. Salesbury's own quatrains, written between 1655 and 1659, bear a superficial resemblance to the Vicar's verses but do not have the didactic vitality and overwhelming sense of zeal that permeate the Vicar's work. Salesbury's quatrains are more personal and have a sad, elegiac quality that reflects, perhaps, the personal tragedies that beset him after a lifetime of striving:

> Fy Nuw, di a roist im fwy na rhan
> O dda'r byd bychan, nwyfus;
>   Cymer fy nghalon, Un Duw tri,
> I'th foli Di'n awyddus.

[My God, you gave me more than a share/ Of the goods of the small, passionate world;/ Take my heart, three in one God,/ To worship you eagerly.]

>Bu farw'r hen gymdeithion
>Oedd gynt yn gywir galon;
>>Nid oes heddiw yn eu lle
>Ond haid o lancie ffolion.

[The old companions have died/ Who were once of true heart;/ Today, there is instead of them/ Only a flock of foolish lads.]

Vaughan was the most innovative and yet the most derivative of the four; an accomplished translator of prose, he also adapted one of the great morale-boosting poems of the king's cause, Martin Parker's *When the King enjoys his own again*, published in 1643, as *Nes caffo Charles ei eiddo ei hun*. Two of the verses are direct translations, but Vaughan added two extra verses to Parker's original five:

>Llawn ddeugen mlynedd yn ddiwad
>Bu'n gwisgo'r goron, fo a'i dad
>Ar dair teyrnas ymhob man
>Heb neb yn gofyn hawl na rhan;
>>Pwy ddyle fod yn ben i'r nod
>>Ond rhain sydd gyfion aer bob un?
>>Bid siŵr na bydd mo'r byd yn rhydd
>>Nes caffo Charles ei eiddo'i hun.

[Full forty years the royal crown
Hath been his father's and his own;
And is there anyone but he
That in the same should sharer be?
>For who better may the sceptre sway
>Than he that hath such right to reign?
>Then let's hope for a peace, for the wars will not cease
>Till the King enjoys his own again.]

The bitter *Cân neu ddameg pan dorrwyd pen y Brenin 1649* (A song or parable when the king's head was struck off) belongs to a popular genre of describing historical incidents as a game of cards, but there is no exact parallel with this poem which immediately presents itself.

Vaughan's best political poem is undoubtedly *Gyrru'r gath trwy Feirionnydd* (Sending the cat through Merionethshire) in which his innovative skills are apparent. He adapts the old Welsh motif of a *llatai* (messenger, often a love-messenger) by sending his cat from Caer-gai in Penllyn to the besieged castle at Harlech, with messages of encouragement and news for the garrison. He outlines the journey from Penllyn to Harlech and tells the cat which Royalist households to visit and which areas to avoid:

> Hwi! dos y ffordd yr archa'
> At weddw lân o'r fwyna';
>   Y Rhiw Goch yw pen dy daith
> Yr ai di y noswaith gynta'.

[Hwi! go the way I tell you/ To a fine lady of the gentlest;/ Rhiw Goch is the end of the journey/ You go on the first night.]

On the bare uplands however, the cat must take extra care:

> Tra bytho'r dydd yn olau
> Carlama dros y pyllau
>   I gael ymborth, gwen ei phryd
> Llygota 'r hyd y Creigiau.

[Whilst the daylight lasts/ Hasten over the puddles/ To receive sustenance, white her face,/ Catching mice along y Creigiau.]

This is a delightful poem as the cat never loses its feline characteristics, although it carries the burden of all the worries of the Royalists as they watched their cause declining visibly in the winter of 1646–7.

In the following year, 1648, John Gruffydd gives an eyewitness account of the attack by the Roundhead army on Anglesey; he blames the arrogance and sinful conceit of the islanders for the defeat that followed:

> A ni yn amharod a'r milwyr mewn cychod
>   Yn dyfod, a'n pechod a'i parai;
> Pan oeddem ni yn cysgu yn esmwyth ar fanblu
>   Hwy ddaethant i fyny tros Fenai.

[And we were unprepared and the soldiers in boats/ Were coming, and it was our sin that caused it;/ Whilst we were sleeping comfortably on down/ They came up over the Menai [straits].]

The consequences of the defeat and the overthrow of the old order is portrayed vividly in his *Cân a wnaed yn amser Oliver Cromwell* (A song made in the time of Oliver Cromwell). In this long poem the structure is simple— a series of descriptions of ordinary craftsmen who have usurped the position and manners of their 'betters':

> Y mae'r cwriwr berrau brain
>   Fu gynt yn hoffi'r gyllell fain,
> Yn awr mae'n yfed gwin a sac,
>   Ni lefys undyn ddwedyd 'cwac';
> Y mae'r sparc yn cadw parc
>   A chantho geirw, lawer un;
> Mae'n noblaf syr â'i ffan a'i ffyr
>   A rapier feindlws wrth ei glun.

[The currier [leather worker] with crow-like shanks/ Who used to like the slender knife,/ Now he drinks wine and sack [sherry],/ No one dares say 'Quack!';/ The spark keeps a park/ And he has deer, many a one;/ He is the noblest sir, with his fan and fur/ And a pretty, slender rapier on his thigh.]

The thresher, swineherd, weaver, fuller, tinker, miller, tanner, barber, cobbler, cooper, slater, saddler, glover, butcher, innkeeper, hatter, joiner, mason, glazier and the fiddler, are all satirized in language Ellis Wynne would have been proud to have written. The poem gives a vivid picture of 'a world turned upside-down'; this had been a rural society self-sufficient in all its needs which had been totally devastated by the Civil War, and the lost world of the pre-war period is viewed, no doubt, with rose-tinted spectacles; in short:

> Fe aeth y gweision bob yn fil
>   A'r morwynion wrth eu sgil . . .
> Yn well eu hynt na'u meistriaid gynt

[The servants in their thousands/ Followed by the serving wenches/ . . . Have become better their lot than their erstwhile masters.]

Gruffydd's most interesting poems are probably the dialogues between himself and his uncle, Richard Bulkeley, Cleifiog (d. 1659), a skilful poet in his own right, who wrote some charming love poetry. In these dialogues, the first written during the Civil War and the second during the days of Cromwell's ascendancy, the nephew asks his uncle whether the old world would ever return.

> A ddaw'r brenin i'w gyfiawnder?
> A ddaw'r eglwys i'w hen arfer?
> A ddaw'r deyrnas yn heddychlon?
> A ddaw byth y byd a welson?

Ni ddaw heddwch i'r teyrnasau,
Ni ddaw'r eglwys i'w hen ddeddfau,
Ni ddaw'r brenin yn ben llywydd
Nes cael cymod Duw o newydd.

[Will the king come to his justice?/ Will the church come to its old custom?/ Will the kingdom become peaceful?/ Will the world we saw ever come [back]?

Peace will not come to the kingdoms,/ The church will not come to its old rules,/ The king will not become chief ruler/ Until we are reconciled to God anew.]

Despite the fact that he could and did write in the strict metres, Gruffydd was conscious of the distance between himself, an amateur, and the professional bards; he mourned the death of the 'last' of the bards when Gruffudd Phylip died in 1666—*Darfu'r henfeirdd heirdd a'u hurddas—i gyd* (The excellent old poets and their dignity have all died); as an *uchelwr* he did not consider himself a bard in the same way as one of the Phylipiaid of Ardudwy. Similarily, Phylip Siôn Phylip, in his elegy on Wiliam Phylip, was anxious to stress that Wiliam Phylip was not an itinerant poet singing for profit, *Nid clerwr chwant cael arian / Ydoedd y glwys wawdydd glân*, but that he belonged to the same class as Vaughan and Salesbury, although by the end of his life he nowhere near matched them in wealth, as his will testifies. Wiliam Phylip's free-metre poetry again reflects the norm—he wrote pious, religious verses adhering strictly to Anglican teaching, such as *Carol o gyffes pechadur* (A sinner's confession carol):

Cyffesu 'rwy i'th unig Fab
  (Ac nid i'r Pab a'i senedd)
Fy mhechode a gofyn gras;
  Gwna Di â'th was drugaredd,

[I confess to your only Son/ (And not to the Pope and his curia)/ My sins and ask for grace;/ Deal mercifully with your servant.]

More interesting to us today, however, is a poem such as *Carol o ffarwel i'r dafarn* (A farewell carol to the tavern), which pictures a man leaving the merry company of the tavern for the delights of the woodlands and the companionship of the birds!

> Ffarwel godi'r fflagon las,
> Ffarwel gymdeithas ffyddlon;
> Ffarwel hefyd i bob ffrind,
> 'Rwy'n meddwl mynd yn hwsmon.

[Farewell to raising the blue flagon,/ Farewell faithful company;/ Farewell also to every friend,/ I am thinking of becoming a husband-man.]

Like Edward Morris he is most anxious to point out that it was not the drink as such which was the attraction of the tavern, but rather the companionship found there,

> Nid am gwrw meinir ffraeth
> Mae fy hiraeth creulon
> Ond cymdeithion glân di-fâr,
> Y sawl a gâr fy nghalon.

[It is not the beer of the saucy slender one/ that I long for cruelly/ But the fair, good tempered companions,/ Those whom my heart loves.]

Many other poets could be mentioned and discussed at length—interesting poets such as Mathew Owen, Llangar (d. 1679) whose *Carol o gyngor, yn galennig ir Cymru* (A carol of counsel as a New Year's gift to the Welsh) was published in Oxford in 1658; Dafydd Llwyd, Sybylltir (*c.* 1580–1657/8), who wrote some charming love poetry; Robert ap Huw (d. 1665), who combined the work of a harpist with that of a poet—and many, many others—but space does not permit.

Before ending, reference must be made to the lower order of poets whose poems are recorded in the manuscripts. There are many anonymous poems but quite a few bear the names of their authors, such as Siôn Rhosier y Gwŷdd, Dafydd ap Huw'r Gof, Wmffre Dafydd, Clochydd Llanbryn-mair, and many others who did not depend wholly or even mainly on their poetry for their livelihood. They usually wrote in strict metres as well as free metres, and often practised the whole gamut of genres, eulogies, elegies, begging poems, love poetry, bawdy verses, comic verses recording funny adventures in a particular vicinity, or religious poetry such as the *halsingod* (<ha(i)lsing = 'greeting, farewell'). The *halsingod* were a form of religious verse peculiar to the environs of the Teifi Valley,

and confined in time mostly to the years between the Civil War and the Methodist Revival. There are about forty named authors of these poems and many were clergymen, following in the path of the Vicar Prichard, since the *halsingod* had a definite didactic purpose, mainly teaching basic biblical knowledge to the illiterate and socially deprived. Some told Bible stories, others were prayers and supplications and all concentrated heavily on the themes of doom and destruction. Crude though most of these poems are in their poetic structure, it cannot be denied that they helped to prepare the way for some of the most profound changes in Welsh social life in the following century, particularly the Methodist Revival, and metrically they, together with the quatrains of Rhys Prichard, showed one of Wales's greatest poets, William Williams of Pantycelyn, the way to the nation's heart.

BIBLIOGRAPHY

Very little of the poetry of the seventeenth century has been published. A small selection can be found in the following volumes:

Nesta Lloyd, *Blodeugerdd Barddas o'r Ail Ganrif ar Bymtheg*, rhan 1 (Abertawe, 1993). (Rhan 2, due to appear in 1997, will be devoted to the poetry of 1650–1700.)
Thomas Parry, *The Oxford Book of Welsh Verse* (Oxford, 1962).
T.H. Parry-Williams, *Canu Rhydd Cynnar* (Caerdydd, 1932).

The works of individual poets can be found in the following volumes:

T.E. Ellis, *Gweithiau Morgan Llwyd o Wynedd*, I (Bangor, 1899).
David Jenkins, 'Bywyd a Gwaith Huw Morys (Pont y Meibion) (1622–1709)' (unpubl. University of Wales MA thesis, 1948).
Idem, 'Carolau Haf a Nadolig', *Llên Cymru*, 2 (1952–3), 46–54.
J.G. Jones and G.W. Owen, *Gweithiau Morgan Llwyd o Wynedd*, III (Caerdydd, 1994).
Nesta Lloyd, *Cerddi'r Ficer* (Abertawe, 1994).
Gwenllian Jones, 'Bywyd a Gwaith Edward Morris, Perthi Llwydion' (unpubl. University of Wales MA thesis, 1941).

The historical background is discussed in:

Geraint H. Jenkins, *Literature, Religion and Society in Wales, 1660–1730* (Cardiff, 1978).

CHAPTER 5

WELSH HUMANIST LEARNING

BRANWEN JARVIS

The attitude of the Welsh humanist scholars to learning was not a cold, dispassionate thing; nor was learning pursued in a spirit of self-interest. The scholars were fired rather by two great ideals: that of service to God and that of service to language and country. They laboured, in the words of Edward Kyffin, *er gogoniant i Dduw ac er mawrhad i'n hiaith* (for the glory of God and for the elevation of our language). They had other goals, too. In particular, they desired that ordinary people should be allowed to share in the new learning, both religious and secular, that they were working to promote. Much of their work therefore is, in a broad sense, educative in its nature and intent. William Salesbury expressed this desire to uplift ordinary people in words which have become famous as one of the keynote passages of Renaissance thought: *oni fynnwch fyned yn waeth nag anifeiliaid, mynnwch ddysg yn eich iaith* (unless you wish to become worse than animals, insist on having learning in your language).

The field in which these three ideals became as one was that of translating the Scriptures. The humanist scholars of northern Europe regarded the translating of the Bible into the vernacular tongues as the pinnacle of scholarly endeavour, and in this Welsh scholars were no exception. The full story of that endeavour is told in another chapter, but no discussion of Welsh humanist learning would be complete without noting the primacy of this aim. The scholars themselves, time and time again, give expression to the overriding importance of this work in their eyes. So William Salesbury, near the beginning of the Renaissance period, introduces his collection of Welsh proverbs, *Oll Synnwyr Pen* (All the Mind's Wisdom) (1547), a collection originally made by the poet Gruffudd Hiraethog, with an impassioned plea that the Scriptures be made available in Welsh. *Oll Synnwyr Pen* is not a religious work, but Salesbury gives priority in his introduction to emphasizing the necessity of having the Bible translated into Welsh. Only then does he set about explaining the importance of proverbs. Similarly, Maurice Kyffin, in 1595, introducing the translation he had made of Bishop Jewel's *Apologia Ecclesiae Anglicanae*, returns constantly in his introduction not to the importance of the tract he has translated but to the significance of the Welsh Bible of 1588: 'But since the book of God's word has now been translated into Welsh and printed, it no longer avails any of the Devil's children to try to darken the light of Wales'.

For Bishop Richard Davies, who translated part of the New Testament in 1567, to have the Scriptures in Welsh was 'a magnificent supremacy' (*ardderchog oruchafiaeth*). Some of the poets, too, expressed their gratitude that this great work had now been done. Siôn Tudur, in his *cywydd* of praise to William Morgan, describes the feeling of the times when he states that no nation can claim to possess learning without having the Bible in its own language:

> Pa ynysoedd? pa nasiwn
> Heb bwyll fawr hap y llyfr hwn ?
>
> [Which islands? which nations
> Have great learning without this book?]

Such examples could be multiplied. It is important to note here that we are not simply faced with two generations of humanist scholars paying lip service to the importance of scriptural translation and, secondarily, of works ancillary to the scripture-based Protestant movement. In this matter, by their fruits do we indeed know them. When the works produced by Welsh humanists are listed, beginning with the first printed book in Welsh, *Yn y llyfr hwn* . . . (In this book . . .) by Sir John Prys of Brecon (1546), and ending around 1632 with the *Dictionarium Duplex* of Dr John Davies (these being the generally recognized termini), a pattern emerges.

Of the works produced by the Welsh humanists, over two-thirds are religious in nature. However, a change, both in the number of works produced and in their content, can be discerned after the publication of the complete Bible in 1588. Up to 1588, humanistic writings, both religious and otherwise, are fairly thin on the ground. Pre-eminent amongst them however are the works of William Salesbury, and, notwithstanding the diversity of his scholarly interests, there is no doubt that the main thrust of his work is scriptural and Protestant in nature. The Catechism and the Book of Common Prayer, in translations by Salesbury and others, figure prominently in the list, but the most important work is undoubtedly the New Testament of 1567, translated by Salesbury, Bishop Richard Davies and Thomas Huet. The most extended piece of polemical writing in this period is Richard Davies's preface to the Testament, written in the form of a letter addressed to the people of Wales. This important work, too, identifies profoundly with Protestantism, and expounds upon the theme of vernacular scriptures as the most necessary product of learning.

By 1588, what may be termed the basic texts of religious scholarship, in a Protestant sense, were available. Thereafter, a marked change occurs. There is a great increase in the number of works produced, almost as though the appearance of a complete Bible had opened a floodgate. Moreover, these are no longer works of textual and liturgical scholarship. They are now devotional, explanatory and homiletic in content, and they join a small number of pre-1588 works of this nature produced by Welsh Catholics. It is these works which form the great bulk of Welsh Renaissance prose. Incidentally, the same comment can be made on the nature of the bulk of contemporary writing in England.

This, then, is the first thing that needs to be said about the work of Welsh Renaissance scholars: that these scholars themselves, both in their stated opinions and in the work which they produced, gave pride of place to fulfilling the need for religious works in the vernacular, and to biblical and liturgical translation first of all. The second thing is that Protestantism, as a movement, has humanist ideals of scholarship at its very core. Biblical scholarship is the most obvious example of one of the primary tenets of humanism, namely that 'new' learning should be based on the truths and glories of the past. In terms of biblical scholarship, this can be interpreted as a search for early sources and a sound knowledge of the languages of original texts. In more general European terms, this meant a resurgence of respect for the languages, literatures and ideas of the Ancient World, in particular the culture embodied in Latin, Greek and Hebrew writings. The translation of classical texts into contemporary languages is one of the most important facets of humanist learning throughout Europe. In Welsh, the influence of the Classics is most clearly seen in the dissemination of classical thought in the prefaces and dedications written by noblemen and men of letters to introduce their own books or those of their protégés. In these prefaces they are able, within the bounds of certain conventions, to give free expression to ideas and beliefs which are important to them. They are therefore a very valuable repository of contemporary thought. That thought is shot through with frequent references to classical literature and to the ideas expressed therein, 'the endless re-expression of the commonplaces of ancient ethics', as Douglas Bush, writing of English authors, described it.

There is, however, little direct translation of classical texts into Welsh. The best-known example, for modern readers, is Gruffydd Robert's translation of part of Cicero's *De Senectute*, but this work was little known in Wales during the sixteenth century. However great was the humanists' professed admiration for classical literature, however highly skilled they were as Latinists (and in some cases as scholars of Greek and Hebrew), the 'past' was for the Welsh humanists overwhelmingly a Welsh one. They were steeped in traditional Welsh learning. Their command of the Welsh language, the cornerstone of so much of their achievement, was the result of their immersion in their native linguistic and cultural inheritance. Thus, many of the religious terms used by William Salesbury, for example, are not contemporary inventions, but can be traced back to the medieval text known as *Llyfr yr Ancr*, the Book of the Anchorite.

The flowering of Welsh humanist learning resulted from the pollination of this Welsh seed by outside influences. Welsh humanist scholars were educated at the universities of Oxford and Cambridge, where they found themselves profoundly influenced by contemporary thought. Sir John Prys, William Salesbury, the historian and geographer Humphrey Lhwyd, the grammarians and lexicographers Thomas Wiliems and Henry Salesbury, Dr John Davies, to name a few of the most important, were all Oxford men; Edmwnd Prys, poet and scholar, and William Morgan were Cambridge men. The connections with the new grammar schools and with Oxford and Cambridge, it should be noted, were not always to the good. Some young Welsh scholars were influenced by their education to forget their linguistic roots, as Thomas Wiliems complains. He criticizes the 'scholars of the universities of Oxford and Cambridge' and warns them that they should 'feel shame, and remember their own country, when they speak a foreign tongue to their compatriots in preference to their delightful mother tongue, the sweet and mellifluous Welsh language'. However, the connection was, for many, productive and highly influential.

Other Welsh humanists, notably the grammarian Gruffydd Robert and Siôn Dafydd Rhys, grammarian, medical man and Italianist, enriched and broadened their culture by the long periods they spent living on the Continent. Gruffydd Robert lived and worked as a Catholic exile in Milan; Siôn Dafydd Rhys graduated as a Doctor of Medicine in the University of Siena. Welsh scholars of the sixteenth and early seventeenth centuries were open to the influence of the new European learning; were it not so, no body of work which could be described as 'Welsh humanist learning' would have been possible. It was not for nothing that William Salesbury referred to Desiderius Erasmus as 'the most learned and productive author in all Christendom'. The debt owed by Salesbury to Erasmus is but one of a myriad of debts and influences which together brought the European humanist movement to Wales.

However, as has already been noted, these Welsh humanist scholars, almost to a man, were also 'learned' in a purely Welsh sense, and it is important to note that embracing new languages and ideas did not imply the jettisoning of an earlier, native, body of learning. So Salesbury's introduction to *Oll Synnwyr Pen* contains passing references such as these (he is speaking of others before him who have interested themselves in proverbs): 'As did the rest of the learned scholars who were gathered to write the Law of Hywel Dda. And as did the learned poet who composed the *englynion* to the snow: and Aneurin Gwawdrydd who composed the *englynion* to the months, all these are full of proverbs.' The references here are to the work of the poets, but they are also to the body of Welsh medieval law known as the Law of Hywel. Salesbury's words remind us that learning, in a Welsh sense, was not confined to the bardic schools; it embraced also a body of prose-writing which was partly narrative, partly religious, and partly technical in nature.

However, for the Welsh humanists, the main guardians of past learning were the professional poets. Their literary and linguistic status was extremely high. Even in their present impoverished state, says Siôn Dafydd Rhys, 'there is no need for them, within their own literary forms, to yield anything to the Latin and Greek poets'. Much of their learning was included in what was known as *Tri Chof*

Ynys Prydain, the three 'memories' of the Isle of Britain. These were the history of the Welsh, or Britons; the Welsh language; and the genealogies of noble families. In other words, the poets were not simply learned in the field of traditional metrics and what may be called poetic rhetoric and stylistics; they were also scholars of Welsh history and of the Welsh language. Their role as guardians of the language was magisterial and was firmly based on centuries of traditional linguistic usage: they were, in the words of Dr John Davies, *vetustae linguae custodes* (the guardians of the traditional language).

It is significant that Welsh humanist scholars, who were themselves writers of prose, adopted this linguistic tradition in their own work rather than the standards and usages of the medieval prose tradition. Medieval writing was based largely on southern usage and is characterized by its liveliness and flexibility. The humanists chose rather to adopt the language of the poets, which was more closely allied to northern usage. The differences, however, should not be exaggerated. They are in no way comparable to the differences encountered by Italian humanists, who were faced with substantial dialect differences and the need to establish a new language from a far wider and less standardized base. The decision to choose Tuscan as a basis for literary Italian was made, at least in part, for the same reason as the lesser decision made in Wales: it was the language of the poets, and Dante in particular.

We should not forget, either, that the prose style of Welsh humanists is in many ways a new creation. It owes a great deal to contemporary influences, particularly in its emphasis on a complex rhetorical style and ornate phraseology. Rhetorical style was no mere ornament; it was an integral part of the armoury of a learned language, and both William Salesbury and Henri Perri produced handbooks on the subject, works which were greatly influenced by contemporary continental writings. Any analysis of the language actually used by the Welsh humanists would have to conclude that its most important features are this rhetorical, and sometimes laborious, complexity, and the striking richness of the vocabulary at the command of many of the humanists. Humanists complained at what they saw as a lack of 'learned' words in Welsh; what strikes the modern reader most often, however, is the abundance of what might be called 'traditional' words at the command of a writer such as Siôn Dafydd Rhys. The often magnificent showiness of many humanist writers however remains firmly based on their analysis of the grammar and usage of the poets. The grammar published in 1621 by Dr John Davies, the work which many would regard as the crowning glory of Welsh Renaissance scholarship, is just that. He describes, says G.J. Williams, 'the literary language, the language as it had been preserved in its purity from one generation to the next by the poets'. It is 'the final analysis of the language of the poets'.

The depth of knowledge of the poetic tradition, not unnaturally, varies from scholar to scholar. After all, these men were not professional poets. So insistent, however, were the humanists on the central importance of poetic learning that scholars such as Gruffydd Robert and Siôn Dafydd Rhys included sections on Welsh metrics in their grammars of the language. One or two produced their own separate bardic treatises. William Midleton, soldier and scholar, who produced a metric version of the Psalms, published *Barddoniaeth neu Brydyddiaeth* (Poetry or Metrics) in 1593; Tomos Prys, soldier, adventurer and metricist, wrote his own bardic grammar, which he intended for non-professional use. This, however, remained unpublished.

When scholars, therefore, turned towards the second great task that they had set themselves, that of analysing and enhancing their own language in order to make it a suitable vehicle for wide-ranging humanist learning, they started from a firm base. The Welsh language was no mere collection of dialects, no preserve of low-born illiterates; it was a sophisticated literary language with a generally recognized set of preferred forms and usages. The work of enriching vocabulary, of embellishing style and of classifying and explaining grammar and syntax, however, remained to be done. These tasks they shared with humanist scholars working in other vernacular languages, though the Welsh scholars themselves saw it differently: whatever its glorious past, the present state of the language, in their eyes, compared badly with the state of other modern European languages. Welsh lacked 'learning', in a contemporary humanist sense. This common complaint is really twofold, in that it encompasses both the lack of learned texts in Welsh and the unsatisfactory state of the language itself as a means of learned expression. Siôn Dafydd Rhys, in the introduction to his grammar of 1592, speaks for his fellow humanists when he notes the supremacy of other languages in this respect:

the ordinary languages, such as Italian, Spanish, French, German, English and Scots . . . which have met from time to time with scholars of language and supporters of language, most kindly disposed to protect and nurture and praise, each of them, his own language; so that in the end there is not a single one of all the ordinary languages that I have mentioned which does not have expressed in it all the arts in the world, described and ordered and preserved in print in books which will last as long as the firmament lasts.

Welsh scholars seemed to take little cognizance of the fact that much the same criticism was being levelled at these other languages in their own countries.

Much of the effort of the Welsh scholars, then, was directed towards overcoming this perceived deficit and to making the Welsh language a suitable tool for humanist learning. It was the vocabulary of Welsh which gained most attention. Welsh words, in the first place, needed to be listed and explained and, from the outset, Welsh scholars addressed themselves to the task of producing vocabularies and dictionaries which would fulfil a wider function than some of the earlier word-lists, produced mainly by poets, which existed in manuscript form. Professor J.E. Caerwyn Williams has pointed out that these pre-Renaissance vocabularies are remarkable in being Welsh–Welsh lists; contemporary vocabu-laries in other European languages are almost invariably Latin-vernacular (or vice versa). One conclusion which can be drawn from this is that Welsh was in fact, and was seen to be, a learned language, a language whose educated practitioners, poets, lawyers, doctors, divines, were working within a medium sophisticated and rich enough to require explanatory lists. There is a ring of self-confidence and self-sufficiency about the Welsh–Welsh nature of these lists. They point to a culture in which scholars felt at ease with their own language. Welsh Renaissance scholars inherited this confidence in the Welsh language as a medium of learning. In other words, there is a marked duality in their attitude. They recognized and praised its past glories; and however much they criticized the deficiency of its vocabulary in terms of 'new' Renaissance learning, they remained conscious of the learned traditions of the past and confident of its potential as the vehicle of humanist learning.

When the scholars of the Welsh Renaissance set about producing dictionaries, their intentions were twofold. First, they wished to collect and classify, and to augment where necessary, the lexicographical resources of the Welsh language. Furthermore, they wished to undertake this work in the spirit of openness and breadth of learning which characterizes humanism and to lay open to the world the riches of the Welsh language. To this end, they produced not the Welsh–Welsh lists of their predecessors but Latin–Welsh (and less importantly English–Welsh) dictionaries.

The first of these dictionaries was produced by William Salesbury. Of all Welsh Renaissance scholars, he is the most ambivalent in his attitude towards his native tongue. His great and pioneering work as a scholar of Welsh and as a translator of the New Testament into Welsh testifies to his love and deep knowledge of his language and of his commitment to serving her needs. On the other hand, he is constantly critical of what he sees as the poverty of resources of the language, and compares Welsh most un-favourably with English in this respect. He encouraged his fellow Welshmen to learn English, so that they might partake of the learning to be found expressed in that language, and his Welsh–English dictionary was produced to this end. *A Dictionary in English and Welsh* (1547), is described as a 'guide to reading and understanding the English language, a language today adorned with all kinds of highest learning, a language replete with its gifted supremacy'. Notwithstanding the order implied in the title, the dictionary is Welsh–English. Its primary function, therefore, is not to display and explain the riches of the English language nor to augment the resources of Welsh by seeking to provide 'new' words where deficiencies existed. William Salesbury was later to con-tribute to the work of enriching and enlarging the vocabulary of Welsh, particularly in his *Llysieulyfr* (Herbal) and in his translation of the New Testament, which lists alternatives and which also offers some very effective, newly minted words. Here, he is endeavouring to provide Welsh readers with a means of learning and understanding ordinary English words.

William Salesbury also comments on the pronounciation of English—comments which have, incidentally, been of great interest to phoneticists and historians of the English language. The introduction also reminds us how new the concept of a dictionary was. Mindful of his intended audience, he explains carefully in his introduction what a dictionary is, how it is arranged and how it should be used. Since the order is Welsh–English he must also explain that Welsh words undergo changes in initial sounds, and must be looked for in their proper, unmutated, forms. It is worth quoting some of Salesbury's instructions to his readers, so vividly do they remind us how new his work was and how much his readers needed to learn:

> And so all words which have *a* as the first letter at their beginning have been brought together to the same place; and all words starting with *b* as their first letter have been placed apart; and the words with *c* at their beginning have also been separated and placed apart . . . And in this way have all the others been arrayed to stand under the banner of their initial Captain-letter. And, as a result, when you wish to find the English for some Welsh word, look first of all which letter properly begins that word, and if it is *a* look for it amongst the list of words which begin with *a*, and in that place, corresponding to it in the list of English words, you will find the English for it. But take great care not to be deceived by mistakenly searching for a word out of its proper and appropriate place, as you might search for one of these words in the shape and form in which they lie in this verse, *Mae i mi gangen deg o fedwen* (I have a beautiful birch bough), as it is no use for you when looking for the English for *gangen* to look for it amongst the words beginning with *g*, but you should look rather amongst the words beginning with *c* [*k* in the original orthography], and the English will be alongside it. For the original, unchanged word is *cangen* not *gangen*. . .

William Salesbury's interest in sounds and sound-changes is seen again in a work published in 1550, described as *A brief and a plain introduction, teaching how to pronounce the letters in the British tongue.* The basic aim of this work is the reverse of that of the dictionary: it is to begin the task of describing and explaining the Welsh language to others. It is the earliest treatise on Welsh phonetics, and is therefore a good example of the pioneering nature of much of the scholarly activity of the mid-sixteenth century. Welsh scholars themselves were well aware of the newness of their work. They not infrequently apologize in their introductions for any deficiencies which may be found in their work 'as no-one has attempted to follow this path before us' (Gruffydd Robert), and, in a spirit of humanist generosity, invite others to utilize and improve upon the work which they have begun.

An interest in phonetics is also a feature of a dictionary produced later by another member of the Salesbury family, Henry Salesbury of Dolbeleidr, near Denbigh. His dictionary remained in manuscript form, but seems to have been fairly well circulated, as parts of it are incorporated into later works, in particular a vocabulary

compiled by the important eighteenth-century scholar and poet,
Ieuan Fardd (Evan Evans). The dictionary, to which Henry
Salesbury gives the title *Geirfa Tafod Cymraeg* (The Vocabulary of
the Welsh Tongue) is a Welsh–Latin compilation. Among its most
important features is that Henry Salesbury incorporates more than
the lexicographical and semantic information normally found in
dictionaries. In tabulated form, he also deals with matters of
orthography, grammar and phonetics, though it must be added that
his treatment of these matters is sometimes confusing. Another
feature is that Henry Salesbury is catholic in his attitude to the
words he includes: he appends a list of old words under the heading
Geiriau o hen Gymraeg a'u dehongliad (Words from old Welsh and
their interpretation), but he also devises new words when he sees the
need. Thus, we have words like *arnofio, arsgrifen, arsyth*, using the
prefix *ar*. Salesbury also draws from the bardic vocabularies and
from dialect sources. It also appears that he added to his work after
seeing the *Dictionarium Duplex* of 1632. His work was a continuing
labour, which remained incomplete and unpublished at his death
around 1637.

There is a sense of urgency about the work of several of the
Welsh Renaissance scholars, a sense of huge tasks needing to be
done. That it is better that these tasks be done inadequately to begin
with than to wait overlong for perfection is a recurrent theme. This
sense of urgency is palpable in the early writings of William
Salesbury: he insists that unless the work of perfecting and
enriching the Welsh language is undertaken in his own generation,
it will be too late thereafter—*bydd ry hwyr y gwaith wedyn*. His
Welsh–English dictionary, strange as it may seem on the face of
things, was part of his urgent scheme. By teaching English, which
he saw as a 'learned' tongue, to his fellow countrymen, he hoped to
educate them in humanist ideas. This newly embraced, humanist
learning could then be transferred to the Welsh language, thus
saving it from becoming no better than the 'twittering of wild birds
or the roaring of beasts and animals'.

Nearly sixty years later, the same sense of urgency and impatience
can be found in the work of another lexicographer, Thomas
Wiliems, author of *Trysor yr iaith Ladin a'r Gymraeg* (The Treasure
of the Latin language and the Welsh). His urgency is partly personal:
'my age increases, and warns me, to gather my bits and pieces ready
for my journey towards my true home, out of this present vale of

sadness'. He did indeed write his dictionary within the space of four years between 1604 and 1608, having, he says, given up hope that other Welsh scholars, whom he names as Dr John Davies, Henry Salesbury, Henri Perri (or Parry), and David Powel, were about to fulfil their intention of publishing dictionaries. He must, he says, do his duty by his people: 'I am bound . . . to work to the uttermost limit of my ability for my country and my natural mother tongue and my dearly beloved fellow countrymen throughout the whole of Wales'. However, the Latin–Welsh dictionary of Thomas Wiliems, which fills three thick manuscript volumes, had in reality been far longer in the making. 'For thirty years and more, constantly from that time to this', he tells us, he has been 'gathering a huge collection of Welsh words, old and new . . . to preserve our language for ever (if God sees it fit), to the shame and discomfiture of Judas and all enemies of the shining British tongue.'

The evidence of his long, hard labour has survived in manuscript collections. Gwenogvryn Evans describes part of the contents of Peniarth 188, a manuscript in the hand of Thomas Wiliems, as 'materials for a *Welsh Dictionary*, consisting of vocabularies, glosses, a very considerable number of illustrative quotations from the poets, the Welsh Laws, the prose Romances, etc.'. We also have versions, enlarged upon by Thomas Wiliems, of Wiliam Llŷn's vocabulary (corrected by William Salesbury) and of a vocabulary by the scholar and collector of manuscripts, Roger Morris of Coedytalwrn. The completed dictionary also draws upon Thomas Wiliems's own wide stock of Welsh words, including local and dialect words.

Professor J.E. Caerwyn Williams has shown how interdependent Welsh, and other, dictionary-makers of the Renaissance were. Lexicography was a new and developing art, a matter of 'devising, making a pathway and cutting the ice', as Thomas Wiliems has it. He himself, as we have seen, drew upon the work of earlier scholars and collectors of Welsh words; he also found a structural pattern for his work in the Latin–Latin dictionary of Ambrosius Calepinus, *Dictionarium Decem Linguarum* (so named after its illustrative examples from ten languages) and, in particular, the *Dictionarium Linguae Latinae et Anglicanae* of Thomas Thomas, which itself was based upon Calepinus. Thomas Wiliems set himself the task of finding, or where necessary inventing, a Welsh equivalent for the Latin words in Thomas Thomas's dictionary; a very considerable task which drew on all the resources available and which resulted in a wide-ranging work which included many archaic words, adaptations and neologisms.

In turn, Thomas Wiliems's dictionary constituted a source-book for the Latin–Welsh half of the celebrated *Dictionarium Duplex* of Dr John Davies, published in 1632. Dr Davies acknowledged his debt to Wiliems and his long labour, but is highly critical of his work and careful to point out that his own dictionary is more of a remaking than a wholesale borrowing: 'As for the Latin–British Dictionary, that of Thomas Wiliems, you will see it here, not directly copied from his manuscript, but having had added to it as many British equivalents of Latin words as was possible; cleansed of the almost endless faults of which it was full; so that it might be more concise and perfect . . . it could indeed be considered something new and different'.

John Davies explains in what regard in particular he has pruned and edited Thomas Wiliems's work. He has sought to weed out all words which are derivatives of root forms: for example, where an adverb is derived from an adjective, the adjective only is listed. He is similarly stringent in his choice of Welsh words for inclusion in the second half of the dictionary, including only a sufficient number of composite words, which he rightly extols as one of the glories of the Welsh language, to provide exemplary patterns. This disciplined, scientific approach to the matter of derivatives and compounds is typical of John Davies: he was a profoundly scholarly man, the most authoritative of all Welsh Renaissance writers in the field of language and literature.

He was also a highly conservative scholar. His instinct always is to look to the past. His prescription for the perceived paucity of words in seventeenth-century Welsh is to search for those words which already exist; new inventions will in most cases be found to be unnecessary. His defence of historical precedent in matters of vocabulary is vigorous. His work, he informs us, is based upon careful study of manuscript sources, and in particular upon the work of the poets: 'for, in order that this laborious work be more complete, I have read almost everything written in British, and especially the work of the poets, who claim for themselves (and that in every language) authority over words . . . they were of the greatest help to me concerning writing British words correctly and looking into their true meanings'.

John Davies's comments in his erudite and considered introduction to the *Dictionarium Duplex*, written in Latin, are the most
important manifestation of the conservative viewpoint in the
struggle to provide for Welsh a 'learned' lexicon. Other scholars,
particularly in the earlier part of the Welsh Renaissance, have a
more liberal approach, and are more conditioned than John Davies
to answering the need for the dissemination of learning among
ordinary Welsh readers. As the author of *Y Drych Cristnogol* (The
Christian Mirror) (1585), says:

> For if I selected old Welsh words which are not in use, not one in a
> hundred would understand half of what I was saying, although it were
> good Welsh . . .

To use old, scholarly words would therefore be an irrelevance
(*amherthynas*), and he deliberately uses words in common usage,
borrowed words and 'a mixture of the words of the South and of
Gwynedd', in order that 'ordinary people may understand the book
for their own good'. The same utilitarian argument is still heard at
the end of the period, in 1630, when Robert Llwyd, the translator of
a similarly hortatory work (Arthur Dent's *The Plain Man's
Pathway to Heaven*), declares that he has 'avoided, to the best of
my ability, words not in current use, settling on such well-used
words as the ordinary people of the country recognize and are
familiar with'. The result, incidentally, is a minor classic of lively
prose.

The arguments heard are not merely utilitarian, however. Other
scholars lay emphasis on the principles of the historical
development of languages, and stress that words which are in
common use, however debased (*sathredig*) they may seem, should
be accepted as being natural and inevitable. Both Gruffydd Robert
and Maurice Kyffin advocate the same procedure: choosing first a
word in common use, whether 'debased' or not; and then borrowing
from other languages to remedy deficiencies. Kyffin puts the matter
succinctly:

> I thought it best to omit the old Welsh words [margin: It is not the
> practice of any learned person to resurrect such obsolete words in any
> language in the world], those which have outgrown the knowledge and
> the usage of ordinary people amongst themselves, and have chosen the
> easiest, most accessible and well-used words that I could in order to

make the run of the expressions used clear and free of stumbling blocks for those who know only habitually-used Welsh. But for essential words, the substance of whose thrust or the significance of whose meaning could not be shown in Welsh, I have, according to the custom of the English language, French, the language of Italy, the language of Spain and a host of other languages, taken such from the Greek or the Latin, in the way in which it has been customary in most countries in Christendom for a long time.

Similarly, Gruffydd Robert emphasizes not just the need for borrowing, but its acceptability and its inevitability. One of the most important scholarly contributions made by him was his methodical and pioneering study of Welsh loans from Latin, which he used as a basis for devising new borrowings from Latin source-words.

Both these broad tendencies, the conservative/historic and the realistic/innovative, can be seen elsewhere in Renaissance Europe. In England, by the late Renaissance, there was in existence a school of linguistic scholars whose views correspond more or less to those of John Davies in Wales. The views of this school are partly a rebellion against the excesses of constant borrowing from Latin and other languages by those who are 'so Latin their tongues, that the simple can not but wonder at their talk, and think surely they speak by some revelation', in the somewhat satirical words of Thomas Wilson, and partly an awakening of pride in native linguistic resources as a result of a resurgence of esteem for all things Saxon. Richard Verstegan, for instance, claims that to bring in borrowed words corrupts the proud Saxon heritage of the English language, which is rich enough in itself to meet all demands:

. . . if ourselves pleased to use the treasury of our own tongue, we should as little need to borrow words from any language, extravagant from ours, as any such borroweth from us: our tongue in itself being sufficient and copious enough, without this daily borrowing from so many as take scorn to borrow any from us.

On the other hand, the views of such scholars as Gruffydd Robert and Maurice Kyffin are closely paralleled by such English scholars as George Chapman, the celebrated translator of Homer, who wrote:

All tongues have enriched themselves from their original (only the Hebrew and Greek which are not spoke amongst us) with good neighbourly borrowing, and as with infusion of fresh air and nourishment of new blood in their still growing bodies, and why may not ours?

The battle for learned words was fought from similar standpoints in both England and Wales, but this should not obscure the fact that there were important differences between what happened, and what was said, in both countries. When an overall survey is made of the opinions of English and Welsh scholars, it appears that the opinion of different schools of thought is more polarized in England than in Wales. There is a strong underlying unity of opinion amongst Welsh scholars which transcends any 'conservative' or 'innovative' approaches. This unity is rooted in a common respect for the recognized standards of the Welsh literary tradition, and for the linguistic resources of the poetic tradition in particular. This common ground prevents some of the excesses of theory and practice seen in England.

It must also be said that the effects of the Renaissance revolution in vocabulary proved to be more far-reaching on English than on Welsh. It is estimated that the vocabulary of English increased by one third during this period. Whatever complaints were voiced against 'inkhorn terms' or 'hard words', the end result of Renaissance linguistic endeavour was a language immensely enlarged and enriched. Welsh, too, was a richer language in 1650 than it had been in 1550, but its expansion was limited. No detailed study has yet been made of the vocabulary increases which occurred; none the less, it can safely be asserted that the enlargement of the Welsh lexicon was of a far smaller order than that of English.

Words did not just need to be revived, translated, or created anew; they also needed to be written down. Welsh scholars devoted part of their energy to the matter of orthography. The spread of printing had given impetus to the call for revision and standardization. A revised orthography was also considered a necessary aspect of elevating Welsh to the status of a learned language. It is noteworthy however that the attitude to orthography differs fundamentally from the attitude to enlarging vocabulary. In the case of the latter, emphasis is constantly laid upon custom and precedent in the matter of coining new words; in the case of orthography, the emphasis is rather upon reform based on rational and aesthetic principles.

Experimentation, therefore, is seen in the work of several important scholars. So radical were some of William Salesbury's reforms in the New Testament of 1567 that much opposition was engendered, and they may partly account for the fact that the translation as a whole did not receive the acclamation that later opinion accords it. He attempted to convey Latin affinities, some of them spurious, in the way Welsh words were written. One important innovation has survived to this day, although based on a false etymology. The singular and plural forms of the third person possessive pronoun, written as *y* in Middle Welsh, are written as *ei* and *eu* by Salesbury in an attempt to show that they are derived from the forms of *eius* in Latin. Other scholars were influenced by aesthetic considerations. So, Gruffydd Robert in his Grammar places a dot under *d* to convey *dd* [ð] or under *l* to convey *ll* [ɫ], 'in order to be rid of the unseemliness of doubling them' (*i ymwared â gwrthundra eu dyblu*). Others again wished to suggest morphological changes; Henry Salesbury thus writes *f* / *v* as *bh*, or *dd* as *dh*. The various reforms suggested by Renaissance scholars, of whom the above are examples, were incorporated into their own individual writing but did not in fact gain general acceptance. Maurice Kyffin, who, like Thomas Wiliems at a later date, opposed experimenting with orthography, knew that such efforts could not succeed: 'it is taking too much upon himself for one man, whoever he may be, to give out new letters and orthography and to believe that it behoves everyone to follow him'. The establishing of Modern Welsh orthography in reality proved to be a gradual and organic process, and ultimately owed little to dramatic innovations by individuals—sensible though some of these innovations undoubtedly were.

The drive to improve and standardize orthography is in fact part of a larger plan: that of making Welsh an ordered and regulated language. It was in an effort to achieve this end that several scholars set about producing grammars. The aim of Renaissance grammarians was, in the words of the first of them, Gruffydd Robert, to lead the language to the privileged status of art, *ei dwyn i fraint celfyddyd.*

Gruffydd Robert's *Gramadeg Cymraeg* (Welsh Grammar) whose publication was begun in 1567, has, improbably as this may seem given the subject matter, a romantic, almost an exotic air to it. Not only is it set in an Italian garden, it was actually written in Italy when its author, a Recusant clergyman, was a member of the household of the famed cardinal archbishop of Milan, Carlo Borromeo. The Grammar is framed as a conversation between Gruffydd Robert and his friend and fellow-Recusant, Morris Clynnog. The work is conceived and written in a form and style deeply influenced by the court culture and Ciceronianism of Renaissance Italy. Their conversation is leisurely and discursive: the friends take time to describe their surroundings and to complain at the fierce heat of the Italian summer, 'which is heavy for those brought up in a country as cold as the land of Wales'.

The elaborate sentences and conversational framework do not, however, mask the serious purpose of this book. It is in essence a technical treatise, and the dialogue form, used by classical writers and revived during the Renaissance, is a useful device for setting forth arguments and counter-arguments. It is a device particularly suited to Gruffydd Robert's work. His Grammar was a pioneering study. He explored avenues of knowledge which were new or barely trodden: it is a tentative work in many respects, and it is useful to have the testing mechanism provided by the dialogue form.

It is not only in style and format, however, that we discern the influence of the high Renaissance culture of which Gruffydd Robert was able to partake in Milan. His work was directly influenced by the ideas of the innovative Renaissance grammarians of Italy and France. It is not only in Welsh terms that Gruffydd Robert's work is to be considered new; it is noteworthy in that it predates similar 'new' grammars in England. To use a modern turn of phrase, Robert's work is at the cutting edge of sixteenth-century linguistic learning. It is, as G.J. Williams has pointed out, a combination of new ideas and of Gruffydd Robert's own incisive and original analysis of the language:

> But although he follows a pattern that he had seen in Italian and French grammars, yet, as far as I can judge, his work shows that he possesses more of the grammarian's talent for discerning what is important and to order his subject-matter than hardly any of his contemporaries.

Grammars, of a kind, had existed in Wales long before this. These were the bardic grammars intended as a digest of required learning and a kind of training manual for young poets. The best known of them, the *Pum Llyfr Cerddwriaeth* (The Five Books of the Poetic Art) of Simwnt Fychan, largely based on the work of Gruffudd Hiraethog, was in fact produced later than the first part of the *Welsh Grammar*, around 1570. From the point of view of comparison, and of what is meant in Welsh terms by 'traditional' and 'new' learning, a few points may be made. First, the bardic grammars, although intended as guidebooks for young poets, are in fact sparse in the information they give about the bardic craft. The poets' professional expertise was jealously guarded, and most bardic learning was transmitted orally. Second, the sections dealing with what we today would define as 'grammar' are based upon traditional Latin grammars. Third, in matters of approach and style they are prescriptive, direct and plain.

Gruffydd Robert's very different style has already been described. In the other two respects also, his approach differs greatly from that of his predecessors. Like them, he considered matters of metrical and poetic craft to be part of Welsh 'grammar' but he is motivated by different considerations. His wish is to disseminate knowledge of the bardic craft to ordinary Welsh readers. He is very much aware that he himself is not a trained, professional poet and that there are, therefore, many gaps in his knowledge. He complains too that, exiled as he is, he has no means of collecting and studying manuscript sources. So aware is he of his deficiencies that he says that 'it is better for Welsh people to seek education orally from the poets amongst them'. However, since the poets do not recognize this duty of educating ordinary people and explaining the intricacies of their craft to them, 'it is necessary for someone other to take it upon himself to set it out, if it is desired that knowledge of it should be spread over the whole country and imparted to all who desire it, so that every learned, godly and poetical man may have instruction in the fashioning of songs and *cywyddau* which are spiritually uplifting and virtuous'.

Gruffydd Robert's analysis is, unsurprisingly, deficient in terms of traditional bardic learning. However, the two sections of the Grammar which deal with poetry are significant in the newness and the originality of the comments made. Gruffydd Robert's vision for the future of Welsh poetry was not restricted by the hallowed yet confining rules of traditional metrics. He wished to see, in Welsh, poetry in the classical tradition, a tradition which a poet such as

Ariosto had harnessed for use in the vernacular. This could only be achieved by using the lowly 'free' metres, 'taking no account of any of the *cynganeddion*', and by giving content precedence over form. Two centuries later, the poet Goronwy Owen, exercised by the same ambition for the future of Welsh poetry, was forced to the same conclusion. But Gruffydd Robert's words went unheeded (and to a great extent unheard) by his own, and succeeding, generations. Goronwy Owen's words, too, fell on deaf ears. It was not until the middle of the nineteenth century that 'free' poetry was generally seen as a vehicle prestigious and elevated enough for the fulfilment of the highest poetic ambitions.

The greater part of Gruffydd Robert's work deals not with poetry, however, but with grammar in the more usual sense. As has been noted, the sections in the bardic textbooks dealing with conventional matters of grammar were in the medieval, Latinate tradition. Gruffydd Robert is once again new and radical in approach. Although he follows the bardic grammars in some matters, and uses their terminology, he sets out to do something which had not been done before, namely the description, by analysis and observation, of the living tongue. He aims at the general reader, or rather, the reader with an amateur's interest in reading and writing Welsh, not at the scholar, and he therefore writes in Welsh.

His considerable intellect, together with a particular bent for linguistic analysis, produced a description of contemporary Welsh which is frequently highly perceptive. Many of the most important features of Welsh grammar were noted for the first time by Gruffydd Robert.

Other grammars of Welsh were later produced by Henry Salesbury and Siôn Dafydd Rhys, but it was Dr John Davies who, in 1621, produced the definitive Welsh Renaissance grammar. Indeed, Dr John Davies's work remained the definitive grammar of the language until the early twentieth century, when Sir John Morris-Jones, product of the new scholarly interest in Welsh and other Celtic languages at Oxford and the newly founded University of Wales, published his major study of the language, *A Welsh Grammar, Historical and Comparative* (1913). John Morris-Jones saw himself as heir to the tradition of John Davies, of whom he said: 'the author's analysis of the Modern literary language is final; he has left to his successors only the correction and amplification of detail'. In the opinion of G.J. Williams, the greatest historian of the

Welsh scholarly tradition, Dr John Davies's Grammar is the crowning achievement of the Welsh Renaissance.

Antiquae Linguae Britannicae . . . Rudimenta differs greatly from the Grammar produced half a century earlier by Gruffydd Robert. This is a work for scholars, written in Latin so that the world might know of the Welsh language and its glories. The preface written by John Davies, in the form of a dedication to his fellow humanist and churchman Edmwnd Prys, is a discourse upon the great antiquity of the Welsh language, its richness of style and vocabulary and its ancient status as a tool of learning. It provides an insight into John Davies's motivation for producing such a grammar, whose publication, he says, is the culmination of over thirty years' study during his leisure hours.

The Grammar is, then, a work of mature scholarship. That maturity has two aspects. First, John Davies wrote it at the end of an era. For eighty years, the Welsh language had been the object of study, analysis and steady enrichment by a body of humanist scholars whose devotion to it was remarkable and whose great efforts, variable in quality though they may have been, had laid some of the groundwork for John Davies. To say this is not to belittle his personal achievement in any way: his Grammar stands as the work of a prince among scholars. Second, John Davies's own thorough and painstaking preparations meant that he himself, after such lengthy study, was properly equipped to undertake the work.

His method is based to a great extent on careful use of manuscript sources. These sources were of fundamental importance for the whole field of humanist learning in Welsh. The printing press, for all its significance for the future, had thus far been used to publish a limited number of books, and most of these were religious in nature. The most important sources for the study of Welsh language and literature remained in manuscript form: no printed collections of prose or poetry, for instance, were published. Thus, any scholar who desired, as John Davies did, to publish a definitive and detailed study of the literary language had to have access to as wide a collection as possible of manuscript sources.

In this, he was fortunate. He was a native of Llanferres, on the eastern edge of the Vale of Clwyd, the major centre of Welsh scholarly and literary activity during the sixteenth and early seventeenth centuries. During his youth, he was able to read, and sometimes borrow, manuscripts collected by such important antiquaries as Roger Morris of Coedytalwrn, Richard Langford of Trefalun, and, later, his own contemporary, John Jones of Gellilyfdy—all of whom were natives of this north-eastern part of Wales. Later, many of these collections began to be dispersed. Fortunately, Robert Vaughan of Hengwrt near Dolgellau acquired many of them, and John Davies, who became rector of Mallwyd nearby in 1604, was again well placed to continue his researches.

Many of the manuscripts in the Hengwrt collection carry marks made by him. It is significant that it was the manuscripts of poetry which received by far the greater part of his attention. His analysis of the Welsh language is firmly based on the traditional usages of the professional poets, who, as we have seen earlier, were considered the guardians of the highest linguistic standards. Thus, this influential Grammar became a very important link in the chain of conservative linguistic usage which stretches from the later Middle Ages to the earlier part of the twentieth century.

For John Davies, as for earlier Renaissance scholars, the manuscripts in circulation at the time formed the tip of an iceberg. It is a constant refrain among Welsh humanists, from Sir John Prys and William Salesbury onwards, that the work of making Welsh a modern, learned language is hampered by the paucity of the historical materials to hand: they considered that, hidden away in cupboards and dark corners in the homes of careless and uncaring members of the gentry were hoards of books and manuscripts which would give weight to their dearly held belief that Welsh, in the past, had been a language of great richness and high learning. They also believed that much had been lost in fires and upheavals in times of struggle against the English. Bishop Richard Davies, for instance, urges his readers 'to recall to memory the loss of books of many kinds by the Welsh, books of art, of history, of genealogy, of blessed Scripture: all Wales has been entirely despoiled of them. For when Wales was subjugated to the English Crown by force of arms, there is no doubt that many of her books were destroyed in that struggle'.

It will be noted that Richard Davies believed that a Welsh translation of the Scriptures had been in existence in earlier times. This too was a commonly held humanist belief, a belief which was allied to the theory that, before the missionaries of the Roman Church came to Britain, the British (or Welsh) Church existed in a form untainted and unsullied by the corrupt practices of Rome.

Such an idea (which was also held in a more anglicized version by Archbishop Parker and other leaders in England as a belief in the existence of an *Ecclesia Anglicana*) served to support and uphold the restoration of a non-Roman Church in Britain. For the Welsh, who considered themselves the true heirs to all past British glories, the English being but latecomers to this island, a belief in the existence of such a Church was a boost to self-esteem and to that sense of pride which is a hallmark of so much of their writing.

There is a third strand also to this sense of pride in past glories. To their belief in linguistic and religious greatness in earlier times, the Welsh humanists added their belief in an ancient and elevated lineage: 'we, the nation of Britons of the exalted nobility of Troy', as the chronicler Ifan Llwyd ap Dafydd has it. Welsh humanists believed that their lineage could be traced back to Troy, and that their heritage included the glorious history of Arthur. Their history was also one of constant battle against the English, and of honour even in defeat against such an enemy. So, Richard Davies talks proudly of the 'dignity, respect, and worldly honour' due to the Britons, and of the 'valour, bravery, victories and adventures of the Welsh in former times'. The idea of Welsh history embraced by the humanists, and constantly referred to in their writings, is in fact that expressed in Geoffrey of Monmouth's *Historia Regum Britanniae* in the twelfth century.

The ideas of Geoffrey's history were roundly attacked by the Renaissance historians Polydor Vergil and William Camden, among others. The English, who for a long time had taken the greater part of the panoply of British and Arthurian history as their own, began to take a more critical view of the past and to emphasize their Saxon historical inheritance. By 1612, Michael Drayton, in his long topographical poem *Polyolbion*, could declare:

> The Britons chant King Arthur's glory
> The English sing their Saxons' story.

Drayton's words are, of course, an oversimplification. The ideas of 'British' history continued to hold sway among many in England, while in Wales, many of the details of Geoffrey's history were questioned and it was conceded by some that there was a grain of truth in a number of assertions made by Vergil and Camden. None the less, the idea of such a British history remained an extremely potent part of the intellectual stock of Welsh humanist scholars.

When Welsh sixteenth-century historians write, the defence of this history is their primary concern. Sir John Prys, in his *Historia Brytannicae Defensio*, published posthumously in 1573 through the offices of his son Richard, defends Geoffrey against the attack in Vergil's *Anglica Historia* of 1534. Humphrey Lhwyd, the most important historian among the Welsh humanists, also defends the tradition vigorously. In his three main works, *De Mona* (which was appended to the *Defensio* of Prys), *Cronica Walliae a Rege Cadwalader ad Annum 1294*, later used as a basis for the *History of Cambria* by David Powel of Rhiwabon (1583), and the *Commentarioli Britannicae Descriptionis Fragmentum*, translated into English by Thomas Twyne as the *Breviary of Britain* (1573), his main thrust is the defence of his nation's traditional history. In the words of Ieuan M. Williams, 'he consecrated . . . his life to the task of trying to interpret—and defend—his nation's past'.

These works of history were written in Latin. Like other products of Welsh humanist learning, they were directed at what Benedict Anderson described as the 'wide but thin stratum' of Latin readers in Renaissance Europe. It is somehow ironic that works such as these, which are at the very heart of the Welsh humanists' striving for a highly regarded and all-encompassing definition of themselves, their language, their religion and their history, should be directed mainly at scholars outside Wales. It is even more ironic to find versions of Lhwyd's work published in English, but not in Welsh. It is not that publishing scholarly works in Latin necessarily militated against the furtherance of native culture: recognition outside Wales was regarded as a *sine qua non* of progress. It is rather that the resources were not available to present the interested, but non-classically educated, Welsh reader with works which were as important in the much-desired development of the Welshman's pride and self-knowledge as in the educating and cultivating of outside opinion. To have had these works in Welsh as well as in Latin would have furthered the humanists' ambition considerably. Siôn Dafydd Rhys's ambitious attempt to write such a work in Welsh was doomed to remain in manuscript.

We are here at the crux of the problem faced by Welsh humanist scholars. They had set themselves a mission, which this chapter has sought to analyse and describe. Commentators have usually seen that mission as ending in ultimate failure, albeit a glorious one. The humanists did indeed fail to produce a wide-ranging body of learning in the Welsh language. Outside the fields of religious and linguistic scholarship, the harvest of humanism is slight. There are a few medical works, such as Elis Gruffydd's translation of Elyot's *Castle of Health* or William Salesbury's *Herbal*, both of which remained in manuscript, but there is little else of substance. Nor did the valuable linguistic groundwork laid by the humanist scholars herald a new crop of writing in diverse branches of learning in succeeding generations. Welsh humanist learning remained confined by the problem of limited human and material resources. Given the constraints imposed by the social conditions of the Welsh language in the sixteenth and seventeenth centuries, it can be seen that the humanists had embarked upon a programme which was nigh on impossible to realize.

In their own terms, therefore, they did not succeed. From a wider historical perspective, however, two great areas of achievement stand out. The first is that they ensured that the Welsh language, whatever use might or might not be made of it in future, was refined and enhanced as a dignified and flexible instrument of learning and creative expression. They were the fathers of the modern tradition of Welsh prose. The second great achievement is less tangible. It is the bequeathing of a spirit of almost fierce love and the conviction that, for the Welsh language, given the right conditions, all things are possible. Such was the inheritance that they passed on to their heirs, the scholars of the eighteenth-century revival of learning. That inheritance of the spirit inspires and influences all scholars who make their acquaintance to the present day.

BIBLIOGRAPHY

The following brief bibliography lists articles of a general nature. A fuller bibliography will be found in Thomas Parry and Merfyn Morgan (eds), *Llyfryddiaeth Llenyddiaeth Gymraeg I* (Caerdydd, 1976), esp. 124–5, 135–40 and 151–4, and in Gareth O. Watts (ed.), *Llyfryddiaeth Llenyddiaeth Gymraeg II* (Caerdydd ac Aberystwyth, 1993), esp. 110–12. Meic Stephens (ed.), *The Oxford Companion to the Literature of Wales* (Oxford,1986) contains useful brief articles, with suggestions for further reading.

Ceri Davies, introduction to *Rhagymadroddion a Chyflwyniadau Lladin 1551–1632* (Caerdydd, 1980).

Idem, 'Erasmus and Welsh Renaissance Learning', *Transactions of the Honourable Society of Cymmrodorion* (1983), 48–55.

O.H. Fynes-Clinton, 'Davies's Latin–Welsh Dictionary', *Bulletin of the Board of Celtic Studies*, 2 (1923–5), 311–19.

T. Gwynfor Griffith, 'Italian Humanism and Welsh Prose', *Yorkshire Celtic Studies*, 6 (1953–8), 1–26.

R. Geraint Gruffydd, 'Wales and the Renaissnace', in A.J. Roderick (ed.), *Wales Through the Ages*, II (Llandybïe, 1960), 45–53.

Idem, 'The Renaissance and Welsh Literature' in Glanmor Williams and Robert Owen Jones (eds), *The Celts and the Renaissance* (Cardiff, 1990), 17–39.

Heledd Hayes, *Cymru a'r Dadeni* (Caernarfon, 1987).

R. Brinley Jones, *The Old British Tongue: the Vernacular in Wales, 1540–1640* (Cardiff, 1970).

Nesta Lloyd, 'John Jones Gellilyfdy', *Flintshire Historical Society Publications*, 24 (1969–70), 5–18.

Enid Roberts, 'The Renaissance in the Vale of Clwyd', *Flintshire Historical Society Publications*, 15 (1954–5), 52–63.

G.J. Williams, 'Hanes Ysgolheictod Cymraeg yng Nghyfnod y Dadeni 1550–1700', in Aneirin Lewis (ed.), *Agweddau ar Hanes Dysg Gymraeg*, (Caerdydd, 1969), 31–81.

Glanmor Williams, 'Dadeni, Diwygiad a Diwylliant Cymru' in *Grym Tafodau Tân* (Llandysul,1986), 63–86.

Ieuan M. Williams, 'Ysgolheictod Hanesyddol yr Unfed Ganrif ar Bymtheg', *Llên Cymru*, 2 (1952–3), 111–24, 209–14, 214–23.

J.E. Caerwyn Williams, *Geiriadurwyr y Gymraeg yng Nghyfnod y Dadeni* (Caerdydd, 1983).

CHAPTER 6

TRANSLATING THE BIBLE

ISAAC THOMAS

The sixteenth- and seventeenth-century Welsh translators of the Bible embarked upon their task confident that the Welsh language had all the literary resources and qualities necessary for a successful version of the Holy Scriptures. Their confidence was not misplaced. On the one hand there was the still living bardic tradition with its colourful vocabulary, well suited to capture the poetic quality of so much of the Scriptures. On the other hand, and perhaps more to their purpose in general, was that remarkable body of medieval prose literature which had encompassed topics as diverse as laws, legends, romances, history, geography, medicine and religion, and had done so with considerable elegance and clarity. Of special interest to them were those religious works, mostly translations from Latin, which were the products of the ecclesiastical reforms of the thirteenth and fourteenth centuries. These contained Welsh renderings of the terms and phrases peculiar to Christian theological discourse, and also translations of some significant passages of Scripture. And, indeed, it is with these that the history of the translating of the Bible into Welsh must begin.

These pre-Reformation translations of portions of Scripture are of various kinds. There are those which appear to be translations of the 'gospels' of the Mass. Thus Luke 1:26–38 was the 'gospel' of the Annunciation of the Blessed Virgin Mary; John 1:1–14 was the 'gospel' for Christmas; and Matthew 26:1–28:7, entitled *y Groglith* (The lesson of the Cross), corresponds very nearly to the 'gospel' for 'the Sunday next before Easter'. It is highly improbable that these translations were ever used as the actual 'gospels' of the liturgy. In the medieval Catholic Church, Latin, and Latin only, was the language of the liturgy; but there was one exception—the sermon, which had to be in the vernacular to fulfil its function. And that is what these translated 'gospels' were: the contents or, at least, the basis of the sermon on the 'gospel'. It will be seen that these three 'gospels' deal with some of the principal doctrines of the Catholic Church and would, therefore, serve admirably to execute the directive of the reforming Lambeth Council of 1281 which required the parish priest, four times a year, on one or more of the holy-days, to expound the doctrines of the Church 'in the vernacular and without introducing any fanciful subtleties'.

Then there are translations of short biblical quotations used to illustrate and sustain a theological argument. This type may be seen in the tract known as *Hystoria Lucidar* (An Explanatory Discourse), a translation of the *Elucidarium* attributed to Honorius Augustodunensis. It contains seventy-six quotations from the Old Testament (including the Apocrypha) and seventy-one from the New. The Welsh translation of these quotations follows the Vulgate text as given in the *Elucidarium* (which differs somewhat from the standard text) and gives, with a few exceptions, a fairly literal rendering of that text.

But in other tracts intended, like the *Hystoria Lucidar*, to supply the homiletic needs of the parish priest, the rendering of the biblical text is not equally faithful. Thus *Llyma pwyll y pater ae dyall val ydyweit hu sant* (This is the sense and import of the Lord's Prayer as Saint Hugh says) discusses the seven deadly sins and the seven principal virtues in the form of a gloss on the text of the Lord's Prayer and the Beatitudes, but it is the explanatory paraphrase of the gloss on these passages, and not the text of Scripture itself, that is rendered into Welsh. Similarly in *Py ddelw y dyly dyn credv y Dyw* (In what manner should a man believe in God), it is not the scriptural Ten Commandments that are translated but the shortened version current in the Church. Again in *Hystoria Adrian ac Ipotis* (The Discourse of Adrian and Ipotis), a theological work in the form of question and answer, the scriptural passages are found to be paraphrases or adaptations which expand or shorten the actual Vulgate text according to the author's purpose.

This rendering by paraphrase, with its expansion or abridgement of the original text, was indeed the accepted method in the Latin Church of spreading knowledge of the Scriptures in the vernacular. A notable example is *Y Bibyl Ynghymraec* (The Bible in Welsh). In spite of its title, this work is not a Bible, but a translation and adaptation of the *Promptuarium Bibliæ* compiled by Peter of Poitiers. As such it belongs to that series of summaries of the historical books of the Bible known as the 'Paupers' Bibles'. It is a storehouse (*promptuarium*) of biblical history to which a cleric of limited means might have recourse. Although not a Bible, it provides a fund of biblical names, phrases and terms which would be of great interest to the later translators.

This Welsh *Bibyl* has one unique feature. It opens with a translation of Genesis 1:1–2:2(3), a passage not found in the *Promptuarium* itself nor in the other 'Paupers' Bibles'. Whether made by the translator himself or by an early copyist, the insertion may well be an expression of Lollard sympathy. At least it can be shown that the version of this interpolation as found in three manuscripts is largely dependent on the earlier and more literal English version associated with the name of John Wyclif.

Another use of Scripture passages is that found in *Ystorya Adaf* (Adam's Discourse), a translation of the Latin *Historia Adam* which relates the legendary fortunes of the 'Tree' (i.e. the Cross) of Christ in its progress from Eden to Calvary. As the legend unfolds it brings the Tree into contact with biblical characters and incidents and in so doing reproduces, or at least echoes, the language of the biblical narrative. This would give the readers, and their audience, some knowledge of the contents of the Bible.

A similar use of Scripture is found in *Y Seint Greal* (The Holy Grail), a translation and adaptation of two French Grail texts. The scriptural passages, taken mostly from the Gospel of Matthew, are used to enhance the story and to point its moral and are freely adapted to this end.

Finally, there is one splendid example of translation into verse. Although it restricted the language of the liturgy to Latin, the medieval church did allow translations of devotional books, including their scriptural content, for the use of the laity. It is, therefore, no accident that *Gwassanaeth Meir* (The Service of Mary), the Welsh translation of the *Officium Parvum Beatae Mariae Virginis*, deploys more Scripture than any other medieval Welsh text. It contains twenty-eight Psalms from the Old Testament, 'The Song of the Three Holy Children' and extracts from Ecclesiasticus, from the Apocrypha, Math. 6:13, Luke 1:26–38, 46–55, 68–79, 2:29–32 and Heb. 2:6, 3:7, 11 from the New Testament. Apart from Psalm 95, the extracts from Ecclesiasticus and Luke 1:26–38, all this scriptural material has been translated into verse. Versification inevitably involves paraphrase, but the unpretentious verse of this translator succeeds remarkably well in conveying the substance and tone both of the Psalms of the Old Testament and the Songs of the New.

But sixteenth- and seventeenth-century Welsh translators, however indebted they might be to these medieval translations, could not but regard them as pitifully inadequate. Their use gave no indication of the supreme authority of the Scriptures. They were based not on the original Hebrew and Greek but on the Latin of the Vulgate, a version whose text was frequently uncertain, its translations often ambiguous, and its interpretative glosses far removed from the plain meaning of the original texts. Moreover, the adaptation and paraphrase, the expansion and abridgement which marked these translations diminished the Word of God. Any attempt at a valid version would have to begin anew. And this, these men of the Renaissance and the Reformation in Wales felt themselves competent and obliged to undertake. They were all *alumni* of the English universities. There they had been introduced to the current revolution in biblical scholarship and had familiarized themselves with its products—the original texts of the Bible and new Latin and vernacular versions printed and published.

The Hebrew text of the Old Testament had been printed as early as 1488 in Northern Italy and thereafter a number of times: in the Complutensian Polyglot Bible at Alcalá in Spain (1514–17), in editions by Daniel Bomberg at Venice (1516/17 and 1524/5), by Sebastian Münster at Basle (1535), by Robert Estienne (Stephanus) at Paris (1539–44) and in the Royal Antwerp Polyglot Bible (1569–72). The Greek New Testament was printed for the first time (1514) in the Complutensian Polyglot, but as that Bible was not published until 1522 the first printed Greek New Testament to be published (1516) is that edited by Erasmus. Following on this 1516 edition, revised editions were published, edited by Erasmus himself in 1519, 1522, 1527 and 1535 (at Basle), by Robert Estienne in 1546, 1549, 1550 (at Paris) and 1551 (at Geneva), and by Theodore Beza in 1565, 1582, 1588 and 1598 (at Geneva).

The sixteenth century saw also the printing and publishing of the two ancient versions: the Septuagint Greek version of the Old Testament and the Latin Vulgate. But the sixteenth-century translators set little store by these versions. The Septuagint departed too often from the exact wording of the Hebrew text and contained writings which had not been accepted into the Hebrew canon, the so-called Apocrypha. And, as we have seen, there were

many reasons why the sixteenth-century reformers rejected the
Vulgate in spite of the much improved text printed in contemporary
editions.

In these circumstances, the reforming biblical scholars became
convinced that a thoroughly revised Latin version had to be made
which would in turn prepare the way for what they saw as much
needed vernacular Scriptures. Thus Erasmus placed his own Latin
translation in parallel columns with the Greek text in all his editions
of the New Testament, and Münster likewise placed a Latin version
of his own parallel with the Hebrew text in his edition of the Old
Testament. Meanwhile (1527/8) Sanctes Pagninus had published a
Latin version of the whole Bible which aimed at giving a literal and
grammatically correct translation without any attempt at literary
embellishment. Unlike its New Testament, the Old Testament of
this version proved very popular and was reprinted, slightly revised,
as the Old Testament of Estienne's 1557 Latin Bible and again
slightly adapted and placed line by line and word by word above the
Hebrew text in the Antwerp Polyglot Bible. In contrast to these very
literal translations, the Zürich Latin Bible (1543) carefully avoids
any wording that contravenes Latin idiom, while Sebastian
Castellio in his version (1551) transforms the language of the Bible
into that of the Latin classics. Beza takes a middle course between
these two extremes in his version of the New Testament, first
published in 1556 in Estienne's Latin Bible, and then, parallel with
the Greek text, in his own editions (1565, 1582) of the New
Testament. The same moderation is true of Immanuel Tremellius'
version of the Old Testament published at Frankfurt (1575–9).
These last two versions fully merited the prestige they acquired in
the latter decades of the sixteenth century, and later.

The series of vernacular versions based on the original texts
begins with Martin Luther's translation of the New Testament
(1522) and of the whole Bible (1534) into German. As the staunch
advocate of the priesthood of all believers his purpose was a
version that would be understood by all. To that end he proceeded
on the principle that in translation the idiom of the recipient
language must prevail. As long as the meaning of the original is
fully conveyed the translator is free from bondage to words. But in
the series of French versions which began with that of Pierre
Robert Olivetan and which continued in revised editions by Calvin
and Beza at Geneva, a quite different principle was observed. In

that the words of Scripture are divinely inspired, a faithful translation requires that they be translated word for word. If any added words are necessary to complete the sense in translation, such inserted words must be indicated by printing them in a different type.

The pioneer of the English versions was William Tyndale. His translation of the New Testament was published in 1526, with revised editions in 1534 and 1535. His Old Testament translations included Genesis, II Chronicles and Jonah. These versions are based on the original languages and are, like Luther's, a rendering of the Bible in the living language of the people. A version of the whole Bible in English was produced by Miles Coverdale in 1535. Coverdale's learning did not extend to Hebrew and Greek, and his version was based on the Latin versions of Erasmus and Pagninus and the vernacular versions of Luther and Tyndale. In 1537 another English Bible appeared which claims on its title-page to have been translated by Thomas Matthew. But actually this 'Matthew's Bible' is a composite work made up of Tyndale's 1535 New Testament, Tyndale's version of Old Testament books, with the rest of the Old Testament, including the Apocrypha, taken from Coverdale.

Although licensed by the king (Henry VIII), there was considerable opposition to these English Bibles: they frequently departed from the familiar Vulgate text and their homely English sounded coarse, if not blasphemous, to ears long attuned to the lofty and sublime sound of the Latin liturgy. A revision was, therefore, decided upon and entrusted to Coverdale. It was published in 1539 and became known, on account of its size, as the 'Great Bible'. It is a revised version of 'Matthew's Bible', its Old Testament brought into line with the more dignified style of Münster, and the New Testament with that of Erasmus. Readings peculiar to the Vulgate are restored, but within brackets and in a smaller type. It was to remain the authorized English version until the appearance of the 'Bishops' Bible'. But meanwhile (1560) another English version had been published at Geneva where a number of English Protestants had found refuge from Mary Tudor's persecuting zeal. Taking advantage of the biblical scholarship available at Geneva they devoted their exile to a revision of the English Bible. Its accuracy in translation and its lively language place this 'Geneva Bible' among the best versions of the period. As might be expected, the translators' method of translation follows that of Calvin rather than Luther. They have, as they themselves claim, 'most reverently kept the proprietie [i.e. the idiom] of the wordes'. But in spite of its excellence as a version and its enthusiastic reception in England after the restoration of Protestantism under Elizabeth I, the Geneva Bible did not find favour with the ecclesiastical authorities, mainly because of the radical and anti-clerical tone of its marginal notes. However, its superiority as a translation made it impossible to continue with the Great Bible as the authorized version. Arrangements were therefore made for a new official version to be undertaken by bishops and other eminent clergy. This so-called 'Bishops' Bible' was published in 1568, but it did not prove a success. It provided little more than an incongruous amalgam of Great Bible and Geneva Bible readings. It could not be the final form of the English Bible. That was to be found in the 1611 'Authorized' Version. According to the Introductory Epistle of the translators the intent was not so much a new translation as the provision, with the help of earlier versions in many languages, of a rendering which would be faithful without being in bondage to words, correct without being obscure, and a means whereby 'the Scripture may speake like it selfe, as in the language of *Canaan*, that it may bee vnderstood even of the very vulgar'. That this version is still in use is proof enough of its success.

It was the good fortune of the people of Wales that they had in their midst, at this juncture in their history, men who could appreciate the remarkable developments in biblical translation outlined above and who could appropriate them to supply what they saw as the desperate need of their countrymen. A faint suggestion of what was to come is found in two works which belong to the first half of the century. In the translation of a few portions of the Gospels preserved in the manuscript, Hafod 22, there is nothing but what we have seen to be medieval practice except that the translation is largely based on Matthew's Bible, a sign that the new influences were beginning to reach Wales. Similarly, what scriptural content there is in *Yny lhyvyr hwnn* (In this book), published by Sir John Prys in 1546, is thoroughly medieval in nature and in scope. But a new note is struck by the author when he calls upon his countrymen to make use of the printing press to speed abroad knowledge of God's words.

This is exactly what William Salesbury had started to do. In 1545 he had received a royal license to print a dictionary and a variety of translations. Armed with this license, Salesbury proceeded to publish a series of works which culminated in the publication of a translation of the 'epistles and gospels' of the 1549 English Prayer Book. It is entitled:

> *Kynniver llith a bann or ysgrythur lan ac a ddarlleir yr Eccleis pryd Communly Suliau a'r Gwilieu trwy'r vlwyddyn: o Cambereiciatl W. S.*
>
> [As many lessons and chapters of the holy scripture as are read to the church at communion,/on Sundays and Holy-days throughout the year: rendered into Welsh,/by W.S.]

In his Latin address to the Welsh bishops which introduces the work, Salesbury begs any assessors of his version to note

> that I have kept to the strict rule of translation and have not used the freedom of one who paraphrases. In Matthew I have been much concerned to follow the Hebrew text, not from any disregard of the Greek, but because the Hebrew phrase resembles our own more closely. But in all else to be translated I have set great store on the Greek, preferring (as is right) the source to the river.

In his claim to have kept to the strict rule of translating, Salesbury is obviously contrasting his own practice with the free and paraphrastic renderings of the medieval translators. His further claim to have translated the 'gospels' from Matthew from the Hebrew text would be in accord with this, for no less a scholar than Erasmus held that the Gospel of Matthew had been written originally in Hebrew. But in fact the Hebrew Matthew which Salesbury had before him was a Hebrew translation of the Gospel of Matthew from the Latin Vulgate made in 1485 by Shem Tob b. Sharprut, a Spanish Jew, and revised and published with a Latin translation in 1537 by Sebastian Münster in a volume dedicated to Henry VIII of England. It is unlikely that Salesbury knew that this Hebrew Matthew was a translation of the Latin Vulgate, for elsewhere in his version he deliberately rejects any peculiar Vulgate renderings.

As to the rest of his version, his claim is not that he has translated the Greek, but that he has set great store by it, by which he probably meant that he had used it as a touchstone in choosing versions to follow. Neither Salesbury nor any other sixteenth-century translator of the Bible dreamt that a version of the Scriptures could or should be attempted without reference to earlier versions. A collation of *Kynniver llith a ban* with the texts and versions available to Salesbury reveals that he took Erasmus' 1535 edition as his Greek text, drew extensively on the Latin version and explanatory notes of that same edition and regularly consulted the Great Bible version as found in the 1549 Prayer Book. His style of translation reflects that of Luther and Tyndale and occasionally he adopts the renderings of the medieval Welsh manuscripts, such as the 'Groglith' and *Gwassanaeth Meir*, but with due care to bring them into exact correspondence with the Greek text. But not infrequently Salesbury goes his own way, and with remarkable success.

In all this, it is clear that Salesbury's guiding principle was fidelity to the original texts. But for him, as for Luther and Tyndale, fidelity did not entail bondage to words. Thus he can disregard connecting particles, introduce Welsh idioms and diverge frequently from the syntax (but not the meaning) of the original sentence. Indeed, in addition to the Protestant emphasis on fidelity, his version seems to have been guided by two other considerations. The first of these may be described as that 'variety of expression' so much esteemed by Renaissance men of letters. Apart from his reproduction of the *paronomasia* (wordplay) of the original, Salesbury rarely fails to vary his translation of a Greek word when it recurs in the same paragraph. And this delight in variety he extends to his syntax and spelling. In addition, he had filled his margins with synonyms of words in the text. The plenitude of vocabulary necessary for this verbal display he achieves by alternating words of Celtic origin with those of Latin origin, and current forms and usages with their medieval equivalents, and especially by coining new word-formations based on the elements of the Greek or Latin original.

Salesbury's other guiding principle may be termed 'dignity of diction'. Believing, as did many of his contemporaries, that the dignity of a language derives from the lustre of its antiquity, he made use wherever possible of the ancient Latin element in Welsh, and of the many old and forgotten words and phrases which he had seen in medieval Welsh manuscripts. Moreover, the structure of his sentence in general follows the age-old literary practice of changing the spoken order (verb/subject/object) into what grammarians call the 'abnormal' order (subject or object or adverb/relative particle/verb). This abnormal sentence observed the Latin rule of concord.

This may have been part of its appeal to Salesbury, although in the interests of variety he does use the normal sentence. Finally, he sought to heighten this archaic effect by devising an orthography which drew attention to the Latin element in Welsh and to older Welsh forms.

In publishing *Kynniver llith a ban* it had been Salesbury's purpose to initiate the process whereby the services of the Church in Wales could be conducted in Welsh. But such a change would probably have been illegal, because a few years earlier the Act of Union of England and Wales had proscribed the use of Welsh in 'any manner office or fees within this realm of England, Wales or other the King's Dominion'. However, the accession of Mary Tudor to the throne and her ruthless determination to restore the Pope's authority meant that any such project had to be set aside. And so it remained until the fifth year of the reign of her successor, Elizabeth I, when Bishop Richard Davies succeeded in getting Parliament to enact (1563)

> that the Bishops of Hereford, Saint David's, Asaph, Bangor and Llandaff . . . shall take such Order amongst themselves . . ., That the whole Bible, containing the New Testament and the Old, with the Book of the Common Prayer . . ., as is now used within this Realm in English, to be truly and exactly translated into the British or Welsh tongue.

The first product of this legislation was the *Lliver Gweddi Gyffredin* (The Book of Common Prayer), translated by William Salesbury and published on 6 May 1567. Its contribution to the history of the Welsh Bible is twofold: a revised version of the Prayer Book 'epistles and gospels', and a pioneering translation of the Psalms.

The 'epistles and gospels' of the 1567 Prayer Book are a thorough revision of *Kynniver llith a ban* by Salesbury himself. Despite the many troubles of the intervening years, it is clear that Salesbury had kept pace with the developments in biblical scholarship. He had learnt what the 'Hebrew Matthew' was and had rejected it. His Greek text now is the one published by Estienne in 1550, and the versions he turns to for guidance are changed to Beza's first Latin version (1556) and the English Geneva Bible, although there are places where he adopts the earlier renderings of Erasmus or the Great Bible and occasions when he offers an entirely independent translation.

It is evident that this revision aimed at a more literal translation. Whereas in *Kynniver llith a ban* he had followed Luther's principle of freedom from bondage to words, he is now, under the influence of the Geneva Bible, much concerned to preserve the exact wording of the original text in order, as he himself explains, 'that God's own word may remayn sincere and unviolate from generation to generation'. This stronger emphasis on fidelity is shown in his extra care to denote 'inserted words' (using square brackets), by substituting more literal renderings for *Kynniver llith a ban*'s rather colourful idioms, and by his constant endeavour to find an equivalent for every particle in the Greek sentence. The various devices which he had adopted in *Kynniver llith a ban* to ensure variety and dignity of expression are indeed used again, but not with the same abandon. These changes certainly give Salesbury's revised version a new measure of exactness, but they also deprive it of some of the colour and raciness which characterized the earlier version.

The other contribution of the 1567 Welsh Prayer Book to the history of the Welsh Bible is the translation of the Psalms found within its covers. Its title reads:

> *Psallwyr/ neu Psalmae'/* Dauid,/*wedy ei Gambereigaw yn/ nesaf ac 'allit, a' chadw'r/ bwyll, ir llythyr E-/ brew: a'i ddosp-/ arth wrth y/ drefn y/ darlleir yn yr/ Eccles.*

[The Psalter/or the Psalms/of *David*,/turned into Welsh as/closely as was possible, whilst keeping/the sense, to the H-/ebrew letter:/and arran-/ged according to/the order/it is read in the/Church.]

The title indicates that Salesbury had translated the Hebrew text and not the Latin Vulgate as was the case with the Psalms of the English Prayer Book. The title also claims that his translation was as literal as possible without obscuring the meaning. In this he is not claiming to have translated directly and independently from the Hebrew. What he is claiming is that the version in its final form, however arrived at, is as literal as was possible consistent with intelligibility.

A collation of Salesbury's version with earlier versions reveals that in over half his text he follows the Geneva Bible, the version which had 'most reverently kept the proprietie of the wordes'. Salesbury does not acknowledge this debt, probably because it might jeopardize the authorization of his work. In that part of his version which is not dependent on the Geneva Bible he appears to have followed Estienne's version in his 1557 Latin Bible, Münster's Latin version and the English Great Bible. And there are passages where he has renderings of his own. These non-Geneva translations all display a more literal rendering than the Geneva Bible. It would seem, therefore, that although his version is greatly indebted to others the principle of fidelity is still dominant. But his two other principles hold their ground. To ensure dignity of diction he continues to deploy archaic words and phrases (clearly, in some instances, taken from the Psalms of *Gwassanaeth Meir*), and to load his vocabulary with words of Latin origin. At the same time, he strives for variety of expression by alternating this with current usages. The same aims account for the archaic and Latin character of his orthography and its protean forms.

The other product of the 1563 Act was the Welsh New Testament, published on 7 October 1567. Its title-page reads:

> *Testament/ Newydd ein Arglwydd/ Jesv Christ./ Gwedy ei dynnu, yd y gadei yr ancyfia =/ ith, 'air yn ei gylydd or Groec a'r Llatin, gan/ newidio ffurf llythyreu y* gairiae-dodi. *Eb law hynny/ y mae pop gair a dybiwyt y vot yn andeallus,/ ai o ran llediaith y 'wlat ai o ancynefin =/ der y devnydd, wedi ei noti ai eg =/ lurhau ar 'ledemyl y tu da =/ len gydrychiol.*

[The New/Testament of our Lord/Jesus Christ./ Drawn as far as idiom permitt =/ed, word for word from the Greek and Latin, whilst/changing the form of the letters of the *inserted words*. In addition/every word deemed to be obscure, whether because of regional dialect or because of the unfamiliar =/ity of the matter, has been noted and ex =/plained in the margin of the same/page.]

The translators are not named on the title-page, but marginal notes indicate that Thomas Huet, dean of St David's, translated the Revelation of John, that Bishop Richard Davies translated I Timothy, Hebrews, James and I and II Peter, and that Salesbury translated all the rest, including the 'arguments' introducing each book and the 'contents' above each chapter (except those that belong to the Epistle of James). As general editor he is also responsible for the various marginal notes (synonyms, variant readings and explanatory notes) and for the change of type to denote the 'inserted words' and the variant forms of a word.

Salesbury, of course had already translated a substantial portion of the New Testament for the 'epistles and gospels' of the 1567 Prayer Book. The greater part of this version is found again in the New Testament unchanged, but the rest has been revised, and it is in this revision alone that traces of the influence of Beza's 1565 Latin version can be seen. With regard to those sections of the New Testament which he now translates for the first time, he uses the same Greek text and the same versions as aids as in his 1567 version of the 'epistles and gospels', and to the same degree, except that here he is much readier to essay an independent rendering. In all this, his constant aim is a version rigorously faithful to the original.

But within the limits of this 'word-for-word' fidelity, Salesbury continues to observe his two other translation principles. To achieve dignity of diction he persists in resurrecting archaic words and phrases, in giving priority to words of Latin origin or connection, and in drawing attention to these marks of antiquity in his orthography. To secure diversity of expression he continues to vary his vocabulary and syntax to the very limits of the Welsh language. And his inventiveness in coining new word-formations is equally evident, as is his 'elegant variation' in spelling. In its faithfulness to the original texts Salesbury's versions must be classed with the very best of his period, but his excessive use of literary embellishments has served only to obscure that achievement and to cause difficulties for the reader, both public and private.

In the manuscript Gwysane 27 there is a translation by Bishop Richard Davies of I and II Timothy, Titus and Philemon. This version is based on the Great Bible, Erasmus's Latin version and his Greek text. As such it would appear to be Davies's first approach to carrying out the requirements of the 1563 Act. But in 1564 Salesbury accepted an invitation by Bishop Davies to take up residence at his palace in Abergwili for the duration of the translating, and this may have led to a new division of labour and a new decision on which earlier versions were to be consulted. In any case, the books actually translated by Bishop Davies were I Timothy, Hebrews, James and I and II Peter, and the text and versions he consulted are the same as Salesbury's: Estienne's 1550 Greek text, Beza's 1556 Latin version and the Geneva Bible. But he can be as venturesome as Salesbury in offering his own renderings. Of these some are excellent, and some not so.

The overriding principle of Davies's translating is, like that of Salesbury, fidelity, to be achieved by a word-for-word rendering. To this end he avoids cumbrous paraphrasing by coining new words, strives for a Welsh equivalent for the many particles in the Greek sentence, limits his use of Welsh idiom and sometimes strains his Welsh sentence into exact correspondence with the Greek. He values diversity in vocabulary and syntax and, even spelling, but is not as extravagant as Salesbury in this regard. And he has none of Salesbury's devices for achieving dignity of diction. On the contrary, his language is marked by non-literary forms and borrowings from English, two things studiously avoided by Salesbury. Whereas Salesbury strives to observe the literary canons of Renaissance letters, Davies is more concerned with the effectiveness of the Protestant mission in Wales and to this end adopts a language much nearer the spoken form. It was this divergence in aims that probably broke up the partnership between Davies and Salesbury and made it impossible for them to go on to produce a version of the Old Testament.

In 1566 Thomas Huet was persuaded to join the translators and undertake the translation of the Revelation of John. In view of the strange Greek of that book it is not surprising that he practically ignored the Greek text and based his translation chiefly on the Geneva Bible with some recourse to Beza's Latin version, the Great Bible and the Vulgate. He was, therefore, not concerned to give a word-to-word translation of the Greek. His object rather was the provision of a version which would run smoothly and be readily understood. In a marginal note Salesbury states that Huet has translated into his regional dialect, giving due warning to the reader that the relative strangeness of Huet's language is because of a phonetic transcription of dialect forms in contrast to the unphonetic literary forms in which he himself delighted. But whatever its defects, Huet's version has succeeded remarkably well in echoing the lyrical qualities of the Apocalypse.

In the Epistle which introduces the 1567 New Testament Bishop Davies had written (in Welsh):

> Here is the one part ready, that which is called the New Testament, while you await (with God's help, it will not be long) the other part which is called the Old Testament.

In fact, it took twenty-one years before this promise was fulfilled, not by Davies and Salesbury but by Dr William Morgan, vicar of

Llanrhaeadr-ym-Mochnant. On 22 September 1588 the Privy
Council informed the four Welsh bishops and the bishop of
Hereford that

> the translation of the Bible into the Welsh or British tongue which by
> Act of Parliament should long since have been done, is now performed
> by one Dr Morgan and set forth in print.

The title of this first complete Welsh Bible reads:

> *Y Beibl cys-/ segr-lan. sef lyr Hen Desta-/ ment, a'r Newydd/ 2 Timoth.*
> *3.14, 15/ .../ Imprinted at London by the Deputies of/ Christopher Barker,/*
> *Printer to the Queenes most excel-/ lent Maiestie./ 1588.*

> [The sacro-/sanct Bible. namely/the Old Testa-/ment, and the New/2
> Timoth. 3.14, 15/.../ etc]

Introductory matter consists of the Dedicatory Epistle to the
Queen, names of the promoters, contents, calendar and tables.
Leaves 1–351 contain the Old Testament, leaves 352–436 the
Apocrypha and leaves 440–555 the New Testament. This brief
description indicates the immensity of the task undertaken by
Morgan. It involved the translation of the whole of the Hebrew Old
Testament (except the Psalms), and of all the Greek and Latin
books of the Apocrypha, into Welsh for the first time, along with a
revision of Salesbury's Psalms and the 1567 New Testament.
Happily, Morgan's scholarship and commitment were equal to the
task.

Morgan gives no information as to his Greek and Hebrew texts
or which versions he consulted, but a collation of his version of the
Old Testament with the texts and versions available to him gives the
following picture of his procedure. Before him would be the seventh
volume of the Antwerp Polyglot Bible. Here he would have a
Hebrew text and above it Pagninus' Latin version adapted to give a
word-for-word translation. A study of these combined texts would
give Morgan the dictionary meaning of every word in the Hebrew
text. But without a knowledge of Hebrew syntax, it would have
been impossible for him to arrive at their sense. And so, to check
that he had properly understood the Hebrew sentence he would
regularly consult Tremellius' lucid Latin version. Should he fail to
be satisfied by Tremellius' rendering, he would consult the earlier

Latin versions of Estienne and Münster. For further confirmation, and to see how a vernacular version expressed the matter, he would usually turn to the Geneva Bible and, occasionally, to the Bishops' Bible. It is this not uncritical use of the best versions of the period which accounts for the scarcity of the places where Morgan's version can be faulted.

The primary source of Morgan's language was the rich idiomatic Welsh of his mainly monoglot community, but to extend and mould this everyday Welsh into the literary forms required by a version of Holy Scripture, he, like Salesbury, had recourse to the religious prose writings of the medieval period. But unlike Salesbury, his use of this material was not uncritical. He rejected words or phrases whose meaning was unfamiliar, or whose theology was Catholic, or whose inexactness as translations of the biblical texts was clear. This loss Morgan made good by drawing upon the vocabulary of the strict-metre poetry, by borrowing a little from Hebrew and English, but chiefly by the use of new word-formations, many adopted from Salesbury, but most coined by himself. These last are frequently modelled on the compound formations of strict-metre poetry and serve to give to his version a poetic tone where required.

In his sentence structure Morgan rarely departs from the 'abnormal' pattern, and it is very rare indeed for him to have a singular verb with a plural subject, the 'normal' but un-Latin Welsh idiom. Indeed, Morgan seems much concerned to bring his Welsh into conformity with the rules of Latin grammar. On the other hand, unlike Salesbury, he makes no attempt to latinize his vocabulary, or his orthography which, with the exception of some oral forms, is that of the strict-metre poetry. In his opinion, there was no need to add anything to the native dignity of the language of the Old Testament. Hebrew is a spare, muscular, direct language, well suited to express the concrete and tremendous realities with which the Old Testament deals. Morgan's achievement is that his version displays these very same qualities.

When he wrote in his Dedicatory Epistle that he had 'translated the whole of the Old Testament' Morgan probably meant that he had translated not only the Hebrew Old Testament, but also the Apocrypha, those books which are found in the Greek Septuagint and the Vulgate versions of the Old Testament but not in the Hebrew. In their commitment to the *Hebraica veritas*, the sixteenth-century translators were uncertain as to the scriptural status of these books and adopted the practice of gathering them from their various locations in the Vulgate and Septuagint versions and placing them together as a separate section of the Bible, usually with a note that they could be read with profit but that they had no doctrinal authority. These doubts had their effect on the translators. Münster omits the Apocrypha from his version; Pagninus, Coverdale and the Bishops' Bible merely reproduce the Vulgate or a translation of it; Luther entrusted its translation to colleagues and Tremellius to his son-in-law, Junius. There are signs that William Morgan's own zeal for fidelity faltered in his version of these books.

The versions consulted by Morgan in translating the Apocrypha are the same as for his Old Testament, except Münster (who did not translate the Apocrypha) and the Bishops' Bible (which reproduces Coverdale's version based on the Vulgate). And there is some evidence that he also consulted Beza's French version. This choice of authorities to consult indicates that Morgan's version is based on the Greek text and not on the sometimes very different Vulgate text. But the most striking feature of the version is the frequency of renderings which are peculiar to Morgan. Some of these are correct translations of the Greek, others derive from Morgan's recognition of the Semitic idiom in the Greek, but most of them are rather loose renderings which Morgan, it would seem, in his haste to complete his immense task did not bother to check with his usual aids. However, in its vocabulary, diction and orthography, the language of his version of the Apocrypha is that of his version of the Old Testament.

As already indicated, Morgan's Psalms and New Testament are revised versions of the 1567 Psalms and New Testament. The revision is of two kinds: a correction of the translation and a 'cleansing' of its language. The revision of the translation is largely dependent on the new Latin versions which had been published after 1567. Thus with regard to the Psalms, Morgan's corrections are mostly derived from the Antwerp Polyglot Bible and Tremellius' version, with a few drawn from the earlier versions of Münster and Estienne and the Great Bible, and there are a number of independent renderings. These revisions have been made to words or phrases in almost half the text of the Psalms and are usually, though not always, improvements.

Similarly in his revision of the 1567 New Testament, Morgan's chief authority was Beza's 1582 Greek text and Latin version. But there are some changes which follow the revised New Testament (1572) of the Bishops' Bible, others which follow Salesbury's versions of the 'epistles and gospels', and a substantial number which are Morgan's own. About a quarter of the text has been revised, but it is questionable whether all its 'corrections' are indeed such.

William Morgan's major contribution to the Welsh version of the Psalms and the New Testament is found in his revision of their language and orthography. Indeed, with regard to the New Testament he states (in his Dedicatory Epistle) that all he has done is 'to have cleansed it of that unreformed method of writing which marked it everywhere'. And, certainly, Morgan's 're-formation' of Salesbury's versions in this area is thorough. It is guided by the following principles: that a translation of the Scriptures should deviate as little as possible from the exact wording and syntax of the original; that variety in expression and especially in orthography should be limited; that the familiar Welsh usage in vocabulary and syntax is preferable to what is archaic or foreign or strange; that new word-formations are acceptable if needed and their meaning readily understood; that the Welsh literary sentence should follow the abnormal pattern and have a finite verb which should always be in agreement with its subject in person and number; that the standard in orthography should be that of strict-metre poetry but that some shortened oral forms were quite acceptable. The same principles seem to have controlled Morgan's revision of the books translated by Richard Davies and Thomas Huet. But in respect of Davies's version he has also rejected its rather frequent English borrowings, and in Huet's version he has changed its recurrent dialect forms throughout. It cannot be claimed that Morgan applied these principles with anything like absolute consistency, but it is certain that his 'reforms' did render the Scriptures much easier to read and understand.

William Morgan's contribution does not end with the 1588 Bible. Indeed it was he himself who started that revision which was to be completed in the 1620 Bible by Bishop Richard Parry and Dr John Davies, Mallwyd. In 1603 the publisher Thomas Salisbury had stated that he had ready for the press the New Testament in Welsh revised again by Bishop William Morgan. But in the disorder in London which followed the great plague of 1603, the manuscript of this revised New Testament was lost. Nevertheless, it is highly probable that substantial parts of it have survived as the 'epistles and gospels' of the revised 1599 Welsh Prayer Book—a revision undertaken by Morgan himself with the assistance of his secretary, the young scholar John Davies (later of Mallwyd). In any case, these 'epistles and gospels' are a revised version of the corresponding portions of the 1588 Bible. In its extent, the revision touches only about 15 per cent of the text, but it provides another example of the ceaseless efforts of the Welsh translators to apply every gain in biblical scholarship to their work, and of their constant striving for greater precision and consistency in language and orthography.

The final form of the Welsh Bible (at least until the latter half of the twentieth century) is found in the 1620 version. It was published under the name of Bishop Richard Parry, but most of the revision has been attributed to Dr John Davies, now rector of Mallwyd and Bishop Parry's chaplain and brother-in-law. The title on the front page reads:

> *Y Bibl/ Cyssegr-lan,/ sef yr Hen Desta-/ment a'r/ Newydd./ 2 Tim. 3.16./ . . ./ Printedig/ Yn Llundain gan Bonham/ Norton a Iohn Bill,/ Printwyr i Ardderchoc-/ caf fawrhydi y/ Brenhin./ 1620.*

> [The Sacro-/sanct Bible,/namely the Old Testa-/ment and the/New./2 Tim. 3.16./. . ./Printed in London by Bonham/Norton and John Bill,/Printers to the Most Excel-/lent majesty of the/King./ 1620.]

The introductory material consists of Bishop Parry's Dedicatory Epistle to King James, Bishop Morgan's Dedicatory Epistle to Queen Elizabeth, calendar, almanac and tables. It is followed by the scripture text: the Old Testament (A–Nnn[6]), the Apocrypha (Ooo–Eeee[5]), the New Testament ([A]–[Y[3]].

In his Dedicatory Epistle Bishop Parry claims that his purpose was 'to do for the Welsh version what had been done so successfully for the English version'. The reference is to the success of the English 1611 version—the so-called 'Authorized Version'. But a collation of the 1620 Welsh version with earlier versions reveals that what was actually done was in the main a revision of William Morgan's version according to the 1611 English Version. In the Apocrypha the English version is the only source of revision; in the Old Testament there are only a few changes not so derived (mostly independent renderings); in the New Testament the English 1611 version is still the dominant source of revision despite a substantial contribution from Beza's 1582 Latin version and by independent renderings. Moreover, the Welsh version's marginal notes are all taken either from the margins or the text of the English version, and its wording of the chapter contents, and also its divisions of chapter and verse, are all brought into conformity with that version.

On the other hand, it has to be noted that the revision has touched only about a third of the text. Of the remainder a goodly part had already anticipated the 1611 version, but the greater part has rejected its renderings. This indicates that Parry and Davies were by no means uncritical in their use of the English version and it can be shown that in choosing between the English and Welsh rendering, their option was strictly controlled by their estimate of its greater fidelity to the original text. In the light of later biblical scholarship, it cannot be claimed that their choice was always right, but in general their revision did help to make the 1620 Welsh version one of the most accurate of the period.

Parry and Davies have deviated from William Morgan's translation principles in two particulars only: they frequently change Morgan's plural verbs with plural subjects into the singular, and they consistently alter Morgan's shortened oral forms into the full literary forms of the strict-metre poetry. Otherwise, their revision consists almost entirely of a more rigorous application of Morgan's principles to his own work. This is especially true of the use of the abnormal sentence structure and the emphasis on as literal a translation as possible.

William Salesbury's linguistic experimentation, its critical 're-formation' by William Morgan, subsequently endorsed and strengthened by John Davies, these, together with the translators' vast scholarship, are the main factors in the production of the Welsh version of the Bible. It was an achievement whose influence on the history of the Welsh people can hardly be overestimated. It showed them that their language had resources which could encompass the experience and thoughts of men whatever their range of complexity. It gave their prose writers a literary standard which ensured that their works would be understood in every part of Wales and which thereby deepened Welshmen's consciousness of belonging together as a nation. Above all, it gave to them that scriptural Christianity which was to shape their religious and social life for many centuries to come.

BIBLIOGRAPHY

Hebrew and Greek texts

Hebraica Biblia latina planeque nova Sebast. Munsteri tralatione . . . (Basileae, 1534, 35).
Biblia Sacra, Hebraice, Chaldaice, Graece & Latine . . . (Antuerpiae, 1569–73).
Nouum Testamentum iam quintum . . . recognita a Des Erasmo . . . (Basileae, 1535).
Της Καινης Διαθηκης 'απαντα . . . Ex officina R. Stephani (Lutetiae, 1550).

Iesu Christi D.N. Nouum Testamentum . . . ([Geneva], 1565, 1582).

Latin Versions (16th century)

[All the above Hebrew and Greek texts, except *Της Καινης Διαθηκης 'απαντα*, have an accompanying Latin version.]
Biblia Vtrius Testamenti . . . Excudebat R. Stephanus . . . ([Geneva] 1557, 56).
Testamenti Veteris Biblia Sacra . . . ab Immanuele Tremellio & Francisco Junio . . . (Francofurti ad Maenum, 1579, 77).

English Versions

The Byble . . . translated into English by Thomas Matthew . . . ([Antwerp], 1537).
The Byble in Englyshe . . . truly translated . . . (London, 1539).
The Bible and Holy Scriptures . . . (Geneva, 1560).
The. holie. Bible. (London, 1568).
The Holy Bible . . . Appointed to be read in Churches . . . (London, 1611).

Welsh Versions

Manuscripts: Gwysane 27; Hafod 22; Jesus College Oxford 119, 134A; Llanstephan 117; Peniarth 5, 11, 20, 253; Shrewsbury School XI. [Note that Hafod MS. is at South Glamorgan Libraries, Cardiff; unless otherwise indicated, all the others are at the National Library of Wales, Aberystwyth.]
Kynniver llith a ban . . . Imprinted at London . . . *MDLI.*
Lliver gweddi gyffredin . . . Imprinted at London . . . 1567.6.Maij.
Lliver gweddi gyffredin . . . Printiedig yn Llundain . . . 1599.

Testament Newydd ein Arglwydd Jesu Christ . . . imprinted at London, 1567. Octob 7.
Y Beibl Cyssegr-lan . . . imprinted at London . . . 1588.
Y Bibl Cyssegr-lan . . . Printiedig yn Llundain . . . 1620.

Recent Critical Studies

R. Geraint Gruffydd, 'The Welsh Book of Common Prayer', *Journal of the Historical Society of the Church in Wales*, 17 (1967), 43–55.
Idem, 'William Morgan', in G. Bowen (ed.), *Y Traddodiad Rhyddiaith* (Llandysul, 1970), 149–74
Idem, 'Richard Parry a John Davies', ibid., 175–93.
Idem, *The Translation of the Bible into the Welsh Tongue* (London, 1988).
W. Alun Mathias, 'William Salesbury—Ei Ryddiaith', in G. Bowen (ed.) *Y Traddodiad Rhyddiaith* (Llandysul, 1970), 54–78.
Idem, 'William Salesbury a'r Testament Newydd', *Llên Cymru*, 16 (1989), 40–68.
Isaac Thomas, *William Salesbury and his Testament* (Cardiff, 1967).
Idem, *Y Testament Newydd Cymraeg 1551–1620* (Cardiff, 1976).
Idem, *William Morgan and his Bible* (Cardiff, 1988).
Idem, *Yr Hen Destament Cymraeg 1551–1620* (Aberystwyth, 1988).
Idem, 'Y Cyfieithiadau', in R. Geraint Gruffydd (ed.), *Y Gair ar Waith* (Cardiff, 1988), 41–65.
Glanmor Williams, *Bywyd ac Amserau'r Esgob Richard Davies* (Cardiff, 1953).
Idem, *Welsh Reformation Essays* (Cardiff, 1967).
Idem, 'Bishop William Morgan and the First Welsh Bible', *Journal of the Merioneth Historical and Records Society*, 7 (1976), 347–72.
J.E. Caerwyn Williams, 'Medieval Welsh Religious Prose', *Proceedings of the International Congress of Celtic Studies* (Cardiff, 1963), 65–97.

CHAPTER 7

ANGLICAN PROSE

R. GERAINT GRUFFYDD

It cannot be too strongly emphasized that the chief glory of Welsh Anglican prose-writing during the period *c.* 1546–1700 was the Welsh translation of the Bible, a translation which has been fully described and evaluated in the preceding chapter. To some extent, however, Anglican writers were able to build upon the foundations laid down by the biblical translators and produce a body of prose-writing which, although limited in volume, was at its best of sufficiently high quality to provide further justification for the claim of Welsh to be regarded as a learned language—one of the main objectives of the humanists described in chapter five—and also to secure for itself classic status, in that it became the norm by which Welsh prose-writing was judged until the great *débâcle* of the early nineteenth century. It is true that none of the prose-writers mentioned in this chapter can compare in originality and profundity of thought, let alone literary genius, with the Puritans Morgan Llwyd and Charles Edwards, the subjects of the following chapter, but this does not mean that they do not have their quieter and no less wholesome virtues. What follows is a highly selective account, since no mention will be made of prose works which remained in manuscript (many of which, however, are listed in the first section of the last chapter), nor of items which do not appear to be particularly significant, nor of those which once existed and are now lost. Somewhat paradoxically, the best and most influential Anglican prose-writings of the period are translations, but some interesting original work was done as well, and we shall look first at this.

ORIGINAL WRITING

Sir John Prys's *Yn y llyfr hwn . . .* (In this book . . .) of 1546, a devotional manual, and William Salesbury's *Ban wedi ei dynnu air yng ngair allan o hen gyfraith Hywel Dda* (A case extracted word for word out of the ancient law of Hywel Dda) of 1550, a bilingual contribution to the current debate on the marriage of priests, represent the exiguous first-fruits of Anglican prose-writing in Welsh (although Prys, strictly speaking, was a reforming Catholic rather than a Protestant). Although they are insubstantial, they are far from uninteresting. Far more substantial was Bishop Richard Davies's lengthy introduction to the Welsh New Testament of 1567 (with uninvited contributions from William Salesbury) in which he argues that Anglicanism is nothing but a reversal to the old faith of the Welsh people, conveyed to them immaculate either by St Joseph of Arimathea *c.* AD 60 or by the missionaries of Pope Eleutherius in the second century AD, and held steadfast by them until they were forced by English power to submit to the corrupted faith brought by St Augustine of Canterbury to England *c.* AD 600 (Davies's date). All was desolate after that, and in particular all the books which enshrined the learning and devotion of the Welsh, including the Welsh Bible, were lost in various catastrophes. Davies argues strongly that there was once a Welsh Bible on such grounds as the existence of Welsh proverbs which summarize biblical truth, and the fact that Welshmen in early medieval times used to give their children biblical names, as members of the Reformed Churches on the Continent did in Davies's day. The conclusion was obvious: Welsh people should welcome the New Testament (and the Old, which was soon to follow it) as a treasure which had once been theirs but of which they had been forcibly deprived. Davies's argument, which was in line with thinking within the English church at this time, was to prove hugely influential and was accepted not only by Anglicans but also by Puritans (although not, of course, by Roman Catholics). The argument is conducted with vigour and verve and draws not only upon classical and patristic sources but also upon Reformed theology and traditional Welsh learning. As might be expected, the influence of classical rhetoric is everywhere apparent. Broadly speaking, Welsh Anglican prose follows closely the example set by Davies: it is learned, in the sense that its authors had almost all received a classical education (and were generally not averse to showing it); it is rhetorical, although the devotion of its authors to classical rhetoric tends to vary according to their theological standpoint; and it is profoundly grounded in the Welsh literary past. In one respect only does Davies not set the norm for subsequent writing: his orthography and grammar are far from regular, not only because he was a pioneer, but also because he, like Salesbury, adhered to the humanistic doctrine of *copia* which could be, and was, interpreted as licensing variety in matters linguistic. This, however, is superficial criticism (as it is when applied to Salesbury's case also) and Davies's introduction contains many passages notable for both clarity and eloquence. He has a splendid extended simile comparing the state of religion to a vegetable garden but this, unfortunately, is too long to quote. The following passage, lamenting the avarice of his fellow-countrymen, is part of his disquisition on the proverb *Heb Dduw, heb ddim: â Duw, â digon* 'without God, we have nothing: with God, we have everything'.

> Consider the way of the world, there you will find vexation. So great is the lust of the world today for field and fallow, for gold and silver and wealth, that rarely does one find a single person who trusts in God and in his promises. Violence and robbery, perjury, deceit, treachery and oppression: with these as with rakes every sort of man gathers and draws to himself. God will not drown the world again with the water of the Deluge, but desire for the world's goods has drowned Wales at this time and has caused the destruction of all commendable qualities and good disposition. For what is office in Wales today but a hook to draw to himself the fleece and crop of his neighbour? What are skill, knowledge and discernment in law but thorns in the neighbours' sides to cause them to shy away? Frequently in Wales, although the law takes no notice of it, is the gentleman's hall a refuge for thieves.

So alarmed was Salesbury by this attack that he immediately inserted, perhaps at proof stage, a sentence which sought to justify it.

For the next thirty years or so, the energies of Anglican prose-writers were mostly devoted to the task of translation. Then, *c*.1595, a Pembrokeshire clergyman named Robert Holland published the first of a number of small books designed to further the Anglican cause in Wales. (Holland came from north Wales and was educated at Cambridge, but spent most of his professional life in the diocese of St David's.) His book of *c*. 1595 was *Ymddiddan Tudur a Gronw* (A Conversation between Tudur and Gronw), which survives only in a manuscript copy and in a second edition of 1681. It is a pamphlet against witchcraft and as such is almost unique among the writings we have to consider in this chapter. The

question of witchcraft had for some twenty years engendered a
lively literary debate in England (a debate to which Robert
Holland's brother Henry had contributed in 1590) and *Ymddiddan
Tudur a Gronw* must be seen in this context. As the title suggests,
Holland's pamphlet is cast in the form of a dialogue between two
friends, Tudur and Gronw, who meet in a far country and find
themselves discussing witchcraft, taking the common proverb *bwrw
cath i gythraul* 'casting a cat to the devil' as a starting-point.
Holland, through Gronw, who is very much in charge of the
conversation, steadfastly upholds the Puritan hard line on
witchcraft, advocating the execution of witches by the state and
denying the distinction between black and white magic; it was in
fact this last matter which most preoccupied him, since it is clear
that common country-people regarded white magicians as
beneficent and considered that recourse to them was legitimate. In
spite of its sombre outlook, however, and notwithstanding its
brevity, in *Ymddiddan Tudur a Gronw* Holland produced a
sparkling piece of work. Because it was seemingly aimed at the
common people as well as the gentry, it makes effective use of
proverbs, and succeeds in conveying through its dialogue something
of the flavour of common speech, as the following short quotation
may show. Gronw is here reporting a conversation he had had the
previous year in 'Albania' (Scotland):

> 'Does your neighbour', I asked, as wise as the stupidest person there,
> 'cast a cat to the devil, and sacrifice to him on Mayday eve?' 'I don't
> know', the little girl said, 'ask my mother'. And then a handsome elderly
> lady that was by the fire (and as far as I know she was the mother of the
> little girl) responded: 'Woe to the person who gets a bad name while
> young! The gentleman of whom that pert little madam speaks has had a
> bad name for a long time for resorting to the devil and bestowing upon
> him many a fair ox. And I heard (when I was the same age as that saucy
> and talkative little thing over there) the old man my father, who had been
> a great traveller and knew a good deal about all countries, say often that
> he once knew a man who lived somewhere between Brittany and
> Scandinavia who used to offer a sacrifice to the devil in the same manner
> as our neighbour, so that the account you have heard is neither new nor
> strange, and he (so my father used to say) was rich enough.'

So brilliant are the gifts displayed in this *opusculum* that it is a
matter of great regret that Holland wrote no further original works
in Welsh, apart from a treatise on prayer, which was published in

Oxford in 1600 but of which all copies have disappeared. From now on Holland's talents were to be devoted almost exclusively to translation.

During the next thirty years or so there is little evidence of activity among writers of original Anglican prose in Welsh, but around 1630 the picture changes somewhat. In 1629 there appeared an anonymous *Rheol o gyfarwyddyd i'w harfer wrth ymweld â'r claf* (A method of instruction to be used when visiting the sick): it belongs to a well-known genre and in fact makes liberal use of material drawn not only from the Book of Common Prayer but also from popular manuals of devotion by Christopher Sutton and Lewis Bayly. As is common within the genre, it includes prayers for the sick person, some instruction regarding the theological and spiritual significance of his condition, and a series of questions designed to ascertain that he is not only right-thinking but also properly repentant of his sins and desirous of forgiveness. The absolution and *osculum pacis* follow, together with further prayers, an exhortation to the sick person to make his will and take communion, a committal of his soul to God, and prayers for those present, that they might be suitably warned and edified by what has happened. Although the book is basically a compilation, its author has selected and combined his material with great skill, and in those few passages which seem to be original rather than derivative he shows himself to be a prose-writer of high quality. There is some slight evidence that he may have been Humphrey Davies, the Cambridge-educated vicar of Darowen in Montgomeryshire, who was a notable transcriber of Welsh manuscripts (see the first section of the final chapter). If this identification were to be proved correct, it would indeed explain the high quality of the *Rheol's* prose. On the face of it, however, it would not explain another noteworthy feature of the book, namely its unmistakable Laudian (or High Church) emphasis, as contrasted with the Calvinism of the bulk of the material already discussed. The following few sentences from a seemingly original prayer for the sick man, however, have little to do with theological differences:

> Lord, do not hold against him that which he has said or done amiss at any time during the whole course of his life, but sustain him in hope. Speak comfortably to his soul. Lead him by means of your Spirit to the treasure-house of your mercies. Take away from him the fear and

heaviness of death. Subvert the stratagems of his spiritual enemies who have taken up their stations all around him. Give him strength to repulse the attacks of the devil so that he may obtain total victory.

A year after the *Rheol* was published, an Anglican author of very different persuasion made his first appearance. This was Oliver Thomas, an Oxford-educated Montgomeryshire man who appears to have spent the years before the Civil War as an itinerant preacher in the northern Marches, basing himself at West Felton near Oswestry. This fact at once suggests that Thomas was a man of Puritan conviction, although he appears to have remained a member of the Church of England until the Civil War set him free to identify himself as a Presbyterian. He appears to have published four books in all: a catechism for children in 1630, a substantial treatise exhorting people to read the Bible in 1631, another catechism, this time in collaboration with Evan Roberts, in 1640 (reprinted *c*.1688) and a brief description of various kinds of Christians in 1647 (reprinted in 1677). His treatise of 1631, *Carwr y Cymry* (The Friend of Welshmen), was inspired by the appearance the previous year of the first portable Welsh Bible, the publication of which was made possible by the munificence of various London-Welsh merchants, notably Sir Thomas Myddleton and Rowland Heylin, and their clerical collaborators. Thomas's book is dedicated to these generous sponsors, and consists of two introductory letters to the Welsh clergy and the Welsh laity, followed by a dialogue between the Welshman and his well-wisher in which the well-wisher (who is Thomas himself) instructs the Welshman in such topics as who is to read the Bible (everyone), what part of the Bible is to be read (all of it), when the Bible is to be read (at all times, but specifically twice a day), how long should this practice continue (all our lives), what benefits are to be had from searching the Scriptures (spiritual graces including individual salvation) and how the Scriptures are properly to be searched (in this section various common objections to the practice are countered). The book ends with various appropriate forms of prayer. Thomas's style, as befits a Puritan, is essentially plain, with little overt display of learning and sparing use of rhetorical devices; it is, nevertheless, effective and challenging. The following passage is atypical in its figurative density; in it Thomas explains why diligence and application are needed in order properly to search the Scriptures.

It is in the deep that the wonders of the Lord are to be seen. The juice is in the root and the fruit is in the kernel, not in the branch or the husk or the shell. The marrow is not in the skin but in the bone: similarly the power and sweetness and goodness are to be found not in the letter but in the secret understanding of the spirit. Gold and silver ore and the priceless treasures are not found on the face of the earth but in the depths of the earth, and because of this one must dig deep and descend into the abyss before they are brought out: in the same way the Scriptures must be searched, and searched closely and assiduously, in order that people may obtain the treasures of wisdom and knowledge to the comfort of their souls.

The Civil War which swept Oliver Thomas to some prominence was generally deeply damaging to the Anglican prose-writers discussed in this chapter. Indeed, it was not until the early eighteenth century that Welsh Anglicanism was to produce, in Ellis Wynne, a prose-writer of high talent if not genius. However, a small band of Anglican authors kept the torch of their cause burning fitfully throughout the second half of the seventeenth century. Thomas Powell, deprived rector of Cantref in Breconshire, published in 1657 his *Cerbyd Iechydwriaeth* (The Chariot of Salvation), a book of elementary religious instruction; its most notable feature is the concluding prayer composed in 1655 'upon entering a ruined church, where there had been no sermon or service for many years' (Powell, incidentally, published the same book simultaneously in English). With the return of happier times in 1660, Anglican authors were ungagged, but it is noticeable that few of them attempted to denigrate systematically the regime under which they had suffered. In 1662 Edward Wynn, a Cambridge Doctor of Divinity and rector of Llangeinwen and Llangaffo in Anglesey, published for the benefit of his parishioners *Trefn ymarweddiad gwir Gristion* (A true Christian's mode of behaviour), essentially a sequence of prayers for various occasions, with a catechism and some metrical psalms appended. Thirteen years later Randolph (Rondl) Davies, vicar of Meifod in Montgomeryshire, published his *Profiad yr Ysbrydion* (Trial of Spirits), a forceful attack on sectaries of all kinds, but particularly the Roman Catholics and Quakers: he is noticeably more lenient in his attitude towards Presbyterians and Independents. John Thomas, a native of Montgomeryshire who graduated from Oxford and held various livings in his native county, published in 1680 a sermon on Philippians 4:6 entitled *Ymarferol Athrawiaeth*

Gweddi (Practical Teaching on Prayer). The text and title (which, incidentally, Thomas gives in Latin also) indicate the matter of the sermon, but give no hint of the vigour with which Thomas writes. A far more substantial piece of work was Bishop George Griffith of St Asaph's *Gweddi'r Arglwydd wedi ei hegluro mewn amryw ymadroddion neu bregethau byrion* (The Lord's Prayer explained in various short declarations or sermons) which was written, according to internal evidence, *c.* 1655 but not published until 1685, nineteen years after Griffith's death. A product of Westminster School and Christ Church, Oxford, Griffith's evident learning is not allowed to stifle his overriding desire to communicate with his readers. At the very end of the century, in 1700, we have an anonymous *Cyngor bugail i'w braidd* (The shepherd's advice to his flock) in which a newly-appointed incumbent lectures his future parishioners to good effect on their need to have regard for their souls and to prepare themselves for his ministry. Finally, Dafydd Maurice, an Oxford-trained and much-beneficed clergyman in the diocese of St Asaph, published *c.* 1700 a fine sermon on Matthew 12:20, *Cwnffwrdd i'r gwan Gristion* (Comfort for the weak Christian), which is sometimes mistakenly said to be a translation from Theophilus Dorrington. The last five or six works mentioned, although their number is pitifully small, are nevertheless of high quality and demonstrate conclusively that by the second half of the seventeenth century the tradition of Welsh Anglican prose-writing had achieved stability and maturity.

TRANSLATION

As mentioned above, the best and most influential Anglican prose-writings from our period are translations, and in bulk they far outweigh original writings in prose by Anglican authors. This should occasion no great surprise. Anglicanism was, after all, a peculiarly English manifestation of Protestantism, and all its foundation-texts, with the exception of the Bible, were in English (or Latin). In addition, it gave rise to a prolific secondary literature, the translation of a selection of which seemed an obvious *desideratum* to those anxious to advance the Anglican cause in Wales. (Whether Anglicanism would have stood its ground in the face of alternative continental models of Protestantism had it not been backed by the full power of the English state is of course another question, which need not concern us here.) Oliver Thomas once ascribed the dearth of original Anglican books in Welsh to a lack of zeal among the clergy, and in view of the far higher proportion of original prose-writings produced by Roman Catholic and Puritan authors, he may have had a point. The deficiency is all the more to be regretted in view of the generally high quality of the dedications and prefaces with which many of the translators introduced their work; it has long been recognized that these dedications and prefaces, collected together, constitute an impressive body of original prose.

We begin with what I have called the foundation-texts of Anglicanism. The most important of these was the Book of Common Prayer. William Salesbury's translation was published on 6 May 1567, five months before his New Testament (to which Bishop Richard Davies and Precentor Thomas Huet also contributed). Although marred by Salesbury's humanistic zeal for archaic and varied spelling, his translation of the Book of Common Prayer must nevertheless be accounted his masterpiece. In particular, Salesbury renders triumphantly Archbishop Thomas Cranmer's beautifully modulated prose in his Orders of Service and prayers, paying strict regard to the requirements of cadence and euphony. In general he translates with almost complete fidelity to the original, the only notable exception being at the end of the collect for the Feast of the Conversion of St Paul, where Cranmer's 'the holy doctrine which he taught' becomes *dy fendigedig ddysgeidiaeth yr hwn a adawodd efe yn ysgrifenedig er athrawiaeth Cristnogion* (thy holy doctrine which he left in written form for the instruction of Christians)—a clear expression of Salesbury's abhorrence of the Roman Catholic doctrine of unwritten tradition which had recently been endorsed by the Council of Trent. The second edition of 1586 reproduced that of 1567 virtually unchanged (it is unlikely that Salesbury had anything to do with it). In 1599, however, Bishop William Morgan produced a revised third edition which removed Salesbury's linguistic eccentricities, thus revealing more clearly than before the intrinsic splendour of his version. Some further revision was undertaken for the fourth edition of 1621 and the seventh of 1664; thereafter the Welsh Book of Common Prayer remained virtually unchanged until our own century. There were further editions in 1678, 1683, 1687 and 1700.

Dependent upon the Book of Common Prayer were such elementary handbooks of religious instruction as the ABC and Catechism and the Primer (known in Welsh as *Llyfr Plygain* (Matins Book)). The earliest extant ABC and Catechism is that published by Rhys Prichard (see Chapter Four) in 1617, but four years later Dr John Davies, rector of Mallwyd in Merionethshire, produced a version which was reprinted at least three times during the course of the seventeenth century. The earliest extant Primer is that edited by Daniel Powel in 1612, but it is clear that at least three previous editions have disappeared. Powel's version is not fully typical of the norm in England (and for that reason is all the more interesting), but in 1633 Dr John Davies of Mallwyd produced a normalized version which remained standard thereafter. It should be mentioned that in 1682 the Puritan Charles Edwards (see the following chapter) produced his own version of both Catechism and Primer, but these were repudiated by Thomas Jones the following year. One uncommon feature of Daniel Powel's Primer of 1612 is that it reproduces a translation made in 1578 by Dr Siôn Dafydd Rhys of Brecon of Dean Alexander Nowell's Least Catechism—itself an authorized Anglican publication—rather than that of the Book of Common Prayer. Catechisms were thought important during the period, and several examples of the genre were either compiled in Welsh or translated into Welsh. Another basic Anglican text was the Thirty-Nine Articles of Religion, and these too were translated by Dr John Davies of Mallwyd; surprisingly, his translation was not published until 1664, twenty years after his death. Edward James's version of the Books of Homilies will be mentioned briefly below.

Following the publication of Bishop William Morgan's Bible of 1588, a number of Welsh Anglican translations appeared. In 1595 Bishop John Jewel's *Apologia Ecclesiae Anglicanae* (Defence of the Church of England) was finely translated by Maurice Kyffin, a gentleman from Oswestry who spent most of his career as an army administrator. He was not university-trained but as a writer he far outshone most of those who had received such an education. In the same year Huw Lewys, who had been to Oxford and was to spend his working life as a clergyman in the diocese of Bangor, published a workmanlike translation of Bishop Miles Coverdale's version of a work of spiritual consolation by Otto Werdmüller, a minister of the Gospel at Zürich (and therefore, naturally, a Zwinglian): this was

Ein Kleinot von Trost und Hilfe in allerlei Trübsale (A pearl of comfort and help in various troubles). It is refreshing to find this product of the continental Reformation appearing in Welsh. Lewys's translation was dedicated to Richard Vaughan, soon to become bishop of Bangor, Chester and London in rapid succession, and Vaughan may also have encouraged the ambitious plans of Robert Holland, whom we have already met, and the London stationer Thomas Salisbury, to publish a number of Welsh Anglican translations during the late sixteenth and early seventeenth centuries. These translations were mainly to be of highly popular works by the great Puritan preachers William Perkins and Henry Smith, but of them only a treatise and a catechism by Perkins appeared and these only survive, somewhat mutilated, in later editions. The crowning glory of this phase of Anglican translation, however, was Edward James's version, published in 1606, of the official Books of Homilies of the Church of England, which were mostly the work of Archbishop Cranmer and Bishop Jewel. James, a sometime Fellow of Jesus College Oxford, who ended his career as chancellor of Llandaff Cathedral, may well have been urged to undertake the task by William Morgan when he was bishop of Llandaff between 1595 and 1601. He certainly took Morgan's version of the Bible and Book of Common Prayer as his model and produced a body of prose of comparable excellence to Morgan's: indeed, in the view of that percipient critic Robert Ambrose Jones, 'Emrys ap Iwan', his Welsh is superior to Morgan's. In the work of Kyffin and Lewys, nine years earlier, biblical linguistic usage had not yet had time to exercise its regularizing influence, but in James's work this influence is everywhere apparent, although it does not preclude the welcome appearance of various south Walian linguistic features from time to time.

The next phase of Welsh Anglican translation begins some years after the appearance of Bishop Richard Parry and Dr John Davies of Mallwyd's 'authorized' version of the Welsh Bible in 1620, and their corresponding version of the Book of Common Prayer in 1621. This phase in fact straddles the publication of the first Welsh portable Bible of 1630, which was paid for (as we have seen) by two London aldermen, Sir Thomas Myddelton and Rowland Heylin. These two, and the group of like-minded merchants and ministers of the Gospel which they gathered around them, may have had something to do also with the publication of some of the books with which we are concerned, as well as Oliver Thomas's *Carwr y Cymry* (already discussed), but such a connection is difficult to establish with any certainty. In 1629 Robert Llwyd, vicar of Chirk (and therefore in a sense Myddelton's pastor) published his translation of Arthur Dent's *Sermon of Repentance*, followed in 1630 by his version of Dent's *Plain Man's Pathway to Heaven*. Dent, like Perkins and Smith, was an Anglican clergyman with Puritan leanings, and his writings and preaching were deservedly popular. Llwyd, like Kyffin, had not been to university, but, again like Kyffin, he is a great master of Welsh prose; in particular, because the *Plain Man's Pathway* is cast in dialogue form, he is given the opportunity to show himself capable of reproducing the rhythm and flavour of common speech as well as producing on occasion passages of exalted oratory. Rowland Vaughan, a Merionethshire gentleman who had been to Oxford, published in the same year as the *Sermon of Repentance* his translation of Bishop Lewis Bayly of Bangor's *Practice of Piety*, an extraordinarily popular handbook of devotion. Vaughan was a poet in both the 'strict' and 'free' metres and was also well-versed in the Welsh prose tradition, but his version of the *Practice*, although thoroughly competent, cannot quite match Llwyd's work for brilliance: it was, however, reprinted twice during the seventeenth century (1656, 1677), whereas Llwyd's *Sermon* and *Plain Man's Pathway* reappeared only once (in 1677 and 1682 respectively). Nevertheless it can be argued that both Llwyd and Vaughan were surpassed as prose-writers by Dr John Davies of Mallwyd, whose translation of *A book of Christian exercise appertaining to resolution*, Edmund Bunny's Protestant version of a popular work of exhortation by Fr Robert Persons SJ, appeared in 1632 bearing the simplified title *Llyfr y Resolusion* (Book of the Resolution). In this book John Davies, almost certainly the chief author of the final version of the Welsh Bible and by far the greatest scholar of Renaissance Wales, shows himself also to be a consummate master of Welsh prose: *Cymraeg cyfoes, coeth, clasurol* (contemporary, refined, classical Welsh) as Saunders Lewis once put it.

Welsh Anglican translation, and indeed Early Modern Welsh prose generally, reaches a summit with *Llyfr y Resolusion*. Welsh Anglican translators, however, were not inassiduous in building upon Davies's achievement, and rather more than forty titles were produced by them between the appearance of his book and the end of the seventeenth century. Only a few of the most notable will be mentioned here. The years of the Civil War were naturally inauspicious times for Anglican writers, but shortly afterwards John Edwards, deprived rector of Tredunnock in Monmouthshire, produced a translation of Edward Fisher's *Marrow of Modern Divinity* (1651) and a mysterious 'WLMA' a version of Henry Valentine's *Private Devotions* (1652); while Rowland Vaughan, although much embittered by his experiences during the Civil War, published in 1658 no less than six translations of works by such authors as Jean D'Espagne, William Brough and John Prideaux. Soon after the Restoration, Elis Lewis produced his version of Fr Jeremias Drexel SJ's *De aeternitate considerationes* (Considerations upon eternity) as Englished by Ralph Winterton, and John Langford his translation of Richard Allestree's enormously popular *Whole Duty of Man* (1672). During the seventies and eighties of the seventeenth century there was considerable co-operation between Anglican clergymen and Nonconformist ministers, led by the eirenic Stephen Hughes, in the matter of publishing Welsh religious books and providing elementary education for Welsh children (see further Chapter One). This co-operation is best symbolized by the 'Welsh Trust' of Thomas Gouge, a London Nonconformist minister and philanthropist, which operated most effectively between 1676 and 1681. However, although such co-operative efforts as the Welsh Trust brought about the reissue of some earlier Anglican books, their main output was of translations of works by the Puritan Richard Baxter and by Thomas Gouge himself (not forgetting the first Welsh version of John Bunyan's *Pilgrim's Progress*, published in 1688 by Stephen Hughes and three collaborators). Translations of purely Anglican works during the final decades of the seventeenth century are better exemplified by John Jones's version of John Songhurst's *Epistle of love and tender good will* (1683), Thomas Williams's version of William Sherlock's *Practical discourse concerning death* (1691) and, finally, Dafydd Maurice's version of Theophilus Dorrington's *Familiar guide to the right and profitable receiving of the Lord's Supper* (1700). Within a year of the appearance of Maurice's book, and strictly within the same tradition, Ellis Wynne was to publish his translation of Bishop Jeremy Taylor's *Rule and Exercise of Holy Living*, the precursor of his ground-breaking *Gweledigaethau* of 1703.

BIBLIOGRAPHY

Eiluned Rees, *Libri Walliae* (Aberystwyth, 1987) lists all the books mentioned.

M. Stephens (ed.), *The Oxford Companion to the Literature of Wales* (Oxford, 1986), has entries on many of the authors mentioned, as does J.E. Lloyd *et al.* (eds.), *The Dictionary of Welsh Biography down to 1940* (London, 1959).

G. Williams, *Recovery, Reorientation and Reformation: Wales c. 1415–1642* and Geraint H. Jenkins, *The Foundation of Modern Wales 1642–1780* (both Oxford and Cardiff, 1987) have much information about the literature of their respective periods as well as about the historical background.

For those who read Welsh, Thomas Parry and Merfyn Morgan, *Llyfryddiaeth Llenyddiaeth Gymraeg* (Caerdydd, 1976), 122–54 and G.O. Watts, *Llyfryddiaeth Llenyddiaeth Gymraeg, Cyfrol 2* (Caerdydd ac Aberystwyth, 1993), 106–19 provide authoritative guidance to the secondary literature on the field.

CHAPTER 8

SEVENTEENTH-CENTURY PURITAN WRITERS: MORGAN LLWYD AND CHARLES EDWARDS

M. WYNN THOMAS

The year 1630 is a very important, if neglected, date in modern Welsh history. It marks both the inauguration of a new phase in the history of Welsh literary culture and the beginnings of a proto-modern sense of national identity. These were the long-term, and wholly unintentional, consequences of an event of momentous *religious* significance that year, when the standard Welsh Bible of 1620 (a revised edition of the great original translation of 1588) was for the first time published in a form (the little Bible) and at a price (the five-shilling Bible) that made it available to 'Welsh families, who never enjoyed it before this time in the like manner and measure'. Those are the appreciative words of Oliver Thomas (*c.* 1598–1652), a Puritan lecturer, whose *Car-wr y Cymru* (Affectionate friend to the Welsh, 1631) was a devotional work expressly designed to capitalize spiritually on the appearance of the little Bible. Indeed, it would be fair to say that, although Puritanism did not arrive in Wales with the 1630 Bible, it entered Welsh literature very largely thanks to that Bible's publication, which immediately inspired devout reformers to produce accompanying spiritual exercises of their own. Unremarkable or humbly derivative though most of these books and tracts were, they worked cumulatively to transform Welsh culture in ways that eventually made possible the appearance of religious writers of undeniable genius, such as William Williams (1717–91) and Ann Griffiths (1776–1805). These were neo-Puritan writers of the eighteenth-century Methodist Revival, hymn-writers whose talents came to be enthusiastically honoured in the nineteenth century by the formidable Nonconformist culture which they had helped form. However, in Morgan Llwyd (1619–59) and Charles Edwards (1628–91?) seventeenth-century Puritanism also produced two figures of imposing spiritual stature and literary genius, and the majesty of their best prose works was an unconscious tribute to the power of the little Bible to produce a great grandeur of spiritual imagination.

Just like that five-shilling Bible (which had been financed by wealthy London Welshmen), Puritanism was a 'foreign' product imported into Wales from England. Throughout the seventeenth century the Welsh remained as attached to the Anglican Church as they were to the English monarchy. Puritanism had little impact either on the gentry or on the bulk of the common people. As it spread along the trade routes, permeated the border region, and took firm hold in such prosperous burgher towns as Wrexham, Cardiff, Swansea and Carmarthen, it remained very much the preserve of the anglicized middle classes. Welsh Puritans constantly lamented the moral sloth and spiritual backwardness of a people that seemed so content to spurn salvation. The contrast with spiritually progressive England, where Puritanism was such a vigorously challenging presence, seemed humiliatingly clear. But paradoxically, this very contrast served to emphasize the irreducible 'otherness' of Wales. Obviously, this otherness was inseparable from the Welsh language, to which Puritans paid particular attention since it was the medium through which they could hope to transform Welsh moral consciousness. But equally obviously, the Welsh were a people historically distinct from the English, a fact which made sense to the Puritans as it had done to earlier Welsh Protestants, as Richard Davies (1501?–81) demonstrated in the great, immensely influential, Epistle to the Welsh People that prefaced the Welsh translation of the New Testament published in 1567 (see the preceding chapter). After all, the Old Testament clearly showed how a historic 'people' could be a social body very close to God's heart, and how a nation's history could be providentially ordained. Ever conscious of the example of Israel, the early Puritans found it natural to think of the Welsh as a separate people under God, and to find evidence of this throughout Welsh history, from the very earliest times. When Oliver Thomas published a prayer for Wales in his Puritan tract of 1631, it was to the song of Simeon that he turned for words to express his vision of a specifically *national* salvation:

> I praise thee for thy goodness, and thy wonders to my dear nation. And when my eyes see thy salvation coming in this manner to the dwellings of my dear people, then I sing the song of Simeon; namely

lettest thou thy servant depart this hour in peace, Lord, for my eyes have seen thy salvation.

The works of Morgan Llwyd and Charles Edwards are consciously addressed to an entire nation. 'O people of Wales!', wrote Llwyd in 1653, 'my voice is directed at you . . . The dawn has broken and the sun has risen on you. The birds are singing; awake (O Welshman), awake; . . . behold, the world and its pillars are shaking. The earth is in turmoil, there is thunder and lightning in the minds of the peoples.' Writing as he was when the radical sectarians were in confident control of government through the Parliament of the Saints, Llwyd had every ecstatic reason to suppose that the day of Christ's second coming was near at hand, and his visionary prose resonates to his millenarian excitement. By contrast, Edwards's greatest work developed under circumstances of domestic unhappiness, religious persecution and deep disillusionment with his nation. In its original form (published 1667), *Y Ffydd Ddi-ffuant* (a title borrowed from 1 Tim 1:5, *faith unfeigned*) was the product of years of enforced idleness following his removal, shortly before the Restoration, from the parish of Llanrhaeadr-ym-Mochnant. Having faithfully served alongside the likes of Llwyd, Walter Cradock (1610–59) and Vavasor Powell (1617–70) in the Welsh Puritan administration (1649–59), Edwards now found that, in spite of his ostensibly meek submission to the new religious and political order instituted by the Restoration, he was nevertheless required to pay the price. It turned out to be a heavy one, since in 1666 persecution took its toll on his immediate family, leading to the death of one of his children and the estrangement of his wife. In both the later, greatly augmented, editions of his book (1671 and 1677), he therefore found it natural to identify passionately with Gildas, the sixth-century monk who had so excoriated the Welsh for their moral corruption in his *De Excidio Britanniae*. Edwards, too, can excel at lament that modulates into a rhetoric of disgust:

> But at present, since scarcely any provide good examples to be followed, and that the gospel has grown old, and the strange gifts of the spirit to produce miracles and visions have ceased to such a degree, and so much of the work of converting the peoples has been completed, and worldly satisfaction has grown so proud, it cannot be but that gospel godliness has ebbed greatly compared to what once was.

Y Ffydd Ddi-ffuant everywhere bears the marks of Edwards's erudition. Educated at the then Royalist stronghold of Oxford, he continued throughout his life to read widely in Welsh, English and classical authors, and the opening section of his ambitious work, in which is traced the history of the great religious faiths of the world (with pride of place naturally going to Christianity), consists very largely of a synthesis of materials from a wide variety of scholarly sources. Similarly, Edwards is indebted in the later sections of his book to the considerable reading he had done in both the important and the popular English theological texts of his period, including Samuel Purchas's *Purchas his Pilgrimage* (1613), Richard Knolles's *Generall Historie of the Turks* (1603), William Bedwell's *Mahommedis Imposturae* (1615) and, most notably, Foxe's famous *Acts and Monuments* (1563–70)—that key text in the construction of an English Protestant nation. By comparison, Llwyd's formal education seems relatively slight. Although he had attended grammar school in Wrexham, most of the important influences on his mental development had been not only extra-curricular in origin but also strikingly unorthodox and heterogeneous in character. From his home background in remote, rural Gwynedd (where his family had for centuries been respected minor gentry) he derived his knowledge of fabulated Welsh history and his grasp of the skills of *barddas* (the ancient tradition of *cynghanedd* writing, requiring a mastery of the demandingly elaborate rules of strict-metre poetry). Following his religious conversion in Wrexham at the age of sixteen, he was supplied from England and the Welsh borders with an understanding of Puritan experience which he was later to enrich through his readings in the works of the highly unorthodox German mystic and pietist Jacob Böhme. And he may well have been pointed in this adventurous intellectual direction by the many restlessly questing individuals (collectively known as 'seekers') he met during his time as peripatetic chaplain in the militarily disciplined but intellectually turbulent ranks of the New Model Army.

In addition to this difference in educational background and personal circumstances, there is also the difference of spiritual temperament to consider when pairing Llwyd with the fiery yet frequently politic Edwards. Llwyd was much the more inward of the two, a man whose whole character was profoundly keyed to the deep, secret harmonies of his serene inner life. In an English letter

he spoke with sweet plainness of the root and ground of his entire
being: 'I finde that the Lord Jesus is as a golden mine in our own
fields, under our owne earth, and is in Saints as the soul in the eye,
or Sun in the Firmament, or fire in the inward furnance, or
inhabitant in a house.' The sequence of tropes is not simply
decorative, but essential for articulating the complex dynamic of the
spiritual experience with which Llwyd is here concerned. The
presence of Christ is the great hidden potential in, and of, every
human existence: it alone can bestow the power of authentic vision
upon the eye, centrally illuminate the interior universe of the soul,
supply the vital energies of being, and convert a rudimentary
human structure into a real dwelling place of the spirit. But
eloquent though Llwyd is on this subject in English, it is through
the great diapason of his Welsh prose that he most fully succeeds in
suggesting the sublime magnitude of the intimate mystery of
Christ's Immanence:

> For the new man is one with God, and that man alone shall be saved.
> Therefore do not rest (through fleshly faith) in this, that Christ has died
> for you, or in this either, that Christ is beginning to rise in you, and the
> signs of God's grace appearing. But understand the fountainhead of all,
> which is the Father in you, for thy life is hidden in God Himself with
> Christ, just as the life of the tree is hidden in its root throughout the time
> of winter. This is the root of all knowledge, and the sum of the eternal
> Gospel. Enter into your secret chamber, which is the light of God within
> you.

The passage opens with a simple sentence that summarizes the
mystical Pauline message about the indwelling Christ. The
remainder of the passage takes the form of an unfolding of the
meanings of that sentence, as Llwyd first employs a discriminatory
syntax that instructs the mind in spiritual finesse, before
demonstrating the firm logical links in the descending chain of his
central mystical argument (if Christ is in man and God is in Christ,
then man is actually united with God through Christ). The passage
then concludes with a quietly recessive image which links back to,
and lyrically reinforces, the opening statement.

Tropes seem to have been integral to Llwyd's distinctive mode of
understanding spiritual experience, so much so that at key points he
seems to 'reason in metaphor', as was once memorably said of
Edmund Burke. Images were, perhaps, for Llwyd, the most
compelling example of language's simultaneous power and poverty

as a vehicle of spiritual expression. Even at their most heuristically profound, tropes can never wholly dispel the pathos of their status as mere figures of human speech: even metaphors are only similitudes masquerading as facts. 'All of this is nothing', says the Dove in *Llyfr y Tri Aderyn* (The Book of the Three Birds, 1653), 'but a hurried glimpse in a mirror, or a rose that wilts even as we smell it'. The allusion here to Paul's famous image of the darkling glass is as suggestive as it is obvious, for Llwyd shared the Apostle's passionate eschatological belief that we shall shortly look upon the whole truth face to face. In other words, Llwyd's millenarian expectations are deeply inscribed in his discourse, in the sense that they determine the deep structure of his thinking and his writing. As a recent theological commentator has pointed out, the Vulgate version of Paul's great passage reads as follows: *Videmus nunc per speculum in aenigmate, tunc autem facie ad faciem.* This brings out the significant derivation (from 'mirror') of the verb 'to speculate', and all its related forms.

But if Llwyd is clearly haunted by the merely 'speculative' nature of images (along with all other human forms of understanding), relative to the definitive truth that will ultimately be revealed, he is equally clearly attracted to the surpassing cognitive powers of the image, compared with other forms of human articulation. He might conceivably be brought to agree, albeit guardedly, with the great post-Symbolist aesthetician Ernst Cassirer that 'only in the mobile and multiform [image], which seems to be constantly bursting its own limits, does the fullness of the world-forming logos find its counterpart'. Whereas many of Llwyd's Puritan friends and contemporaries primarily valued what Walter Cradock called 'the spiritual reason', he himself seemed instinctively inclined to trust and empower another faculty, which might be termed the spiritual imagination. The opening sentence of his very first book *Llythur ir Cymru Cariadus* (A letter to the beloved Welsh people), is driven and directed by similes: 'Books are as fountains, and teachers as a multitude of lights among some people at this present time.' And within a very few sentences he is again multiplying tropes in order to mediate truths:

> Almost all respect the bats under the sun more than the eagles, try to raise the spirit of man above the spirit of God, follow their own candles in ignorance of the heavenly sun in the high firmament.

> And alas, alas, alas, that many of the Welsh too, the wise as much as
> the unwise, are living in the sieve of vanity, and in the bile of bitterness,
> lying in the bonds of untruth in the bed of Babel, grazing in the
> meadows of the devil to feed the flesh, without knowing the invisible
> God who made them or the blessed God who bought them or the kind
> God who is crying at their doors to enter into them to dwell in them.

Here images are part of the very substance of the original
thought, as well as an effective means of communication. It is in
this latter way, though, that tropes primarily function in Charles
Edwards's prose. His work is noted for the figures of speech used to
clarify meaning through illustration and, as one would therefore
expect, one of his favourite devices is the extended simile—a
comparison developed in such a detailed, leisurely and expansive
way that it allows the reader to keep both vehicle and tenor
constantly in mind:

> When the winds buffet the corn as it flowers, despite the flimsiness of
> the wisp that holds the flower yet because man cannot live without
> nourishment God causes the grain to maintain its grip in spite of strong
> opposition; in the same manner God's providence may be seen to keep
> the corn of the soul.

Alive as he is to the homiletic power of the simile, Edwards often
deliberately turns, for his examples, to homely aspects of the
contemporary world. So the residual presence of God in the
corrupt soul is likened to the sheen that rubbing can still produce
from an old silver coin, long after the king's image has been worn
away. Deploring the way the Gospel had for centuries been available
only in Latin, he pithily notes that 'for the common people it was
like food locked away, with a step-mother as custodian of the key'.
And his attractive alertness to everyday experience is also
occasionally evident in other aspects of his writing. Whereas the
Welsh are reluctant, he complains, to spend money on buying the
Scriptures, the Bible is to be seen in the hands of English children
almost 'as often as bread and butter'.

As these examples suggest, Edwards is clearly a notable exponent
of the 'plain style' that had been so beloved by many Puritans
(including the Welshmen Oliver Thomas and Walter Cradock) from
the very beginning; and of the various kinds of Puritan discourse
(many of them, like Llwyd's, radical and innovative) that had been
practised during the turbulent Commonwealth period, it was

obviously this older, direct and accessible, style that was best suited to the cool rational temper of the Restoration period in which Edwards began to write. Indeed, it is not surprising that Llwyd's work tended to go out of favour with Nonconformists after 1660. He had himself had profound misgivings about the obscurity of his writings, even going so far as to accuse himself, at one arresting point in *Llyfr y Tri Aderyn*, of not fully understanding what he was trying to say. However, his had been an ecstatic, mystical rhetoric wholly appropriate to the apocalyptic times in which many had then felt they were living. There had been a widespread belief in progressive revelation, so that people like Llwyd could legitimately suppose that mysterious figures of speech were the harbingers of profounder understanding. It was this spiritual climate that fostered the extraordinary early writings of George Fox, the greatest of the founding fathers of the Quaker sect (to which several of Llwyd's followers were eventually attracted), and nothing illustrates the dramatic change of temper that followed the Restoration better than the startling difference between Fox's intensely questing original tracts (of the early 1650s) and the monumentally rational exposition of the Quaker faith published by Robert Barclay in *An Apology for the true Christian divinity* (1678).

As has recently been noted, Charles Edwards wrote much of *Y Ffydd Ddi-ffuant* in such a way that the opening sentences of successive paragraphs would, if removed from context and placed in sequence, constitute a clearly developing argument:

> The creation of the world should also persuade you to acknowledge that there is a God . . . And it is not incredible that God created the world from nothing, since there is as great a difference between living and unliving as there is between matter and nothing . . . The Creation also informs us like Moses that there is but one God . . . Moreover, The Holy Trinity is not without its impression on many.

As can be seen, Edwards likes to follow the common Puritan practice of first carefully subdividing a topic and then considering each of its elements separately. He habitually highlights a subject, such as the wholesale corruption of man's being that has resulted from the Fall, and then proceeds to deal with it comprehensively by analysing it into its component parts—the universality and inescapability of sin (as suffered by all peoples, of all ages, and all degrees), its power over all of man's powers and faculties, its essential character as the antithesis of the divine, and its invariable harmfulness to man. Such an exhaustive analysis of evil is, of course, prologue to his equally methodical explanation of how grace alone can vanquish sin. And, unlike Llwyd, he is always ready to employ the classical Puritan terms for distinguishing between the different steps involved in the process of salvation, carefully drawing the customary distinction, for example, between such categories as justification and sanctification.

Compared to Llwyd, Edwards is a systematic thinker and it is accordingly easy to determine what his views are on key points of doctrine. The difference between them in this respect may very largely be a matter of temperament, but it may also again partly derive from their respective historical situations. Although Edwards outwardly compromised with the new authorities to a degree that has prompted some modern historians to brand him a contemptible trimmer, he began to write at a time when the powerful Puritans had been newly turned, following the Restoration, into proscribed, harassed, and sometimes persecuted, Nonconformists. It was therefore a period when distressed believers needed to be rallied and their faith reinforced, and when the full power of the Gospel's message of salvation had to be authoritatively communicated to what Edwards regarded as an arrogantly unredeemed world. Under such circumstances clarity of doctrinal explanation, complete with telling 'proofs' (both experiential and logical), was obviously highly desirable.

That Edwards was himself very conscious of the spiritually remedial work his age so urgently required is evident from the many years he spent in London overseeing the translation of several of the classic works of English Puritanism into Welsh. Yet underlying, and perhaps secretly powering, all this steady, dedicated labour were psychic tensions that eventually resulted in Edwards's mental breakdown. As has frequently been noted, the autobiography he wrote towards the end of his life bears signs that suggest he may by then have been suffering from paranoia, a condition that may well have been the outcome of years of secret mental struggle with a hostile world. To realize this is perhaps to read *Y Ffydd Ddi-ffuant* in a more sympathetic spirit. One now notices how the drama of the writing derives as much from Edwards's need to convince himself as from his missionary efforts to convert others. So, for instance, the opening part of the book, outlining the Christian view of history from the Creation to Edwards's own time, is more than the sum of the many learned sources from which it has been so assiduously assembled. It is a psychologically heroic attempt to construct, in the face of present desolating disappointments, a master narrative of history that proves it to have been providentially designed, after all, to culminate in the perfected, Puritan version of the Protestant religion. Edwards's indefatigable search (in the approved Puritan fashion) for every scrap of evidence (typological and otherwise) that confirms the teleology of history can seem faintly risible to a modern reader. In particular his narrative can seem 'over-determined', as if he were excessively concerned to clinch his case at every conceivable point. However, the pathos of passion in the writing becomes apparent when one sees it as deriving, like Milton's *Samson Agonistes*, from an attempt to compensate for the historical defeat of the cause to which the author had devoted his life.

Since his feelings of oppression were denied open expression, Edwards vented them indirectly by dwelling almost pruriently, for instance, on the agonies of torture suffered by the martyrs whose bloody stories he had read in John Foxe's famous *Acts and Monuments*. Much more affecting, though, are the explorations of psychological distress in the later parts of his work, where he deals with the condition of the individual soul:

> Hard weather without aggravates the heat of guilt within; and while the worldly conditions are cloudy, lightning often shoots through the mind. Sins that are not perceived in the successful warmth, and the muggy atmosphere of wantonness, appear as numerous as stars when the heart begins to cool.

Moreover, Edwards was exceptionally sensitive, like Llwyd, to the emotional charge of the Welsh language itself, excited by the sensuous interaction between its open vowels and hard consonants. He argued that Welsh must have originated in the Middle East, since 'when spoken it is very like Hebrew, coming from the regions of the heart, from the very root of the jaws, and not, like English, from the tip of the tongue'.

He went so far as to append to *Y Ffydd Ddi-ffuant* a table supposedly demonstrating the close correspondences between a long list of Welsh and Hebrew words. This 'evidence', for which he was heavily indebted to such earlier Welsh scholars as William Salesbury (*c.* 1520–84?), Maurice Kyffin (*c.* 1555–98), John Davies

of Mallwyd (*c.* 1567–1644) and Thomas Salusbury (1612–43), was
meant to confirm the theory (to which Llwyd also subscribed) that
the multiplicity of modern languages dated from the disaster of
Babel, when the original single language of the spirit (Hebrew) had
become fractured.

Absurd though this theory may seem to us today, it is probable
that it contributed substantially to the development of the genius of
both Edwards and Llwyd as prose-writers, since it gave positive
spiritual sanction to their instinctive, sensual love of the phonetic
patterns and phonic dynamics of the Welsh language. They then
proceeded to exploit these aspects of their medium to produce
morally powerful effects, as in the following sentences by Edwards:
*Y mae brunti pechadurus yn llawn o nadroedd, a'u colynnau yn eu
cynffonnau. Yn niwedd direidi pechod y mae mileindra, a chwerwedd
bustlaidd yn gymysc â gwaddod ei win* (Sinful foulness is full of
serpents, with their stings in their tails. At the end of sin's evil there
is ferocity, and bilious bitterness mixed with the dregs of its wine).
Through the liquefaction of sounds, the sentence enacts, or
sonically emblematizes, the malign metamorphoses that guileful sin
contrives: at the last, the serpents display the stings (*colynnau*) in
their tails (*cynffonnau*), and evil (*direidi*) is transformed into
mileindra (savagery).

Remarkable though Edwards's gift is for exploiting the phonic
resources of his medium, it is surpassed by that of Llwyd, who may
well have felt literally inspired to reveal through his writing the
hidden spiritual syntax of the Welsh language. As Nigel Smith has
recently shown, daringly experimental English prose was produced
throughout the 1650s, because so many radical religious writers felt
that only by transfiguring discourse could they adequately express
their visionary experiences. Llwyd's magnificent Welsh prose is a
product of the same spiritual conviction, and it features many of
the innovative devices singled out for comment by Smith from the
work of such radicals and ecstatics as George Fox, Laurence
Clarkson, John Webster and Joseph Salmon. In his relatively
measured and temperate way, Llwyd indulges in word-play,
elaborate internal rhymes, and insinuatingly intimate use of
pronouns, bracketed digressions to suggest an inwardness of
reflection, emblematic variations in typography, and many other
means of suggesting an urgently inspired speaking that transcends
the normal rules of expression. In particular, he has many

compelling ways of indicating that his consciousness has been heightened and his tongue liberated by the presence of the Spirit. On occasions it is as if, like the Quakers, he were under an irresistible compulsion to speak:

> This Flesh is the enemy of God, the poison of man, the livery of hell, the image of the beast, the beloved of the sinner, the refuge of the hypocrite, the web of the spider, the merchant of souls, the home of the lost, and the dung-heap of devils.

However, in spite of the power this sentence possesses to convey a rapture of personal insight, it also betrays the debt Llwyd owed to the great rhetorical traditions, the one Welsh the other classical, in which he had been trained. It is, perhaps, the influence of classical Welsh poetry which is most evident in his particular case, as Llwyd constructs a chain of hyperbolic images or conceits after the famous fashion of the *cywyddwyr*—the ingenious artificers of the great strict-metre poetry of the Middle Ages. But if Llwyd's work partly marks the culturally significant point at which the practice of elaborate formal verbal patterning crosses over from *cynghanedd* poetry to Welsh prose, it also partly marks the juncture at which the devices definitively classified in the traditional manuals of classical rhetoric become thoroughly normalized in Welsh practice. Without a doubt, such thoroughgoing assimilation and normalization was made possible only by the majestic examples of religious rhetoric already available in the great Welsh Bible of William Morgan, first published in 1588. But Llwyd may well have been prepared to appreciate these aspects of Bishop Morgan's literary skills by the basic training in classical rhetoric he presumably received at Wrexham Grammar School. As for Charles Edwards, his Oxford education would, of course, have provided him with a thorough grounding in classical rhetoric, and the extent to which he valued such a training, and had benefited from it, is evident from the descriptive list of the main rhetorical figures he appended to the final edition of *Y Ffydd Ddi-ffuant*.

The sonorous dignity of utterance Llwyd could achieve by employing rhetorical figures is evident from the following example:

> Oferedd yw printio llawer o lyfrau; blinder yw cynnwys llawer o feddyliau; peryglus yw dwedyd llawer o eiriau; anghymharus yw croesawu llawer o ysbrydoedd, a ffolineb yw ceisio ateb holl resymau

dynion: ond, O ddyn, cais di adnabod dy galon dy hun, a mynd i mewn
i'r porth cyfyng.

Llawer sydd yn ymwthio, ychydig yn mynd i'r bywyd; llawer yn
breuddwydio, ac ychydig yn deffro; llawer yn saethu, ac ychydig yn
cyrhaeddyd y nod: pawb yn sôn am Dduw ac yn edrych ar waith ei
ddwylo, ond heb weled nesed yw fo ei hunan atynt yn rhoi anadl i bawb,
a bywyd ysbrydol i ni.

[Vain it is to print many books; exhausting it is to embrace many
opinions; dangerous it is to speak many words; inconsistent it is to
welcome many spirits, and foolish it is to attempt to answer all of men's
arguments: but, O man, attempt thou to know thine own heart, and to
enter into the narrow gate.

Many there are who jostle together, few who enter into the life; many
do dream, and few do waken; many shoot and few reach the target: all
speak of God and gaze on his handiwork, but without seeing how near
he himself is to them, giving breath to all, and spiritual life to us.]

Here inversion helps to foreground the elaborate style of repetition
(*repetitio*) which includes reiterated words as well as recycled
syntax. Phrases ending with similar sounds (*similiter desinens*) are
threaded together to form a sequence that generates cumulative
power. The turn from the formal to the familiar (*familiaritas*) is
beautifully contrived, and coincides with the emergence of the new
structural principle of contrast (*contrarium*), which includes single
phrases yoking opposites together and is calculated to emphasize
the essential difference between two contrasting spiritual states
(*dissimilitudo*). Urgency is injected into the passage by the
apostrophe 'O man', which brings the listener into focus alongside
the speaker (*communicatio*).

Charles Edwards was equally familiar with the extensive
schematio of classical rhetoric, as laid out, for instance, in *Eglvryn
Phraethineb*, the Welsh manual of rhetoric published in 1595 by
Henri Perri, a disciple of Ramus. Like Llwyd, he was therefore
capable of making masterly use of a variety of figures; but the
architectonics of his prose is frequently less elaborate, even though
he excels at pithy formulations, epigrammatic phrases and
proverbial expressions of a kind that Llwyd, too, regularly favours:

Dod heibio dy rag-farn, dos at yr scrythyrau i geisio gwybod ewyllys
Duw, nid i gadarnhau dy ewyllys dy hun. Bydd ostyngedig; y pethau a
guddiwyd rhag y beilchion, y ddatcuddir i rai bychain: Ir pant y rhed dwfr
y bywyd. Drwy rigolau'r galon ddrylliedig, y daw goleuni nefol i mewn.

[Put by your prejudice, go to the scriptures to seek to know the will of
God, not to confirm your own will. Be humble; the things that are
hidden from the proud will be revealed to the little ones; the water of life
runs to the hollow. Through the chinks in the shattered heart will the
heavenly light enter in.]

Clearly designed as they are to penetrate the mind and lodge in the
memory, these succinct phrases remind us that the main concern of
both Edwards and Llwyd was to create an affective rhetoric
powerful enough to effect a profound transformation in people's
lives. Their aim was, after all, first to help save souls and then to
help keep them in a state of grace. To this end they employed a
prose style that was infinitely supple, as capable of swelling into
anger as of subsiding into beguiling serenity; one minute intensely
emotional the next rigorously intellectual in its examination of
complex theological issues.

Whereas Llwyd is the more intuitive writer, instinctively alert to
the labyrinthine twists and turns of the troubled human psyche in
its existential travails, Edwards is the better able of the two to map
out the main areas of spiritual concern. His skill in this respect
comes very much into its own in a long work like *Y Ffydd Ddi-
ffuant*, since it enables him to provide the book with a convincing
overall design that makes it an imposingly coherent composition.
His success is all the more remarkable when it is recalled that the
work was actually developed piecemeal, through three successive
editions (1667, 1671, 1677), and there is no evidence to suggest that
Edwards had any idea, when he started, what form his book would
eventually take. Initially he intended only to describe, in Christian
terms, the history of the world from the Creation to his own times.
This historical material was not significantly altered when the book
was later more than doubled in size through the addition of new
sections, but Edwards skilfully integrated it into his new design by
re-presenting it as evidence for the divine origin and character of
the Christian faith. These proofs from history were then reinforced,
in the new sections, by other kinds of evidence, such as the divine
qualities discernible in Christian doctrine and true faith's proven
power to overcome human corruption. One notable consequence of
Edwards's final method is that it allows him to place the struggles of
the individual soul in the context of the whole of history, thus
turning the internal drama of personal salvation into what Marxists
would call a great world-historical event. This correlation of the

psychological and the cosmic was, of course, an essential feature of Puritan thinking, as Milton memorably demonstrated in *Paradise Lost*. The structure of *Y Ffydd Ddi-ffuant* in its final form may thus be said to have profound theological significance, beginning as it does with the Creation of the world and ending with the recreation of the individual human soul.

Of the five classic works of Welsh religious prose published by Llwyd only one, *Llyfr y Tri Aderyn*, is on a scale comparable to *Y Ffydd Ddi-ffuant*. It takes the form of a conversation, primarily about spiritual matters, between the imposing Eagle (representing secular authority), the scavenging Raven (the worldly Anglicans) and the pacific otherworldly Dove (the Sectarians, under the guidance of the Spirit). The opening section of the book is dominated by exchanges between the first two birds, during which the main social, political and religious issues of the day are discussed as the Raven seeks to persuade the Eagle of the dangers of Puritanism and the advisability of returning to the traditional state of affairs in both church and government. The Sectarians are portrayed as illiterate anarchists, secretly intent on the violent overthrow of all properly constituted authority. However, the peevish tone of the Raven's intemperate complaints, the manifest cunning of his partisan arguments, and the vindictiveness of his anti-Puritan remarks, help to disqualify him in the eyes both of the reader and of the Eagle, who scarcely bothers to conceal his impatience and contempt. By such dramatic devices as these Llwyd the skilful propagandist prepares us to listen to the sweet voice of his Dove, who is willing to share its spiritual secrets with us only after the Raven has abruptly departed in a huff.

Both Raven and Dove figure prominently, of course, in the account of the Flood as found in the book of Genesis, and indeed the debate in *Llyfr y Tri Aderyn* is centred on the story of Noah and his Ark, which the early Apostles had taken to be an allegorical representation of God's relationship to his Church. Through the figure of the Dove, Llwyd attacks the traditional claims of both the Catholic and the Anglican Churches to be the true Ark in which sanctuary from sin could be found, and emphasizes instead that it is through Christ alone, and not through any human institution, that man can be saved. This is the true meaning of the profound central mystery of the Ark, and the Dove proceeds to elaborate upon it in the second part of *Llyfr y Tri Aderyn* in response to a number of questions put to him by the spiritually humble and enquiring Eagle. The result is a series of mystical meditations on many of the key areas of Christine doctrine, including the nature of the Godhead, the process of Creation, the reasons for the Fall, the operations of the Spirit and the offer of Salvation. While never clearly departing from, let alone directly challenging, orthodox Puritan teaching on these matters, Llwyd develops such a highly unconventional and densely suggestive discourse—in which St Paul's language of faith is blended with that of Böhme, and typological imagery is combined with Llwyd's own inventive figures of speech—that the impression given is of a strikingly original religious vision. The arcane or esoteric aspects of this vision are offered by the Dove as evidence of the supra-human profundity of the matters being contemplated, which can at present be apprehended only partially at best, and then only by the redeemed; but there is the further, millenarian, implication that these mysteries will very shortly become more intelligible to the saints, when Christ returns to earth. The rhetoric of *Llyfr y Tri Aderyn* serves therefore both to signify the enticingly special understanding already available to the spiritually initiated, and to adumbrate the perfected understanding which will shortly be theirs.

Particularly interesting is the way Llwyd regards human sinfulness as a perversion of creative energy resulting from the arresting of spiritual development. Energies that originally found complete expression in the context of a worshipful, self-transcending relationship with God, turned destructive at the Fall when they were used instead merely for the gratification and the aggrandizement of the Self. Indeed for Llwyd, as for Böhme, the original sin of man is the sin of ruthlessly narcissistic self-regard. Selfhood is the root of all evil, so that 'almost all while on earth . . . have a striving in their secret bosom between two Monarchs, Christ and Satan, Self and Selfhood, Flesh and Spirit, Conscience and Corruption'. Salvation therefore involves the destruction of Selfhood, through the power of grace, accompanied by a regeneration of spiritual life as man discovers his true Christocentric identity—the latent presence of Christ in the deepest ground of his inner being. But until he is saved man will continue to live unwittingly and complacently in a state of chronic self-alienation:

[he] lives as if on a beach shore, where the ebb and flow of flesh and blood works incessantly, without thinking that he is on a precipice, and on the crag of eternity, going in to the world that lasts forever, but sleeping under the paws of the cat of hell and talking entertainingly in his sleep and his slumber.

'Awaken (O Welshman) awaken . . . look about you and see', Llwyd wrote in *Gwaedd Ynghymru yn Wyneb pob Cydwybod* (A cry in Wales in the face of every conscience), another of the great works he published in 1653. Together with *Llythur ir Cymru Cariadus* (A letter to the beloved Welsh, 1653) and *Cyfarwyddid ir Cymru* (Instructions for the Welsh, 1657) this forms a group of shorter works that are eloquently evangelical in character, and given the difficulties Llwyd (unlike Edwards) clearly experienced in sustaining a work of the length of *Llyfr y Tri Aderyn*—a book which may in many ways best be regarded as an impressive compilation of brief meditations—it could be persuasively argued that his genius is actually to be seen at its greatest in these magnificent devotional tracts, which are the closest Welsh Puritanism came to producing mystical-theological writings of the kind and quality associated with the great Rhineland mystics Meister Eckhart and Johannes Tauler.

Since these tracts are specifically designed to win men to salvation, they are psychologically searching and emotionally affecting as well as spiritually enquiring, and they include passages of exceptional lucidity as Llwyd endeavours to demonstrate the profoundly simple economy of the divine scheme. By contrast, his book *Gair o'r Gair* (A Word from the Word, 1656) is a complex design of meditative arabesques on the subject of the Logos. Little attracted by the Evangelists' narrative of the Word made Flesh, who dwelt among us, Llwyd is primarily fascinated by the Word as it was in the beginning, and as it continues, through the resurrected Christ, to inhabit every person who comes into the world. In this latter respect his Christology is, of course, very Pauline in character, following as he does the apostle's example in explaining 'the mystery which hath been hid from ages and from generations, but now is made manifest to his saints. To whom God would make known what is the riches of this glory among the Gentiles; which is Christ in you, the hope of glory' (Col 1: 26–7). But Llwyd's related, Johannine understanding of the Word in its original and eternal Trinitarian aspects is developed very much under the influence of his readings of Böhme in English translations, two of which he himself further translated into Welsh. The Lutheran had evolved his own idiosyncratic doctrine, according to which the Trinity consisted of an eternal dynamic of intergenerative relationships between the expressing, energizing Father, the expressed, energized Word and *its* expression as the creative power of the Spirit. Böhme seems to have thought of these interdependent relationships as constituting a kind of spiritual chain-reaction, and he emphasized that each of these participating powers truly existed only in and through its relationship with the others. Once the chain-reaction was interrupted (which happened within man's being in the Fall) then the power of the Father, no longer mediated through the Word and Spirit, could only be experienced in human terms as fiercely destructive. Llwyd followed Böhme in using this psycho-spiritual model to explain both the nature of the Fall and the nature of redemption.

Such subtle speculations about the Logos are a very far cry indeed from the simplistic belief in a triumphalist 'King Jesus' that characterized the Fifth Monarchists, the renegade group of millenarian insurrectionists with whom Llwyd briefly sympathized in early 1654, following the disillusioned Cromwell's angry dissolution of the Parliament of the Saints. Quickly regretting his rashness, Llwyd reverted, in the face of uncongenial political developments, to an emphasis on *inner*, purely spiritual reformation, an emphasis that is as evident in his best English works (*Lazarus and his sisters discoursing of paradise*, 1655 and *Where is Christ?* 1655) as in his Welsh writings. His submission to what he regarded as the legally constituted authority of Cromwell, and his quietist belief in letting history run its preordained course, is made clear in *An Honest Discourse between three neighbours* (1655).

In 1655 Llwyd was counselling himself and others to 'look no more too much at your windows upon Time and the flowers and motions of time, but look in upon Eternity in your own chamber, that ye may come to the ground of all things, and of yourselves'. These are the words of a time-scarred man, who had lived through violently turbulent times and whose original faith in the divine pattern of contemporary history was eventually deeply shaken by events. Tradition has it that squabbles within his own church deepened his misgivings over the next few years so that he died a disappointed man. However, his death in 1659 saved him from the anguish that befell Charles Edwards, who had in a sense to re-evaluate his faith in the light of the triumphant restoration of the previously anathematized Church and king. But what must strike us now is how dramatically circumstanced both Llwyd and Edwards were, and how deeply their historical situation must have influenced their religious writings. Indeed, it could almost be said that their unacknowledged secular muse was Clio, even though they believed themselves to be writing under the intimate direction of the Spirit. In any case, the outcome was a body of religious work of supreme literary as well as spiritual quality, that continues to offer us compelling evidence of the impressive nature of mature Puritan experience.

BIBLIOGRAPHY

Hugh Bevan, *Morgan Llwyd y Llenor* (Caerdydd, 1954).

John H. Davies (ed.), *Gweithiau Morgan Llwyd o Wynedd* II (Bangor a Llundain, 1907).

P.J. Donovan (ed.), *Ysgrifeniadau Byrion Morgan Llwyd* (Caerdydd, 1985).

T.E. Ellis (ed.), *Gweithiau Morgan Llwyd o Wynedd* I (Bangor a Llundain, 1899).

E. Lewis Evans, *Morgan Llwyd: ymchwil i rai o'r prif ddylanwadau a fu arno* (Lerpwl, 1930).

Geraint H. Jenkins, *The Foundations of Modern Wales* (Oxford and Cardiff, 1987).

Idem, *Protestant Dissenters in Wales: 1639–1689* (Cardiff, 1992).

J. Graham Jones a Goronwy Wyn Owen (eds.), *Gweithiau Morgan Llwyd o Wynedd* III (Caerdydd, 1994).

R.M. Jones, 'Morgan Llwyd—Y Cyfrinydd Ysgrythurol', in idem, *Cyfriniaeth Gymraeg* (Caerdydd, 1994), 39–77.

R. Tudur Jones, 'The Healing Herb and the Rose of Love', in R. B. Knox (ed.), *Reformation, Continuity and Dissent: essays in honour of Geoffrey Nuttall* (London, 1977), 154–79.

Saunders Lewis, 'Arddull Charles Edwards' and 'Y Ffydd Ddi-Ffuant', in R. Geraint Gruffydd (ed.), *Meistri'r Canrifoedd* (Caerdydd, 1973), 172–82, 164–71.

Derec Llwyd Morgan, 'A Critical Study of the Works of Charles Edwards (1628–1691?)' (Oxford, D. Phil. thesis, 1967).

Idem, *Charles Edwards* (Caernarfon, 1994).

Idem, 'Charles Edwards', in Geraint Bowen (ed.), *Y Traddodiad Rhyddiaith* (Llandysul, 1970), 213–30.

Idem, 'Defnydd Charles Edwards o ddelweddau yn *Y Ffydd Ddi-Ffuant*', in J.E. Caerwyn Williams (ed.), *Ysgrifau Beirniadol*, 4 (Dinbych 1969), 471–4.

Merfyn Morgan (ed.), *Gweithiau Oliver Thomas ac Evan Roberts* (Caerdydd, 1981).

G.F. Nuttall, *The Welsh Saints, 1640–1660: Walter Cradock, Vavasor Powell, Morgan Llwyd* (Cardiff, 1957).

Goronwy Wyn Owen, *Morgan Llwyd* (Caernarfon, 1992).

L.J. Parry, 'The Book of the Three Birds' (a translation of Morgan Llwyd's *Llyfr y Tri Aderyn*), in E. Vincent Evans (ed.), *Winning Compositions in the Llandudno Eisteddfod, 1896* (Liverpool, 1898), 195–274.

Nigel Smith, *Perfection Proclaimed: Language and Literature in English Radical Religion, 1646–1660* (Oxford, 1988).

M. Wynn Thomas (ed.), *Morgan Llwyd: Llyfr y Tri Aderyn* (Caerdydd, 1988).

Idem, *Morgan Llwyd* (Cardiff, 1984).

Idem, *Morgan Llwyd, ei gyfeillion a'i gyfnod* (Caerdydd, 1991).

Idem, 'Morgan Llwyd a Hanes y Presennol yn y Gorffennol', *Y Cofiadur*, 57 (Mai, 1992), 4–15.

Idem, '"No Englishman": Wales's Henry Vaughan', *The Swansea Review*, 15 (1995), 1–19.

G.J. Williams (ed.), *Charles Edwards: Y Ffydd Ddi-Ffuant* (Caerdydd, 1936).

CHAPTER 9

ROMAN CATHOLIC PROSE AND ITS BACKGROUND

GERAINT BOWEN

In 1559, during the first year of Elizabeth's reign, an Act of Uniformity was passed declaring the queen Supreme Head of the Church. Priests were given a choice either to conform or to resign. Any citizen who refused to conform would be allowed to leave the country provided that citizen refrained from visiting Rome. Rather than conform many preferred exile. In 1563 it was further decreed that teachers and graduates were to take a vow to defend the supremacy of the queen and that those who defended papal authority or refused to attend church services could be imprisoned for life, fined or lose all their property.

Morris Clynnog, a graduate in law at Oxford, had experienced some years of exile during the reign of the Protestant King Edward VI as a member of Cardinal Reginald Pole's embassy in Louvain, Flanders, territory held by the king of Spain. Cardinal Pole had attended the opening session of the Council of Trent in 1540 and had frequently sought to persuade the Emperor Charles V to restore England to the Catholic faith by force of arms, and the embassy had been established to that end. Clynnog, from early in his career, was a witness to political conspiracies and military schemes, and this left its mark on his future endeavours. When Edward died in 1553 and the Catholic Mary was enthroned, Pole thought it wise not to attend the crowning ceremony at Winchester and sent his chaplain, Thomas Goldwell, and Morris Clynnog as his deputies. He later returned to England and was consecrated archbishop of Canterbury. He appointed Clynnog as chancellor of Lambeth Palace Court and his private secretary, relieving him of his duties for a short period in 1555–6 which was spent studying in Padua where he acted as custodian of Edward Courtenay, the earl of Devon, who had been exiled for leading an insurrection in 1554.

In the first meeting of Mary's parliament, by the passing of the *De Haeretico Comburando* Act, Edward's religious laws were abolished and papal power restored. Mary's reign lasted for six years and during this period Morris Clynnog, having been ordained priest in 1555, was awarded numerous livings for his loyalty, Llanengan in Llŷn, the churches of St Olave in Catcombe on the Isle of Wight and Orpington in the diocese of Rochester. He was also promoted rural dean of Shoreham and Croydon and canon of York Minster. In 1556 he was presented with the living of Corwen by his friend Thomas Goldwell, the newly appointed bishop of St Asaph, and granted the prebend of Blaen-porth in the diocese of St David's.

On 19 October 1558, a month before Mary's death, Morris Clynnog was nominated bishop of Bangor. He had already embarked on a journey to Rome to gain the assent of the Pope when he heard of her death and the proclamation of Elizabeth as queen. Clynnog remained on the Continent for a year, returning to England as a member of a commission led by Vincenzo Parbaglia set up to ascertain the religious policy of Elizabeth. The commission departed dismayed, and Clynnog left for Louvain, there to assist as overseer of the new Catholic *émigrés*. A number of other Welshmen decided to quit the country, including Thomas Goldwell, Gruffydd Robert, the newly appointed archdeacon of Anglesey, and Owen Lewis, a teacher of law at Oxford. During his stay in Louvain, Clynnog followed a course in law at the university, and in 1561 wrote a letter to Cardinal Morone expressing his conviction that the king of Spain, who had been married to Mary, should be urged to dethrone Elizabeth by force of arms.

In 1561 Thomas Goldwell left for Rome and was appointed *custos* of the long-established Pilgrim Hospice, a post previously held by Edward Carne, a native of Cowbridge, Mary's ambassador to the Vatican. Goldwell had acted as *locum tenens custos* of the hospice for Cardinal Pole on an earlier occasion between 1540 and 1548. By 1563 Morris Clynnog and Gruffydd Robert had also left for Rome, and Clynnog had been appointed *custos* of the hospice where Gruffydd Robert had acted as chaplain for a while before moving to Milan to serve as confessor to Archbishop Charles Borromeo. Thomas Goldwell had been appointed superior of Theatines in Naples and later vicar-general to the archbishop. He attended the Council of Trent held under the chairmanship of Charles Borromeo, the leader of papal reform, prime mover in producing the *Catechismus Romanus* (1566) and a committed

Renaissance humanist. At this Council it was declared that the
teaching of Aristotle in humanistic pursuits had equal authority to
the decrees of the Catholic Church in dogma. Giulio Cesare
Scaligero (1484–1558) of Padua, the most notable advocate of
humanist ideas and a master of the Ciceronian style, had declared
Aristotle to be *imperator noster, omnium bonarum artium dictator
perpetuus*. During his student days at Padua, Morris Clynnog had
undoubtedly been given the opportunity to familiarize himself with
Scaligero's humanist concepts, as Gruffydd Robert had in the
archbishop's palace in Milan. Both these committed Welshmen had
found themselves in the mainstream of both Catholic reform and
Renaissance thinking, and were driven to action by what they
regarded as the sorry religious and cultural state of their home
country.

Owen Lewis, by now canon of Cambrai Cathedral and
archdeacon of Hainault, had been involved with William Allen in
establishing in 1568 the Catholic college in Douai, and in 1574
during a visit to Rome, he was appointed to the key position of
referendarius, the Pope's adviser on political, legal and even military
matters relating to England, and had taken up residence in the
papal court. This was deemed to be an essential appointment, as
there was very little prospect of success for a strictly religious
campaign to restore papal supremacy.

Morris Clynnog, who had not forgotten Pole's efforts to win
support for his military plans against Edward's England, submitted
a memorandum, written in his own hand, to Pope Gregory,
outlining an invasion plan of mainland England via Wales, with
details of recruitment and policy for restoring papal supremacy. It
was written in Latin, but he gave it a Welsh title, *At y pab. Cyngor i
ddal y deyrnas yn y phydd*. At a meeting of 'divers Englishmen to
treat their common cause' held in Rome in 1575, the plan, which
had been approved earlier by Philip of Spain, was discussed, but on
hearing of the insurrections in Flanders against Spanish rule, the
plan was shelved. Two other invasion plans in 1577–8, one a landing
in England from Flanders and another from Ireland, did get the
financial support of the Pope but eventually came to nothing.

At the 1575 meeting, the future of the Pilgrim Hospice was also
discussed and it was decided to convert the hospice into a hostel for
student-priests who would follow courses at the *Collegium
Romanum*. Owen Lewis suggested that it should be called

Seminarium Britannicum, but the 'divers Englishmen' present at the meeting rejected his suggestion claiming that the *Seminarium Anglicum* would be a more appropriate name. Owen Lewis persuaded the Pope to give his financial support to the project. At the same meeting, Morris Clynnog was made rector of the establishment.

The process of changing the hospice into a college led to controversy, as it meant that the chaplains had to abandon their quarters to provide accommodation for new students. Morris Clynnog was also accused of taking in students who showed little intent to return on the English mission and of showing preference for Welsh students. Later students had to make a vow that they would return on the mission. Two Welsh students, Owen Thomas and Rhosier Smyth, who earlier had been a student in Douai, refused and were dismissed. Ultimately the Pope intervened and invited the Jesuits to undertake the administration of the Seminar, and Morris Clynnog was obliged to resign. In 1580 he left Rome, travelled to France, and in Rouen embarked on a ship for Spain. The ship foundered and Morris Clynnog was drowned.

Loyalty to Rome and involvement in papal affairs had led these Welshmen into permanent exile, but they never abandoned the hope that the Roman faith would be restored to Wales and that the Welsh language, through their efforts, not only would become a worthy medium of instruction in the Roman faith but also that it would serve to introduce the Welsh people to classical thought and the humanist learning which they had witnessed blossoming in Italy as they entered the country in the sixties. There they found themselves in cultured circles where speaking and writing were regarded as an art and where members were familiar with the works of the courtier Baldassare Castiglione (1478–1529) and the scholar Pietro Bembo (1470–1547), authors who had advocated the use of spoken Italian in preference to Latin as a medium of modern literature and had used dialogue as the format in their books.

The principal Welsh exponent of these ideas and of Aristotelian thought concerning the nature of the art of speaking and writing was Gruffydd Robert. His Welsh Grammar *Dosparth Byrr ar y rhann gyntaf i ramadeg cymraeg* (A Short Treatise on the first part of Welsh Grammar) was published in Milan in 1567 (with appendices in 1584 and 1594). He rejected the use of *dd*, *ll* and *w* using in their place *d̦*, *l̦* *u̦* and *ph* for *ff*, and he adopted the dialogue form throughout. He condemned the Welsh poets for being conservative, reluctant to change and unwilling to accept the Renaissance way of thinking. The new humanist age, he claimed, called for a new literary medium based on the spoken word, but this new medium had to have refinement and dignity, and due care had to be given to orthography. His Grammar was intended to teach the nation to adapt the living language in such a way as to provide this refined literary medium. Words had to be borrowed and adapted, preferably from Latin, and he provides a guide to the consonantal changes to be applied when borrowing. He seldom refers to the construction of the Welsh sentence or to idioms because, in his opinion, this aspect of the language remained uncontaminated; but he warns against the possible future use of non-Welsh idioms. His Grammar is also intended to assist those who undertook the essential tasks of translating Latin texts on philosophy, for no one, he remarks, should expect the Welsh to produce original comparable works of philosophy. In the final pages he provides his translation of an extract from Cicero's *De Senectute* (Concerning old age) as an example.

Soon after the appearance of the Grammar he received the manuscript of a small Welsh catechism entitled *Athravaeth Gristnogavl* from Morris Clynnog. So pleased was he to find such a 'treasure' in the Welsh language that he decided to publish it in Milan. It was printed in 1568 at Vincenzo Girardone's press, representing *dd* by *d̦*, *ll* by *l̦*, *w* by *u̦*, *ff* by *ph* as in the Grammar. In the preface, Gruffydd Robert congratulates Morris Clynnog on his simple, neat and precise exposition of the doctrine in a way that children and women could understand (*fel y gallo y plant a'r gwragedd eu deallt*), referring to the work as 'your book' and expressing his hope that with God's help he would be able to produce similar books for the benefit of Christians, thus implying that it was Morris Clynnog's original compilation. In actual fact *Athravaeth Gristnogavl* appears to be a translation of *De Doctrina Christiana* by Ioannes Polanco (1517–74), a Spaniard and first general secretary of the Society of Jesus and author of at least eleven books. James Brodrick, in his *Saint Peter Canisius* (1935), mentions that Owen Lewis had written to Cardinal Sirleto in 1579 appealing for financial aid to publish Welsh religious books. Owen explained that only one Welsh book had appeared up until then, namely a translation of Polanco's *De Doctrina Christiana* (*nisi libellus polanci de doctrina Christiana*). This can only refer to *Athravaeth Gristnogavl* (1568). According to *Apparatus Sacri*, by Antonio Possevino (1608), no copy of Polanco's catechism has survived, and there is therefore no means of verifying Clynnog's indebtedness to Polanco's catechism.

There is no suggestion in Gruffydd Robert's preface to *Athravaeth Gristnogavl* that he had in any way amended the text, but one can trace plenty of evidence of the influence of his Grammar in more than one way. The letter *k* is discarded; capital letters are regularly used in definite nouns; the definite article is joined to the pronoun, e.g. *yrhwn*; the possessive pronoun *fy* (my) is attached to the noun, e.g. *fynghalon* (my heart); affixed pronoun to preposition, e.g. *iddynhwy* (to them); preposition to noun, e.g. *ynghaer* (in Chester); personal form of verb to pronoun, e.g. *rowchwi* (you give); and the interrogative *pa* to noun, e.g. *paddelw?* (in which way?). Where necessary, Welsh words unfamiliar to the common folk (*y cyffredin*), but with which an educated Welshman would probably be familiar, are used with a Latin glossary added, which suggests that these were either the equivalent Latin words found in Polanco's text or that devotional Welsh people were already familiar with the Latin, words such as: *gau dduwiaeth* (*idolatria*), *ennaint* (*unguentum*), *canllaw* (*advocata*), *ofergoel* (*superstitio*), *cyfaredd* (*remedium*) and *cyfryngwr* (*mediator*). In the glossary we also find words, mostly abstract nouns, not found in earlier books or manuscripts, such as: *dirgeledd* (*mysterium*), *annirgelu* (*revelare*), *grymhyssedd* (*fortitudo*), *goddefedd* (*patientia*), *cymgadwriaeth* (*continentia*), *galluedd* (*potentia*) and *cymwynasedd* (*benignitas*). We meet words not found in any work prior to the Grammar, e.g. *pwylledd* (*prudentia*), *hygaredd* (*pietas*), and there is evidence that the Grammar guidelines as to the formulating of words borrowed from Latin are followed, e.g. *murfuro* (*murmurare*). Gruffydd Robert's contemporary, William Salesbury, uses *murmuro* in 1551.

The catechism takes the form of a dialogue between master and pupil, dealing firstly with the meaning of the word Christian, and answering such questions as how one recognizes a Christian, who Christ was and what was Christian doctrine, under the following main headings: the sign of the Cross, the customary use of the sign, the destiny of a Christian and how to attain it, the need for faith as manifested in the Creed, hope as expressed in devotions and prayers, perfect love and good deeds shown by loving God and

living according to his commandments and the precepts of the
Church, the Seven Sacraments, the Eight Beatitudes, the Seven
Works of Mercy and the Fifteen Mysteries of the Lord.

In 1578 Owen Lewis, in a Latin letter to Cardinal Sirleto, the
Vatican librarian, requested financial assistance to publish three
Welsh texts to be printed in Milan under the supervision of
Gruffydd Robert, namely two original works, *De ecclesia et
primatis Ro. pontificis* (Concerning the Church and the Supremacy
of the Bishop of Rome), *De Sacramento et Sacrificio altaris*
(Concerning the Sacrament and the Eucharist) and a translation of
Canisius' Catechism, *Catechismi p. canicij versorum in linguam
Britannicam* (The Catechism of Father Canisius translated into
Welsh). These printed books would be sent secretly to England for
distribution amongst the Welsh (*in Angliam dextre mitti et ibi
secreta ratione spargi inter Britannos*). He does not name the
authors and translator, and nothing is known of what became of
them. But one is tempted to suggest that the translation of
Canisius' Catechism was the original draft of a translation by
Rhosier Smyth, which was eventually published in 1609.

Rhosier Smyth *o dref Llanelwy* (from the town of St Asaph) had
been a student in Douai in 1573 but had moved with other students
to the *Seminarium Anglicum* in Rome in 1579, later to be dismissed
during the controversy which had led to the abdication of Morris
Clynnog and his departure from Rome in 1580. In the same year
Owen Lewis left for Milan to serve as vicar-general to Archbishop
Borromeo. In 1588, the year of the Spanish Armada disaster, an
event which did not reflect well on his position as *referendarius*, he
was appointed bishop of Cassano and later papal nuncio in
Switzerland. Smyth, finding himself isolated, left Rome for Rouen,
France. He was introduced to Cardinal Jacques Davy Duperron,
bishop of Evreaux, the leader of the Counter-Reformation in
France and later, following his new patron, he took up residence in
Paris. It was during his stay in Paris that he succeeded with the aid
of Duperron in publishing part of his translation of Canisius'
Catechism in 1609 and the complete work in 1611.

The original Latin text, *Summa Doctrinae Christianae*
(*Catechismus Major*), was first published in Vienna in 1555, and in
1566 a revised edition appeared with additions. There are, for
example, ten additional questions in the second edition, the answers
vary, and there is a further section on Christian Justice (*De Justitia*

Christiana) dealing with the declaration issued by the Council of Trent—*De Hominis Lapsu et Iustificatione Secundum Sententiae Et Doctrinam Concilii Tridentini.* There are also additional quotations from Scripture and from the Christian Fathers. Between the time of publication of the first edition and the second, the Council of Trent had made decrees on subjects such as baptism, the sacrament, annointing, penance, original sin and justification. The Declaration had redrafted Church teaching on the Eucharist, the priesthood, marriage, invocation of saints, relics, images and indulgences.

Following such pronouncements, Canisius had no choice but to publish a revised edition. The original edition appeared fifty times and the revised thirty-nine times. Abridged versions of the original edition had appeared soon after its publication, namely *Parvus Catechismus Catholicorum* (*Catechismus Minor*) (Cologne, 1558) and *Catechismus minimus* (Ingolstadt, 1555). According to Rhosier Smyth, the Catechism had been translated into every European vernacular tongue including Lowland Scots and Breton. He refers here to *Ane cathechisme or schort instruction of Christian religion* possibly by Adam King (Paris, 1588) and *Catechism hac instruction . . . composet en latin gant M.P. Canisius . . . ues a societe an hanu Jesus* by Gilles Kerenpuil (Paris, 1576). An English translation of *Parvus Catechismus* was published in 1579 under the title *Certayne necessarie Principles of Religion, which may be entitled, A Catechisme contayning all the partes of the Christian and Catholique Fayth, Written in Latin by P. Canitius and now amplified and Englished by T.I.*, but the first edition of Henry Garnet's translation of *Catechismus Major* did not appear until *c.* 1592–6. It was printed by a secret press set up in the vicinity of London.

The text (pp. 7–65) of Rhosier Smyth's translation as found in *Crynnodeb o addysg Cristnogawl . . . gwedi gyfiaithu o'r ladin i'r gymeraeg drwy ddyfal astudiaeth a llafur D. Rosier Smyth o dref Llanelwy*, which was published according to the title-page in Paris in 1609, appears again on pages 7–61 of the 1611 Paris edition to which he added a Latin title, *Opus Catechisticum . . . Sef yv Svm, ne grynodeb o addysg Gristionogavl . . . a gyfiaithwyd o'r ladin i'r Gymraeg drvy ddyfal lafyr ag astudiaeth D. Rosier Smyth o dref Llanelwy.* This work is a free translation and in parts a summary of the first and second sections of the original Latin, namely *De Fide & Symbolo* (Of Faith & the Creed) and *De Spe & Oratione Domini* (Of Hope and the Lord's Prayer) and a part of the third, *De*

Charitate & mandatis Decalogi (Of Charity and the Ten Commandments). The section on *De praeceptis Ecclesiae* (Of the Precepts of the Church) has been omitted.

In his preface he expresses his concern that Welsh orthography was far from standardized and that he had decided to adopt the orthography used by Gruffydd Robert in his Grammar. Gruffydd Robert had stated that mutated words should be written as pronounced, as in such words as *ymlhith*, placing the *h* after the *l*, and as in *yngrhog* and *yngrhist* with the *h* after the *r*; also linking preposition and noun should form one word. Rhosier Smyth follows his advice as he does in other matters, such as the spelling of such words as *bowyd* and *towallt*, the joining of the definite article to the pronoun as in *yrhwn*, *yrhain*, a pronoun to a noun, e.g. *fyngobaith*, *fyngorchumynion*, an affixed pronoun to the personal form of a preposition, e.g. *ynomi*, *drosomi* and a personal pronoun to the personal form of the verb, e.g. *ewchi*, *carafyntau*, *ydyminau*.

He uses words coined by Gruffydd Robert and published for the first time in his Grammar, such as *amhetrus*, *cyffyrfau*, *cynglyddu*, *descrifyddu*, *duwioledd*, *egwalyddus*, *ewcharisten*, *gweryddu*, *gwidyddu* and *gwithifen*. He explains that he himself has borrowed a number of words from Latin, adapting them according to the rules provided by Gruffydd Robert in his section on *Cyfiachyddiaeth*, a section of the Grammar not published until 1584. This reference to the section by name is proof that Rhosier Smyth had not completed his translation before that date, or that he had undertaken to revise his earlier translation after consulting the Grammar. Among the words which Rhosier Smyth himself coined we find: *adbresennu*, *canonig*, *cardinol*, *consolyddiad*, *consolyddwr*, *cynghaffael*, *cynghaffiad*, *cyfegwal*, *deleithrwydd*, *ecsberiaeth*, *ecsblicyddu*, *egwalyddus* and *golustraidd*. Smyth also coined new words from Welsh root words. Some of these were later used by other authors, e.g. *aflonyddus*, *amhuraidd*, *astudiaeth* and *gorthrwm*. Others that did not take hold, and they are numerous, included *addasus* and *bywioledd*. His borrowings from English include *canonaidd*, *fform* and *adwltres*.

Rhosier Smyth chose to translate Canisius' Catechism for the obvious reason that both the Emperor Ferdinand and Philip of Spain had prohibited the use of any catechism other than that of Canisius in the territories ruled by them. Antonio Possevino had also recommended it, and it was a set book for all students at Douai College when Rhosier Smyth was a student there in 1576–9. He knew that it was the catechism which Du Perron, bishop of Evreaux, would sponsor, as it was the very means of instruction that the Welsh had longed for, *pueri petunt panem, et non est qui frangat*, especially as forty years had now passed since the publication of Morris Clynnog's *Athravaeth Gristnogavl*.

A year after the appearance of *Opus Catechisticum* Rhosier Smyth published, again in Paris, his translation of Robert Southwell SJ's *Epistle of a religious priest vnto his father: exhorting him to the perfect forsaking of the world*, which was first printed on a private press in 1596/7, a year or two after Southwell was martyred. This was the most famous example of a well-known genre of letters written by Catholic children to their Protestant parents in order to bring about their conversion. Smyth's translation was entitled *Coppi o lythyr crefydhvvr a merthyr dedhfol discedig at i dad ivv ginghori i 'mvvrthod ag oferedh a gvvagedh y byd ag i fedhvvl am y enaid* (A copy of a letter from a religious who was a godly and learned martyr to his father to exhort him to forsake the vanity and dissipation of the world and to have regard for his soul), and the only extant copy of it was recently discovered at the Bibliothèque Mazarine in Paris. It is dedicated to Morgan Clynnog, Morris Clynnog's nephew and leader of the secular missionary priests in southern Wales at the time, who had asked for the translation. As might be expected of Smyth, it is a competent if not masterly rendering of the original, although Thomas Wiliems of Trefriw (of whom more below) thought he could improve upon it, as a letter he wrote to his patron John Edwards of Chirk (NLW 3561) clearly shows.

During his stay at Paris, Rhosier Smyth also translated *Le Théâtre du Monde*, written by the Breton, Pierre Boaistuau, a historian and translator of Italian and Latin texts. It was first published in Paris in 1561. Other editions were printed in Lyon, Rouen, Antwerp and London (in 1595). An English translation appeared in 1663, *Theatrum Mundi, The theatre or rule of the world*, by John Alday.

According to the title-page of the French edition Pierre Boaistuau had written the book originally in Latin: *composé en Latin . . . puis traduict par luy mesme en François*, and according to Rhosier Smyth the Welsh version was a translation from the French. The full title reads: *Theater dv mond sef ivv Gorsedd y byd lle i gellir gvveled trueni a lescni dyn o ran y corph ai odidavvgrvvydd*

o ran yr enaid, a scrifenvvyd gynt yn y Phrangaeg ag a gyfiaethvvyd
i'r gymraeg drvv lafyr Rosier Smyth o dref lanelvvy athravv o
theologyddiaeth . . . A Breintivvyd yn Ninas Paris, 1615. One gathers
immediately from the orthography used in the title-page that he had
ceased to follow Gruffydd Robert's suggestion on the use of *d̦, l̦, u̦*
for *dd, ll, w.* For *w* which was not used in the printing of French, he
used *vv,* but he followed Robert's suggestion as to the spelling of
such words as: *dirmig, bowyd, yrhon, arnafi, gallafi.* Nevertheless
there are obvious signs that other works written later had
influenced his orthography. The following words for instance bear
signs of the influence of the New Testament of William Salesbury:
Iuddeon, pethae, pebae, bestfiliaid, testiolaeth, tuy and the possessive
pronoun *ei.* He followed Gruffydd Roberts's instructions when
borrowing from Latin as evidenced by the examples *ambyddiad* and
acstasis which are not found in any later works. Some of his
formations based on Welsh word roots such as *adrithio, coginyddu*
and *gobeithus* have not been accepted either, but others have, either
by lexicographers or by authors, e.g. *anharddu, diaelodi* and *barbar-*
iaeth. Some of his borrowings from English, including *ecsberiens,*
amffitheatr and *Fenesiaid* were similarly accepted, but others have
been rejected, e.g. *astrologiad, caraterau* and *esensiad.* He borrowed
such words as *cyfnewidiad, cynhemlu, ephaith* and *gweddeidd-dra*
from Gruffydd Robert's Grammar and *blasphemio* from *Athravaeth*
Gristnogavl.

As for content, the book deals with the human condition
according to the teaching of the Church, the abhorrence of the
human body and the dignity of the soul. By obeying and
submitting to the teaching of the Church man shall ultimately enjoy
eternal life. The book is in four parts. The first part (pp. 10–39)
quotes from classical authors and the Church Fathers to prove that
man is the most pitiful of all creatures. The second part (pp.
41–110) seeks to show that man's life is a tragedy from beginning to
end. The only thing that has increased in his time is man's
wretchedness. Everyone becomes bored with his occupation: the
sailor, the worker, the merchant, the soldier, kings, ecclesiastics,
justices and husbands with their wives. The third part (pp. 116–76)
shows how human suffering demands that man submit to God and
acknowledge him. It gives the causes of his sufferings: unorthodox
teachings, poisons, the four elements (water, fire, air and earth rising
against him), the judgements of God, mental illnesses, desire,

avarice, envy, pride, passionate love, death, the grave, judgement and the resurrection of the dead. The final section (pp. 177–219), *Traethiad ar odidavvgrvvydd dyn*, deals with that which is excellent about man. God made the world and created man to take possession of it. He was created in the image of God to lord over every created thing and to glorify God. God also endowed man with a soul. The original magnificence of man was the reason for God's incarnation and his becoming man. It is the godliness in man that explains his beauty and his propriety. He has excelled in the arts: painting, architecture, mathematics, printing, making gunpowder, wings for flying, music, and medicine.

In contrast with his translation of Canisius' Catechism where the sentences are intentionally short and simple in construction as in the original Latin, in *Theater du mond sef ivv Gorsedd y byd* Smyth's sentences are complex not only in the translated text, where this is understandable, but also in the introduction. His style reflects the Ciceronian mode advocated by Gruffydd Robert in his Grammar. One should add that like his mentor he uses the phrase *yr hvvn beth* to introduce relative clauses and the plural of the verb in affirmative relative clauses qualifying plural subjects, e.g. *Mae'r eleirch a'r Eos a fuont*.

One cannot doubt Rhosier Smyth's loyalty and devotion to his country, his language and to Rome, and one can easily believe him when he says:

> If you find faults in this translation, do not be surprised, for I have been away from my homeland for over forty years, in France and Italy and in many other regions, living amongst foreigners without having scarcely any contact with any Welshman at all, without any book or any means to help me, but I was forced to learn their languages to earn a living . . . I have made this [translation] out of love for my country, hoping that I can inspire other members of the gentry to love their country and succour the language, and other revered and learned men to write something worthy for the benefit of their country. As for myself, I am not in any way jealous of anybody who improves on what I do, but I wish every true-blooded Welshman to bear with me, wishing them success and honour in this world and eternal joy in the next, and to pray for me. From the city of Paris 20 of December 1615.

One cannot but conclude from the tenor of these remarks that the exiled Rhosier Smyth was not well informed about the social plight of the Welsh gentry, and was completely ignorant of the religious works and literary and scholarly pursuits of his fellow catholics back in Wales, men like Robert Gwyn, Siôn Dafydd Rhys, Llywelyn Siôn and Thomas Wiliems.

Disrupted by enforced religious uniformity and alien cultural demands, the Welsh gentry appeared to the unfamiliar to be unsympathetic towards the Welsh language and the old faith, but we find evidence in comments made by the lexicographer, Thomas Wiliems of Trefriw, that some noblemen were ready patrons, although perhaps secretively, of Catholic authors and missionary priests. He mentions his relative Maurice Wynn of Gwydir and others like Sir John Salusbury of Lleweni, the brother of Thomas Salusbury, the catholic who was executed in 1586, Robert Puw of Penrhyn Creuddyn, John Edwards of Plasnewydd, Chirk, Sir Edward Stradling of St Donat's and Edward Somerset (Lord Raglan). Other known patrons were Edward and John Gam of Y Drenewydd, Brecon, Morgan Meredydd of Bugeildy, Radnor, William Hanmer of Fenns Hall, Maelor Saesneg and John ap Huw ap Madoc of Plas Pickhill, Bangor Is-coed. Between 1559 and 1609 missionary priests were secretly housed at times in the following homes: Llwyndyrys, Plas-du, Erbistock, Grosmont, Cemais, Machen, Y Fan, Llanharan and Werngochen, Abergavenny. There is evidence that the number of registered recusants increased from eighty-eight in 1574 to 808 in 1603.

One Catholic priest who perfectly understood the religious situation in Wales in 1574 was Robert Gwyn, son of Siôn Wyn ap Thomas Gruffydd of Penyberth. We know nothing about his early education and life, but he himself states that he was in London in 1559 and that he had actually heard John Jewel, bishop of Salisbury, delivering his famous sermon at St Paul's Cross on 26 November (*Onyd oyddwn a'm llygaid yn gwrando*). In his sermon John Jewel spoke as follows:

> If any learned man of all our adversaries or if all the learned men that be alive be able to bring any one sufficient sentence out of any old catholic doctor or father or out of any old general council, or out of the holy scriptures of God or any one example of the primitive church, whereby it may be clearly & plainly proved that there was any private mass in the whole world at that time for the space of six hundred years after Christ, or that there was then any communion ministered unto the people under one kind, or that the people had their common prayer then

in a strange tongue that they understood not, or that the bishop of
Rome was then called an universal bishop, or the head of the universal
church, or that the people was then taught to believe that Christ's body is
really, substantially, corporally, carnally or naturally in the sacrament . . .
If any man were able to prove any of these articles, I would give over and
subscribe unto him.

In 1562 the sermon appeared in print in two separate volumes:
Apologia Ecclesiae Anglicanae and a translation: *An Apologie of the
Church of England.*

Robert Gwyn (*alias* Robert Siôn Wyn) had been brought up to
conform with the Established Church and had entered Corpus
Christi College, Oxford, graduating in arts in 1568. In 1571 he was
persuaded by a relative, Robert Owen of Plas-du, a member of an
obdurate recusant family in Llŷn and a student at Douai College, to
pursue his studies further at Douai. The college register refers to
him as 'Robertus Guinus, Bangoriensis . . . ex antiquorum
Britonum natione'. He gained his BD degree in 1575 and was
ordained priest.

Douai College was established in 1568 by William Allen and
other eminent divines to instruct missionary priests. Allen, formerly
principal of St Mary's Hall, Oxford and head of the new seminary,
had attracted to Douai a number of exiled scholars and theologians
dedicated to the cause of restoring England to Rome, many of them
his former students at Oxford.

Within two years of the appearance of John Jewel's *Apologia*,
numerous books intended to refute Jewel's claims appeared, such
as:

An Answere to Master Juelles Chalenge, Thomas Harding
(Louvain, 1564).
*A Confutation of a Booke intitled An Apologie of the Church of
England*, Thomas Harding (Antwerpe, 1565).
A proufe of Certeyne Articles of Religion denied by M Juell,
Thomas Dorman (Antwerpe, 1564).
Defense and Declaration of the Catholicke Doctrine, William
Allen (Antwerpe, 1565).

Between 1564 and 1568 the Douai authors produced forty books
and between 1570 and 1580 another fifty. There is no evidence in
their writings that they had been influenced in any way by advocates

of the Renaissance idea that literature in the vulgar tongue should imitate classical literature. In fact, one senses a revolt against the epideictic style advocated by Renaissance scholars. This statement by Thomas Harding speaks for all the authors—their intention was 'To make harde thinges easy to be vnderstanded'.

Of these authors A.C. Southern writes:

> Primarily, as must be evident, they were not concerned with literature as an accomplishment at all. Their business was to combat what they believed to be error and to expose the truth, not to produce literary masterpieces, and their writing is altogether directed towards this end . . . It is clear that they aimed at a simple straightforward exposition of their themes, such as would appeal to the unlearned.

To refute John Jewel's challenge and to propagate the Roman faith in simple language to the public in general was the aim of most of the published works.

But there was (as we have already seen) another type of literature, that of letter-writing to relatives and friends, which arose from the custom which William Allen had promoted amongst the students. Initially the letters were not intended for publication, but at least eleven were printed either abroad or in England at secret presses, of which the earliest was *A consolatorie epistle to the afflicted catholics*, Thomas Hide (Louvain, 1579).

Five years before the printing of the first English letter, that is in the month of December 1574, a short time before he sat his final BD examination, Robert Gwyn wrote a long letter to his parents intended to prove 'That there is no other faith but the true faith'. A copy of this long letter has come down to us in a manuscript bearing the title *Lanter Gristnogol* (Christian Lantern) in the hand of William Dafydd Llywelyn, a professional copyist from Llangynidr in Breconshire (NLW 155428B, pp. 61v–311v). Robert Gwyn was obliged to arrange for the duplication of his works by professional copyists as a law passed in 1559 prohibited the printing of Catholic literature. The frontispiece gives the name of the author, Robert Gwyn. It appears from the contents that this was not his first letter, because he refers to two earlier letters. In one the theme was the miracles claimed by the reformers (*Gwyrthiau'r Gwŷr Newydd*) (p. 186) and in the other that Christ's Church is one body (*Fod Eglwys Grist yn un corff*) (pp. 115, 268v).

Gwyn's extant work is an expository treatise on Christian doctrine. It is exemplified by quotations from Scripture and the Church Fathers from the first six centuries in response to John Jewel's insinuations that Catholics could not produce evidence from such early sources in support of some of their beliefs, such as corporality (that Christ's body is present in the Eucharist). He refers to Jewel as a false bishop (*esgobyn ffals*), to his book *Apologia* as fallacious (*celwyddog*), to Latimer as a knave (*cnaf*), to Lutherans as bastards (*bastardiaid*) and to the reformers as *novationes* (*gwŷr newydd*). He criticizes Clynnog for being satisfied with simply providing an outline of Church doctrine in his catechism, *Athravaeth Gristnogavl*, as the heretical state of the Welsh people demanded a more comprehensive explanation. He admits that Clynnog's Welsh is better than his own, but his lack of instruction in the Welsh language was not going to deter him from doing everything he could to deepen the belief of some Welshmen in the Roman faith. Like his fellow students in Douai he uses the familiar language of the hearth and the countryside, and one finds no evidence that his style is in any way influenced by Renaissance thinking on such matters.

The next extant treatise attributed to Robert Gwyn is known as *Gwssanaeth y Gwŷr Newydd* (The Service of the New Men) (NLW 15542, pp. 1–61). This also takes the form of a letter to his parents. As he mentions his father who died in 1575 in the text, he must have begun to write it, unaware of his death, before he left on his mission to England and Wales in January 1576. It was intended to be read to his family and relatives in Llŷn and to be copied for distribution further afield. The topics discussed in this letter are: attending Church of England services; social intercourse with schismatics; no grace outside the Roman Church; attending parish church but not participating in the service; and church vows. There is an addendum on the dangers facing the immoral person.

Robert Gwyn, by now a peripatetic secular missionary priest in Wales, found refuge during the first few years of his mission at Plas-du and at Penrhyn Creuddyn, but later in Werngochen near Abergavenny. His status among missionary priests is evidenced by the facts that in 1578 the right to bless cassocks and consecrate portable altars was granted by Pope Gregory XIII to Robert Gwyn and two other priests, and that two years later he was invited to attend a London meeting to discuss ways and means of putting into effect the right granted by the Council of Trent to priests to set up secret presses to publish Catholic books.

By the year 1583/4 Robert Gwyn had written a six-hundred page treatise called *Y Drych Kristnogawl* (The Christian Mirror) on the Roman Church's teaching on the Four Last Things: Death, the Day of Judgement, Hell and Heaven, with ample supporting evidence from the Scriptures and from the works of the Christian Fathers of the first six centuries and Dionysius Carthusianus (1402–71), whose works have been called a summary of scholastic teaching in the Middle Ages and who himself has been described as the last of the schoolmen. Only one copy of this work has survived, although we are told that several copies were made by hand. The extant copy (Cardiff MS 3.240) is in the hand of the recusant copyist and poet, Llywelyn Siôn of Llangewydd in the Vale of Glamorgan.

Robert Gwyn, like all other students during his final year, pursued a course on religious controversy and the art of preaching, under the guidance of his tutor Thomas Stapleton. Gregory Martin, a fellow student, wrote in 1578:

> We preach in English in order to acquire greater power and grace in the use of the vulgar tongue, and by which the heretics plume themselves exceedingly and by which they do injury to the simple folk.

We should not therefore be surprised to find a contemporary biographer describing Robert Gwyn as 'a learned theologian and a most eloquent preacher', and the fluency of his style in *Y Drych Kristnogawl* is ample proof of this. Robert Gwyn himself explains why he adopted the homiletic style of writing:

> In order to enable the simple folk to understand the book and benefit from it, I have set out my thoughts before them in the most common and vulgar language in use amongst the Welsh.

Such a comment would be unimaginable from the pen of Gruffydd Robert.

He also justifies the use of English words commonly heard from the lips of the Welsh:

> I use foreign words, such as English words and others not related to

Welsh, for I blame the Welsh people for their lack of care for the Welsh language.

The following examples are found in *Y Drych: consydro, entrio, cwmparo, occwpio, kwnterffeto, condisiwn, corekdo*. One feature of his homiletic style is his use of what literary critics term 'doubling the expression' or 'exuberance'. He has numerous examples, e.g. *yn flin ac yn boenus* (angrily and painfully), *clwyfe a dolurie* (wounds and pangs), *myfyrio a meddwl* (consider and think). Here, no doubt, he is imitating the style of his tutor Thomas Stapleton as seen in his translation of Bede's *Historia Ecclesiastica Gentis Anglorum*, where we find some 350 examples, such as 'clearly and evidently', 'aid and succour', 'tempests and storms'.

Robert Gwyn, knowing that priests could publish works secretly, undertook to print *Y Drych Kristnogawl* with the aid of a printer known as Roger Thackwell and six others, including Hugh Thomas of Golch and William Davies of Croes-yn-Eirias, the martyr and author of the carol, *Karol Santaidd i'r Grawys*, in a coastal cave on land owned by Robert Puw of Penrhyn Creuddyn in 1586/7. It appeared entitled *Y Drych Cristianogawl* with the text falsely attributed to G.R. of Milan and the preface to R.S., adding a forged press mark 'Rouen' and the date 1585. This might have led one to believe that the true author was Gruffydd Robert and the writer of the preface Rhosier Smyth, but the style of the language is so different from that of Gruffydd Robert and so obviously that of Robert Gwyn that we must conclude that G.R. is R.G. inverted and stands for Robert Gwyn, and that R.S. stands for Robert Siôn, his *alias*. One gathers from the preface that the author had intended to publish all the text but only the first part appeared in print.

All the other works attributed to Robert Gwyn remain in manuscript. Two copies of *Coelio'r Saint* (Believing the Saints) have come down to us in NLW, MS Hafod 6 (attributed to 'Robert Johns Gwyn') and Cardiff MS 2.82. Both the vocabulary and homiletic style of *Coelio'r Saint* bear the marks of Robert Gwyn with the customary doubling of expressions and a similarity of content to his other writings. The text is set out in readings (*llithiau*) which suggests that each chapter was to be read to Catholic family circles. We have here another attack on John Jewel, Calvin and his descendants (*Kalvin a'i hiliogaeth*), and the enemies of the Eucharist (*gelynion yr aberth*) and a long verbal assault on the false teaching of the reformers (*y gau ffydd newydd*) with the usual ample quotations from the Scriptures and the Ecclesiastical Fathers of the first six centuries in defence of such articles of Catholic faith as the presence of Christ at the Eucharist, communion by means of bread alone, prayers for the dead and to saints, honouring the saints, their relics, their images and those of the cross and pilgrimage.

So far we have dealt with Robert Gwyn's original works, but he also undertook the translation of selections from *Summa Casuum Conscientiae*, a Latin treatise on moral theology based on the teaching of the Ecclesiastical Fathers and on the decrees of the Church Councils, a work composed by Cardinal Francisco Toledo. The manuscript (Cardiff MS Hafod 14) is 126 pages long and deals with such subjects as brotherly love, fasting, the nature of witchcraft, sins against the Catholic faith, the Ten Commandments, adultery, the breakdown of marriage, incest, rape, sodomy, theft, compensation, usury, marriage and confession. The names of owners or handlers of the manuscript and additions to the text point to the fact that the translation was intended for relatives of his in Llŷn. One finds among others the name of John Wyn of Bodwrda, known to the authorities as 'the captain of the pirates of Ynys Enlli', and a comment on the sin of piracy, an addition which is not found in the Latin original. His reference to the art of herring-fishing so common in Llŷn is also absent from the *Summa*. The style of this translation has all the characteristics with which we are familiar in Robert Gwyn's original works.

He also translated from English. The original work which he translated, *A Manuall or Meditation and most necessary Prayers with a Memorial of Instructions right requisite. Also a Summary of Catholike Religion*, was a very popular book of private daily devotions, as evidenced by the fact that it was published on a secret press three times between 1580 and 1592. It was a brief summary of the Christian religion and forms of Confession together with the Jesus Psalter and Golden Litany, specifically designed for recusants. A far from complete translation has survived in two manuscripts (NLW MS Llanstephan 13 and Swansea Town Library MS A1.57), both in the hand of William Dafydd Llywelyn of Llangynidr, Robert Gwyn's regular copyist. The diction is obviously Robert Gwyn's and the exceptionally frequent use of English words in the Welsh translation suggests that it was intended for recusants in border parishes such as Skenfrith and Grosmont where many

English words had infiltrated into spoken Welsh. Robert Gwyn, who had found refuge in Werngochen near Abergavenny, spent a great deal of his last years travelling in this part of the country 'to reconcile the people to the Romishe Religion', and, evidently enough, the purity of the vernacular, the 'old British tongue', was to take second place in his missionary campaign.

It was during his missionary work in this area that he met the grammarian Siôn Dafydd Rhys, a native of Llanfaethlu, Anglesey, an alumnus of Oxford and of Siena where he had graduated in medicine. He later moved to Pistoia, and while there published three books, a Greek grammar written in Latin, a Latin grammar written in Florentine-Italian, entitled *Regole della costruttione latina, Di M. Giovanni Dauid Britanno* (Venetia, 1567), and a Latin guide to the pronunciation of Italian: *Pervtilis exteris nationibvs De Italica Pronvnciatione, & Orthographia Libellus, Ioanne Davide Rhoeso, Lanfaethlensi Autore* (Patavii, MDLXIX). This latter book he dedicated to Robert Peccham, the son of Sir Edmund Peccham, a Catholic émigré and a former member of the Privy Council. Siôn Dafydd Rhys describes Robert as his *patronus* and 'Maecenas'. It appears that he was the patron of a group of Toscan linguists for it is significant that another author, Orazio Lombardelli, also dedicated his book *Della pronvnzia Toscana* to Robert Peccham.

In the section dealing with the pronunciation of the letter V in *De Italica Pronunciatione* (1569) Siôn Dafydd Rhys refers to Gruffydd Robert's Grammar and Clynnog's catechism, which testifies that he was familiar with both Welsh publications before he returned to Wales to be appointed headmaster of Friars' School Bangor in 1574, having taken the necessary vow of loyalty to Elizabeth as head of the Church in 1571. He had resigned from the post by 1576 and spent the next three years at Abergwili assisting Bishop Richard Davies, his cousin, with the translation of the Scriptures. Following the death of his latest patron in 1581, he returned to his profession as a physician with a practice in Cardiff. We gather from a letter which he received from the grammarian, William Midleton, that he had already started composing a Welsh grammar in 1582 when he lived in the house of Morgan Meredydd at Bugeildy in Radnorshire. During his stay in Cardiff he befriended Sir Edward Stradling of St Donat's and it was to him that he dedicated his grammar, *Cambrobrytannicae Cymraecaeve Linguae Institutiones et Rudimenta* which he completed in his secret retreat at 'Y Clûn Hir, ym mlaen Cwmm y Lhwch' in the Brecon Beacons and which was printed in London in 1592. Sir Edward met the cost of printing 1,250 copies.

Siôn Dafydd Rhys wrote his Grammar in Latin so that 'the perfection and magnificence of your language and culture be revealed to the whole of Europe in a language known to all', and to this end he applied the linguistic discipline which he gained during his stay amongst the Toscan Renaissance enthusiasts. Unlike Gruffydd Robert, Siôn Dafydd Rhys deals with *structura* (construction of the sentence), although he discusses only the simple sentence and makes no mention of the complex sentence. More than half the book deals with the art of Welsh poetry, admitting correctly that the section was an abortive mess (*erthyl*) due to the fact that he had been advised by poets whom he had met in pubs and who were themselves uncertain of the rules. He condemns the unreadiness of the poets to make public their poetic secrets and of the Welsh gentry to publish the works of Welsh historians and poets and classical works as other European nations did. He himself translated Aristotle's *Metaphysics* as an example, a copy of which has not come down to us. He appeals to the gentry in another document which he wrote in NLW MS Panton 2, *Cyngor i Feirdd a Dyscedigion Cymru* (Advice to the Poets and Learned Men of Wales), to keep the Welsh language pure but to borrow ideas from other countries. 'The poets should once more visit your homes and keep away from the taverns. They need your patronage so that they can become learned poets and masters of their art.'

Between the years 1587 and 1593 the Anglican Church and the civil authorities suspected Rhys's religious loyalty. The bishop of St David's, Marmaduke Middleton, wrongly accused him of publishing secretly a Welsh translation of *A Christian Directory* by Robert Persons. A house rented by Siôn Dafydd Rhys in the town of Brecon was searched as it was thought to contain a secret press run by David Jones, Robert Gwyn's brother, but no evidence was found. Nevertheless Siôn Dafydd Rhys was summonsed to appear before the court in Ludlow and later in London to face some questioning by the archbishop of Canterbury. He was released on condition that he took the vow recognizing Elizabeth as head of the Church. David Jones was arrested and died in prison. Werngochen was also searched, but Robert Gwyn had escaped to Gwynedd where he probably witnessed the martyrdom of William Davies in

Beaumaris. We know nothing of Robert's fate, but William Dafydd Llywelyn writing in *Lanter Gristnogol* in 1604 refers to him as one the best men from Rome to St Davids in Menevia (*yn un o'r gwŷr gore o Ryfain i dy ddewi, myniw*).

Thomas Wiliems, the lexicographer, like Siôn Dafydd Rhys, had studied medicine. He was ordained deacon in 1573 to serve in Trefriw, but later abandoned holy orders to follow a profession as a physician. In the introduction to his massive unpublished compilation, *Thesaurus Linguae Latinae et Cambrobrytannicae* (NLW Peniarth 228), he refers to the fact that neighbours who suspected his religious beliefs used to attack him as he visited his patients. In 1606 he was summoned to appear before the bishop of Bangor and in 1607 before the archbishop of Canterbury to answer for his recusancy.

He based his dictionary on the Latin–English Dictionary of Thomas Thomas, *Dictionarium Linguae Latinae et Anglicaniae*, which appeared in 1585. It is written in three volumes, with the completion date given as 1607. As one would expect in the work of a recusant Catholic, his sources are all the works of pre-Reformation or recusant authors. He cites from such works as *Athravaeth Gristnogawl*, 'Y Beibl Hen Cymraec', 'doctor davis o Aberhodni' (*Institvtiones*), 'doctor Gr. Robert' (*Dosparth Byrr*), *Y Drych Cristianogavl*, and 'drych huvydhdawt'. Like Siôn Dafydd Rhys and Gruffydd Robert he was motivated, so he says, by his desire 'to do my utmost for my country and my mother's natural tongue and to my loving kin throughout Wales', but he adds that he did not follow the orthography employed by these authors, and the reason he gives is 'that these new letters were devised for the learned'.

His love for his kin also motivated him in another way. He translated into Welsh an English book of Catholic devotions, first published by a secret press run by a Jesuit, Henry Garnet, in London in 1597. A second edition appeared the same year and a third in 1605. The full title of the 1605 edition reads as follows: *A Short Treatise of the Sacrament of Penance, With the manner of examination of conscience for a general confession, for such spirituall or deuout persons as frequent that Sacrament. Set forth in Italian by the Reverend Father Vincent Bruno of the Societe of Iesus.* The title of the original Italian edition reads *Trattato del Sacramento della Penitanza* and it was published in Venice in 1585. Its popularity is evidenced by the fact that it was also translated into Latin, Portuguese and French.

Thomas Wiliems's translation has disappeared. We know of its existence from a letter (NLW 3561) which he wrote to the recusant John Edwards of Plasnewydd in September 1615 enquiring about the translation which he had sent him earlier so that he could make a neat copy of it for him either with a view to printing it or distributing it to neighbours. This is the relevant extract: 'Am y lhyuran or Sacrauen o Benyt a drosais er ys talm, os ailscrivenwyd belhach e vydhe dha genyf gael vy hen vara cras or diwedh er lhes ir annysgedic'. The only known English book of devotions bearing a comparable title to the Welsh, 'Llyuran o'r Sagrafen o Benyd' is the English version of Vincent Bruno's 'Trattato del Sacramento della Penitenza'.

Another member of this recusant circle was Richard Vaughan of Bodeiliog, Henllan, Denbigh who was registered as a recusant in 1585 and 1609. He published in 1618 *Eglvrhad Helaeth-lawn o'r Athrawaeth Gristnogawl. A gyfansodhwyd y tro cyntaf yn Italaeg, trwy waith yr Ardherchoccaf a'r Hybarchaf Gardinal Rhobert Bellarmin o Gymdeithas yr IESV. Ag o'r Italaeg a gymregiwyd er budh Ysprydol i'r Cymru, drwy dhiwydrwydh a dyfal gymorth y penbefig [sic] canmoladwy V.R. Permissu Superiorum, M.DC. XVIII.* The title-page attributes the translation to V.R. In his *Crynodeb or Athrawiaeth Gristnogawl* (NLW 4710) Gwilym Pue of Penrhyn Creuddyn, a Benedictine, explains that the translator was Richard Vaughan of Denbighshire (*wedi Ei Gyfiauthu Eir Gymraeg Drwy waith Rissiart Vychan o swydd Ddinbech*). As was customary, to conceal the authorship it was thought advisable to reverse the initials. The earliest bibliography to mention the book is *Bibliotheca Scriptorum Societatis Iesv* by Philippus Alegambe, 1643. It wrongly attributes the translation to John Salisbury (1575–1625), a Jesuit missionary priest and head of the St Francis Xavier mission in Wales and the Marches, as does the manuscript *Scritture XXX*, dated 1632, deposited in the library of the English College in Rome, and other later bibliographies. It could be that Salisbury arranged for the printing of the book at the secret Jesuit press in St Omer, that is, if the press mark is genuine.

The original Italian edition appeared in 1598 as *Dichiarazione piu copiosa della dottrina Cristiana*. In 1598 Pope Clement recommended that in future only Bellarmino's catechism should be used and the 1603 Rome edition specifically says 'per ordine di N.S. Pape Clemente VIII'. It later appeared in sixty languages, as in English in 1604, *An ample Declaration of the Christian Doctrine . . . translated into English by Richard Hadock*, published secretly in England. Other editions appeared in 1604, 1605, 1611, 1617 and 1624. James Brodrick in his biography of Robert Bellarmino states that he was one of the greatest, if not the very greatest, of the Church's catechists. But it was from the Italian that Richard Vaughan made his translation, as the title-page indicates, and as does the last sentence in the book which reads: *Moliant i'r Iesu ag i'w fam fendigedig Mair burforwyn; a'r Gyfarchiad yr hon, y gorphenned hyn o gyfieithiad o'r Italaeg 25 Martij 1618* (Praise to Jesus and to his blessed mother, the virgin Mary, on whose Annunciation on the 25 of March, 1618 this translation from Italian was completed). And there is evidence that Vaughan kept closer to the Italian text than Richard Hadock.

His Welsh is far from being unblemished. He uses for example the plural form of the verb *bod* as copula, e.g. *A'r strymentau ydynt y Sacrafennau*; the plural form of the verb in affirmative relative clauses, e.g. *plantos a fuont feirw*; a plural verb with a plural subject, e.g. *Gallant yr angylion*; plural nouns after numerals, e.g. *saith Sacrafennau*. He uses words only found in the works of earlier Catholic authors, such as *adrybedd, absolfeniad, ansoddfab, erlidiaeth*; and some words are his own creations, e.g. *amfrudo, balmolew, ailbresennu*.

Huw Owen of Gwenynog, Llanfflewin, Anglesey (1575–1642), a recusant, a linguist and learned in the law, in his will dated 1640, wrote, 'I Hugh Owen . . . give and Bequeath to my son Hugh Owen [*alias* John Hughes] all my books, writings and papers'. According to his son, John Hughes, in his preface to *Dilyniad Crist*, his father was the author of many godly treatises. The first named is 'the latest and most complete edition . . . of The Book of Resolution'. The latest actually edited by Robert Persons was *A Christian Directorie Guiding Men to their Saluation* (St Omer, 1585), but in 1590 another edition appeared: *The Seconde parte of the Booke of Christian exercise, appertayning to Resolvtion Or a Christian directorie guiding men to their saluation, Written by the former Author R.P.* According to A.C. Southern, this 1590 edition had been 'anonymously adapted from "A Christian Directory" for the use of protestants' and falsely attributed to R.P..

In the Cardiff Central Library there are remnants of a comprehensive translation in a manuscript (4.193) written in the hand of John Hughes, entitled 'Directori Christianogol'. The last of the pages bears the number 420. The text on these extant pages has been proved to be a translation of parts of both the above mentioned books. Undoubtedly Huw Owen had been deceived by the false attribution of *The Seconde parte* to R.P. We must conclude that this is the son's copy of the original which was bequeathed to him in his father's will. The copy was intended either to be passed round amongst recusants or for publication. In actual fact John Hughes in *Allwydd Paradwys* (1670) advocates the use of the *Directori* to his fellow recusants:

> Da iawn ac angenrheidiol y fyddai i'r Penteulu, ar amser cynnefin y boreuau, alw y tylwyth ffyddlon oll ynghyd i'r lle-gweddi arferol, ac yno darllain iddynt yn eisteddfod o bobparth (neu beri i ryw vn arall a fedro yn rhwydd ac yn gywraint ddarllain) Pennod neu Wers o'r Directori Christianogol . . .

The second translation attributed to Huw Owen by his son is *Libellus vere aureus* by Vincentius Lirinensis, a work published in 1591 entitled *Vincentii Lirinensis Galli Pro Catholicae Fidei Antiqvitate & veritate adversus prophanas omnium haeresson nouationes, Libellus vere aureus*. There is in the National Library of Wales a manuscript (Cwrtmawr 16) which is a translation, with variations and additions, of this work, bearing the title: *lLyfr prydferth o waith Vincentius, ffranc, monach ac offeiriad o ynys Lirin, ynghweryl henafiaeth a gwirionedd y ffydd gatholic, yn erbyn newyddiaeth pob heresi . . . ac yn awr wedi ei gyfieithu o'r lLadin i'r iaith gamberaec . . . er mwyn denu ac annog y Cymru truain i ymgais a chyrchu at yr hên ffydd gatholic eu henafiaid.* On page 1 the date of translating is given as 1591. However, in view of the following facts: that the manuscript is neither in Huw Owen's nor in John Hughes's handwriting, that John Hughes quotes in Welsh from Vincentius' *Libellus Vere Aureus* in *Allwydd Paradwys* (p. 69) but that the quotation in no way resembles the translation in Cwrtmawr 16, and that Huw Owen was only sixteen years of age in 1591, we cannot ascribe Cwrtmawr 16 to Huw Owen.

The third of Huw Owen's works is *Dilyniad Christ* which was edited by John Hughes and published in London in 1684, with the printing cost met by I.H. (Ioannes Hvgo) (*Gwedi ei imprintio ar gôst I. H.*). It is a translation of *De Imitatio Christi* by Thomas à Kempis as edited from the original manuscript dated 1441 by Heribertus Rosweydus, and published in 1617 and 1627. The translation has the following main headings: *Rhybyddion da i fyw'n ysprydol* (Good counsels to live spiritually); *Rhybyddion yn tynnu at y pethau sydd oddimewn i ddyn* (Counsels concerning those things within a man); *Am gysur ysprydol* (On spiritual comfort); and *Am sacrament yr Allor* (On the sacrament of the altar). Huw Owen undertook the trnslation some time after 1617, probably after entering the service of Henry Somerset, Lord Raglan in 1622. The title *Dilyniad Christ* was chosen in imitation of the popular English translation of Richard Whitford, *Following of Christ*, published in London in 1556. In the preface, John Hughes dedicates his father's translation to the viscounts, lords, baronets, knights and gentry and all the people of Anglesey asserting that:

> It would be unreasonable to seek anyone else to sponsor this translation since the translator comes from the same region and is of the same blood as most of you . . . Indeed nobody in Môn was more welcomed in the halls of Baron Hill, Prysaeddfed and Bodeon than Huw Owen, Gwenynog.

Huw Owen had acted as agent to Sir Hugh Owen of Bodeon and had as a young man been the 'Leader of the Trained Band of Soldiers of the Hundred of Tallabollion'. In Saunders Lewis's judgement, Huw Owen in his translations,

> kept faithfully to the Latin, to the technical terms of the Latin, to the figures of speech and the rhythms of Thomas à Kempis and close to the mind of the author from beginning to end. He deserves a place of honour amongst translators of the Renaissance period. Certainly there are mistakes in his language, in his mutations, in his constructions, and these not infrequent.

John Hughes explains in *Dilyniad Christ* that many a learned and godly man had translated *De Imitatio Christi* into Welsh. He says that he had seen the translations of the Benedictine Mathew Turberville of Castell Pen-llin and of the Jesuit Thomas Jeffreys of Arllechwedd Isaf, Aberconwy, and a part of the translation made by Huw Parry, a secular priest. He adds that they had all died twenty or so years previously, before printing their translations, but that it was right that they should be remembered and praised for trying to do something for the good of Wales.

John Hughes (1615–86) was registered as a student in the *Seminarium Anglicum* in Rome in 1636. He was ordained priest in 1641 and in 1648 joined the Society of Jesus, returning to Wales in 1650 and joining the St Francis Xavier mission with its centre at Y Cwm, Llanrhyddol on the River Monnow. He also served as supervisor of St Winifred's Mission and as keeper of St Winifred's Well, Holywell. In 1670 he published his own compilations of devotions: *Allwydd neu Agoriad Paradwys i'r Cymrv, hynny yw: Gweddiau, Devotionau, Cynghorion ac Athrawiaethau tra duwiol yn mynnu agoryd y Porth a myned i mewn i'r Nef, wedi eu cynnull o amryw lyfrau duwiol, a'i cyfansoddi gan I.H. Yn Lvyck. Imprintiwyd yn y Flwyddyn M DC LXX.* Lvyck, the Flemish for Liège, is a false imprint. The book was actually printed in London. In the preface he says that the devotions were intended to 'kindle godliness' (*ennynnu Duwioldeb*), explaining that:

> Years have gone by now since I first heard many of you sincerely wishing that you had such devotions in your own language. And thus far I have waited for somebody else to collect them, and now that I have found that everyone neglects this work, in spite of my incompetence, I had no choice but to show my good will towards you in the best manner I could . . . If you make good use of this book, it will be easy for you, with the help of God's grace, to open the Heavenly Paradise, and thus gain possession of the Treasure, the Comfort and the Glory that will last for ever.

He emphasizes that the book is not only intended for recusants. It had been compiled for all Welshmen, be they heretics, sectarians or schismatics, but he does refer specifically to his 'dear Brothers and Sisters and my other faithful Friends in Gwent and Breconshire' (*fy anwyl Frodyr a'm Chwiroydd a'm Ceraint ffyddlon yn Gwent a Brycheiniog*). One can understand why, because there were more than twice the number of recusants in those two counties (742) than in the rest of Wales (353) at that time.

The contents are in nine main sections: The Christian Calendar, Christian Doctrine, Daily Prayers, Penance, Holy Sacrament, Extreme Unction, Prayers to the Virgin Mary, Collects and Prayers and Meditations. He attributes the second part of the section on Penance, entitled 'Guide to those guilty of deadly sins' to 'P.C.B.S.I.', namely *Pater Carolus Bacherus, Societatis Iesu*. Charles Baker was the *alias* of David Lewis who was martyred in 1679.

John Hughes's sources include: The Vulgate; The *Breviarum Romanum ex decreto sacrosancti Concilii Tridentini; Missale Romanum ex decreto Sacrosancti Concilii Tridentini restitutum; Officium Beatae Mariae Virginis; Ritual Romanorum; Breviarum Sacrum*; St Augustine's 'De Fide ad Petrum', 'Contra Epistolam Manichaei' and 'De Vera Religione'; *Libellus Vere Aureus Vincentii Lirinensis; Imitatio Christi* by Thomas à Kempis; *Nicetas seu Triumphata Incontinentia* by Hieremias Drexelius; *The little garden of our B. Lady* by François de La Crois; *Martyrologium Romanum; The English Martyrologe* by John Wilson (1608, 1640) which lists the names of forty-five Welsh saints; *Charity mistaken* by Toby Matthews (St. Omer, 1630); *A Manual or Meditation; A Manual of Prayers* (printed twenty-six times between 1583 and 1643); *The treasury of deuotion* by John Wilson (1622). But the volume to which he was most indebted, as he says in the preface, was *The Key of Paradise* by John Wilson, a prolific compiler of English devotions for recusant laymen. Nathanael Sotwellus in his *Bibliotheca* (1676) attributes a number of other books to John Hughes: '1) *De Grauitate Peccati mortalis praesertim Haeresis, sub titulo Verbum Conscientias* (Londini, 1668); 2) *Cathechismus lingua Cambro-Britannica ex Anglicana translatum* (Londini, 1668); 3) *Tractatus ad permouendos Sectarios & Politicos opportunus, edidit Anglicé tacito suo nomine.*' None of these has been traced and they may have been booklets which were later incorporated in *Allwydd Paradwys*. Preserved in the library of Stonyhurst College is an English manuscript of another of his works, 'The Life and Miracles of St Winifred', written in his own hand.

Another missionary serving the recusants of Gwent was Gwilym Pue (c. 1618–89), the third son of Phillip Puw of Penrhyn Creuddyn. He had served as captain in the army of Charles I at Raglan in 1648. In 1660 he joined the Benedictine Order in St Edmund's Paris and was a student in Valladolid in 1670. Returning to Wales in 1677, he followed his profession as a physician and served as 'massing priest' to the Morgan and Bodenham families in Blackbrook, Gwent. Gwilym Pue translated two devotional works, 'Pllaswyr Iessu' and 'Erfynnion neu Littaniav Evraid', both translations from English;

two copies of each remain in manuscripts (NLW 13167B, dated 1674; and NLW 4710B dated 1676).

Jesus Psalter first appeared in 1529 with the title *An invocacyon gloryous named ye psalter of Iesus*, a composition attributed by scholars to Richard Whitford. Numerous editions appeared, mostly entitled *Certaine devout and Godly petitions, commonly called Iesus Psalter*, sometimes as sections in Manuals of Prayers. The work comprises 150 petitions in rhythmic and rhymed phrases and sentences, the commonest rhymes being 'me' and 'Thee'. Gwilym Pue makes no attempt to translate literally or to follow the form of the original. *Erfynnion* is a translation of *The Golden letany in English* by R. Copland (1531), which was later published in most Manuals. Gwilym Pue's version is not an exact translation. He glides over some words and changes the name St Francis to St Gregory, the patron saint of the Benedictine Abbey in Douai.

The Jesuit John Hughes escaped the persecution following the Titus Oates Plot in 1679, when the mission centre at Cwm, Llanrhyddol, was ransacked by agents of the bishop of Hereford who discovered 'great store of divinity books . . . small popish books lately printed against the Protestant religion and some Popish manuscripts' in the building. These books, 'several horse-loads', were moved to Hereford Cathedral and the 'Welsh popish books' burnt outside. William Morgan, the head of the mission, was imprisoned. In 1680 three Jesuit missionary priests were martyred: John Kemble in Hereford, David Lewis in Usk and Charles Mahony in Ruthin. John Hughes, although condemned for high treason according to the Statute of Persuasions, continued with his missionary work mainly in north Wales, probably residing with his cousin in Cwm, two miles from St Asaph, replacing William Morgan as head of the Jesuit mission. He died in Holywell in 1686.

Gwilym Pue, being a Benedictine, was not so suspect. According to the report of the Proceedings of the Definitors for the Union of the Congregation, 1617–19, all members of the Benedictine Congregation would be under severe censure if one spoke or wrote anything which might savour of sedition, contempt or injury against the Kingdom, or concern himself in political affairs. Gwilym Pue, having in his opinion remained loyal to this declaration, ventured to remain in Gwent where he died in 1680.

The 'Welsh popish books' burnt in Hereford probably included the stock of *Allwydd Paradwys* and some Welsh manuscripts stored in the Jesuit Mission centre at Cwm, Llanrhyddol. This depletion of Welsh books created a demand for new translations, and around the end of the century another translation was produced entitled 'Crynodeb Catechism Doway wedi ei gymhwyso at Gyrhaeddiad plant a rhai dilen' which has remained in manuscript (Cwrtmawr 15). It is an unpretentious Welsh version of extracts from both *An Abstract of the Douay Catechism* (Douai, 1697) and from the original catechism *An Abridgement of Christian Doctrine*, attributed to Henry Turberville and first published in Douai in 1649 for the instruction of missionary students at Douai College.

The *Abstract* was also printed in London, bearing a similar title to the Welsh translation: *An Abstract of the Douay Catechism, For the use of children and ignorant people*. The Welsh text includes in part adaptations and translations of sections from both versions— on Catechism, Devotions (The Fifteen Mysteries of the Rosary, Daily Exercises, The Lord's Prayer, The Ave, The Creed, The Confession, Angele Dei, Vias tuas) and Good Thoughts for Every Day of the Week. As in the *Abstract*, the reverse side of the Welsh title-page gives the letters of the alphabet. *Crynodeb Catechism Doway* was the last and best seventeenth-century Welsh translation of works of Catholic doctrine and devotion. But although the Act which had for a century and a half prohibited the printing of Catholic books was not renewed in 1695, the demand for special Welsh devotional books had so declined after the 1678 persecution that this translation, like many others, remained in manuscript.

BIBLIOGRAPHY

Philippus Alegambe, *Bibliotheca Scriptorum Societatis Iesu* (Antuerpiae, 1643).

A.E. Allison and D.M. Rogers, *The Contemporary Printed Literature of the English Counter-Reformation between 1558 and 1640* (2 Vols; Aldershot, 1989–94).

A.C.F. Beales, *Education Under Penalty* (London, 1963).

Geraint Bowen, '"Allwydd neu Agoriad Paradwys i'r Cymru" John Hughes, 1670', *Transactions of the Honourable Society of Cymmrodorion*, 2 (1961), 88–160.

Idem, *Y Drych Kristnogawl* (Caerdydd, 1996).

Idem, 'Catholigion Cymru yn Oes William Morgan', in Glanmor Williams *et al.*, *William Morgan, Y Dyn, ei Gyfnod a'i Feibl* (Yr Wyddgrug, 1988), 31–56.

Idem (ed.), *Gwssanaeth y Gwŷr Newydd* (Caerdydd, 1970).

John Fisher (ed.), *Allwedd neu Agoriad Paradwys i'r Cymru* (Caerdydd, 1929).

R. Geraint Gruffydd, *Argraffwyr Cyntaf Cymru: gwasgau dirgel y Catholigion* (Caerdydd, 1972).

W. Gerallt Harries, 'Robert Gwyn: ei Deulu a'i Dylwyth', *Bulletin of the Board of Celtic Studies*, 25 (1972–4), 425–38.

E. Gwynne Jones, *Cymru a'r Hen Ffydd* (Caerdydd, 1951).

W. Alun Mathias, 'Rhai Sylwadau ar Robert Gwyn', *Llên Cymru*, 3 (1954–5), 63–73.

Thomas Parry and Merfyn Morgan, *Llyfryddiaeth Llenyddiaeth Gymraeg I* (Caerdydd, 1976).

Thomas Parry (ed.), *Theater Dv Mond sef ivv Gorsedd y byd. Rhosier Smyth* (Caerdydd, 1930).

D.M. Rogers (ed.), *Y Drych Cristianogawl* (Menston, 1972).

Idem, *Athravaeth Gristnogavl* (Menston, 1972).

Idem, *Eglvrhad Helaeth-lawn Robert Bellarmin* (Menston, 1972).

John Ryan, 'The Sources of the Welsh Tradition of the Catechism of St Peter Canisius', *Journal of the Welsh Bibliographical Society*, 11 (1973–6), 225–32.

Nathanael Sotwel, *Bibliotheca Scriptorum Societatis Iesv* (Romae, 1676).

A.C. Southern, *Elizabethan Recusant Prose* (London, 1950).

J.E. Spingarn, *A History of Literary Criticism in the Renaissance* (London, 1963).

G.J. Williams (ed.), *Gramadeg Cymraeg gan Gruffydd Robert* (Caerdydd, 1939).

CHAPTER 10

FROM MANUSCRIPT TO PRINT
I. MANUSCRIPT

GRAHAM C.G. THOMAS

The initial impact which the development of printing had on the transmission of texts in the Welsh language was minimal. The bards rejected the printing press outright as a means of disseminating both their poetry and the wealth of native learning and esoteric lore which they had inherited, and they continued to copy and circulate their texts amongst themselves in manuscript. Although certain humanists such as Sir John Prys of Brecon and William Salesbury of Llansannan recognized the importance of the press in promoting their programme to revitalize Welsh cultural and literary life, most humanists, for one reason or another, failed to take advantage of this medium of communication and many texts written by them, either original compositions or translations from other languages, remain in manuscript, unpublished to this day. No doubt many texts have disappeared; for example, only the title-page remains in the hand of the Breconshire scribe William Dafydd Llywelyn of what had been a Welsh translation of George Marshall's *A compendious treatise in metre declaring the firste originall of sacrifice and of the buylding of aultares and churches and of the firste receavinge of the Christen fayth here in England* (1554) (NLW, E. Francis Davies MS 209). Apart from William Salesbury, who published a series of proverbs in his *Oll Synnwyr Pen Kembero Ygyd* (1547), following it with *Trioedd Ynys Prydain* and other texts in a volume published probably in 1567, the humanists made little attempt to publish the traditional literary, historical, religious, legal and pseudo-scientific prose texts which they found in medieval manuscripts and in which they took such great interest. Similarly, they made little attempt to publish the poetry of the *cywyddwyr*. Instead, they chose to transcribe these texts and circulate them in manuscript amongst themselves. It was as a result of such conservatism on the part of both bard and humanist that the manuscript remained the main means for transmitting texts, a position which it was to hold, in the case of some types of text, well into the nineteenth century.

Although by the mid-sixteenth century the bardic order was in decline, the poets were still regarded as the chief authorities on the pedigrees and arms of the Welsh gentry families and a large proportion of the surviving manuscripts written by them during the second half of the sixteenth century and the beginning of the seventeenth century concerns this aspect of their work. The two most important poets of the mid-sixteenth century were Lewys Morgannwg (*fl.* 1520–65) of Glamorgan and his pupil Gruffudd Hiraethog (d. 1564) of Denbighshire. Lewys Morgannwg is believed to have left his books to his pupils Meurug Dafydd and Dafydd Benwyn but these have not survived (see Llanstephan MS 156, p. 10). The only surviving manuscript which until recently was thought to have been in his hand is a collection of pedigrees bound together with other pedigrees including some in Gruffudd Hiraethog's hand (Peniarth MS 132). Morgannwg's pupil, Dafydd Benwyn, also compiled a book of pedigrees (Cardiff MS 2.1 (*RMWL* 10)), but from the late sixteenth century or early seventeenth century onwards, genealogy and heraldry in Glamorgan became the pursuit of gentlemen antiquarians such as Anthony Powel of Llwydiarth, Llangynwyd.

Gruffudd Hiraethog, a native of Llangollen, was raised in that north-eastern corner of Wales which had long occupied an important place in Welsh literary life. It was here that many of the foremost Welsh poets of the late fifteenth and early sixteenth centuries such as Dafydd ab Edmwnd, Gutun Owain, Guto'r Glyn and Tudur Aled were born, learned and practised their craft, and by the mid-sixteenth century, the bardic order had not declined to such an extent here as it had in south Wales. There were still poets to sing and patrons to maintain them, and Hiraethog himself had sufficient pupils to ensure the continuance of the bardic tradition after his death. Hiraethog also held the office of deputy herald for Wales under the College of Arms and the greater proportion of his surviving manuscripts (Peniarth MSS 132–6, 139, 176–8) are genealogical and heraldic in content and reflect his work as a herald bard. On the one hand, he copied the genealogical and heraldic manuscripts of his predecessors, citing as authorities both the poets of south Wales such as Lewys Morgannwg, Morgan Elfael, Ieuan Brechfa and Lewys Glyn Cothi, and of north Wales such as Gutun Owain and Tudur Aled. On the other hand, he copied the pedigree rolls and papers in the possession of the gentry he visited. Other sources included painted glass in churches and monumental inscriptions. As Francis Jones observed, Gruffudd Hiraethog, while representing the continuity of native tradition, developed his own special method of recording the material and handed on a modified tradition to his pupils. Hiraethog died in 1564 and the bulk of his genealogical and heraldic manuscripts were acquired by his pupil Wiliam Llŷn, who added indexes to them. Llŷn in turn, in his will (dated 9 August 1580, proved at St Asaph 7 December 1580), bequeathed 'all the books and rolls that I have' to his pupil Rhys Cain of Oswestry, after whose death they passed to his son Siôn Cain. Large collections of pedigrees and arms based upon the work of their master and his predecessors survive in the hands of Simwnt Fychan (Cardiff MS 4.265, Peniarth MS 74), Wiliam Llŷn (Peniarth MSS 132, 136, 139–42), Wiliam Cynwal (NLW MS 21249) and Siôn Cain (Peniarth MS 149).

The programme which the Welsh humanists set themselves to revivify the cultural life of Wales was based not only on classical learning and antiquities as their counterparts in England and on the Continent sought to do in respect of their own countries' cultures but also upon the Welsh literary and historical past. For them, as R. Geraint Gruffydd has shown, the restitution of Welsh letters was to be achieved by creating a new learned prose style with a translation of the Bible into Welsh, by restoring the poets to their former greatness and making their work more accessible to those outside the bardic order, by producing grammars and vocabularies of the Welsh language, and by studying the history of Wales. In order to accomplish all this, they sought out and copied old manuscripts and records relating to Welsh medieval literature and history, and circulated them amongst themselves. Many assembled sizeable collections of books and manuscripts, for example, John Lewis of Llynwene, Radnorshire, whose manuscripts included 'The Book of Taliesin' (Peniarth MS 2). A number of the more enlightened Elizabethan and early Stuart Welsh landowners spent some of their wealth assembling large collections of books, often important humanist works acquired from the Continent, and manuscripts, many in Welsh or relating to Wales. Some became patrons of the less well-off humanists, allowing them access to their libraries, for example, Sir Edward Stradling of St Donats, Glamorgan, patron of Siôn Dafydd Rhys, and Sir John Wynn of

Gwydir, Caernarfonshire, patron of 'Sir' Thomas Wiliems of Trefriw.

The Welsh humanists tended to come from the ranks of the lesser gentry and the professional classes such as clergymen and lawyers. A large proportion of them congregated in the north-eastern corner of Wales centred on the Vale of Clwyd, a region which G.J. Williams regarded as the cradle of the Renaissance in Wales. They included Jaspar Gryffyth (d. 1614), sometime warden of Ruthin Hospital, Dafydd Johns (*fl.* 1573–87), vicar of Llanfair Dyffryn Clwyd, Richard Langford (d. 1586) of Trefalun (Allington) near Gresford, William Maurice (d. 1680) of Cefn-y-braich, Llansilin, Roger Morris (d. 1607) of Coedytalwrn, Llanfair Dyffryn Clwyd, Rhisiart ap Siôn of Sgorlegan, Llangynhafal, William Salesbury (*c.* 1520–84) of Llansannan, Denbighshire, and John Jones (*c.* 1585–1657/8) of Gellilyfdy, Ysgeifiog, Flintshire. Many were active in other parts of Wales, such as 'Sir' Thomas Wiliems (1545/6–1622) of Trefriw in the Conway Valley, Caernarfonshire, Thomas Evans (*fl.* 1580–1633) of Hendreforfudd near Corwen, Dr John Davies (*c.* 1567–1644), rector of Mallwyd, Humphrey Davies (d. 1635), vicar of Darowen, and Robert Vaughan (*c.* 1592–1667) of Hengwrt near Dolgellau. Another large concentration was in south Wales and included Sir John Prys (1502–55) of Brecon, Siôn Dafydd Rhys (1534–*c.*1619) living at Cwm Llwch near Brecon, and the scribes Llywelyn Siôn (1540–*c.* 1615) of Llangewydd and Ieuan ab Ieuan ap Madog of Betws Tir Iarll in Glamorgan, and William Dafydd Llywelyn of Llangynidr Eglwys Iail in Breconshire. With the possible exception of William Maurice, most of whose manuscripts have been destroyed, the most prolific copyists of texts were Thomas Wiliems and John Jones. Thomas Wiliems, a former Anglican priest turned recusant physician, spent over thirty years assiduously searching manuscripts, transcribing their contents, and noting Welsh words in their context for his Latin–Welsh dictionary. He cast his net widely, copying extensively from manuscripts known to have been in the Vale of Clwyd region as well as from those in the Conwy Valley, especially in the library of his patron, Sir John Wynn of Gwydir. The industriousness with which he set about his task is evinced not only by his monumental dictionary, which still remains unpublished in manuscript (Peniarth MS 228), but also by the large number of surviving manuscripts in his hand and by the marginal notes he made in many of the important medieval Welsh manuscripts. John

Jones's copying activities fell into two periods of his life. From about 1605 to 1610 he copied mainly transcripts of early manuscripts previously made by the humanists of the Vale of Clwyd such as Richard Langford, Rhisiart ap Siôn, and Roger Morris. After a period of seeming inactivity, he resumed copying about 1635 and continued to do so until his death. Much of the work was done in the Fleet Prison, London, while he was serving various terms of imprisonment for debt. By this time, he owned many important medieval manuscripts such as the White Book of Rhydderch (Peniarth MSS 4, 5) (*WBR* hereafter), the Black Book of Chirk (Peniarth MS 29), and *Y Cwta Cyfarwydd* (Peniarth MS 50). He also received manuscripts on loan, especially from his friend, Robert Vaughan.

The availability of texts inevitably dictated what the humanists copied. The wide range of texts copied by the poet Gutun Owain would indicate the presence of a pool of literary, religious, medical, astrological and other pseudo-scientific texts in north-east Wales during the late fifteenth century, probably in one of the abbeys, Basingwerk or Valle Crucis, with which he had connections. It was probably from the same pool or directly from Gutun Owain's manuscripts that Edward ap Rhoesier and Ieuan ap Wiliam ap Dafydd ab Einws, two gentlemen of Ruabon, drew many of the texts which they copied. The former is primarily remembered for his genealogical and heraldic manuscripts (e.g. Peniarth MS 128). He copied the heraldic treatise *Disgriad Arfau* (BL Addl MS 15041) and owned a manuscript written by an unidentified contemporary scribe containing the saint's life *Buchedd Martin Sant* (BL Addl MS 14967 (*RMWL* 23), two texts said to be translations into Welsh made by Siôn Trefor, bishop of St Asaph (d. 1410). Both these texts occur in manuscripts written by Gutun Owain (Jesus College MS 141 (*RMWL* 6)) and NLW MS 3026 (Mostyn MS 88) respectively), but only the former was later copied by the bards, by Simwnt Fychan (Cardiff MS 4.265), Wiliam Dafi (Peniarth MS 183) in 1586, and Hywel ap Syr Mathau who made two copies, one (Llanstephan MS 46) in 1557 on behalf of fellow bard Morgan Elfael, and the other (Cardiff MS 3.11 (*RMWL* 50)) in 1561. Ieuan ap Wiliam, who served as constable of Ruabon in 1554, has left us two large compilations (Llanstephan MS 117 and Cardiff MS 2.629 (Hafod MS 19)) which contain mainly religious, astrological, and medical texts, some in the same tradition as those copied by Gutun

Owain. Roger Morris also had access to some of Gutun Owain's manuscripts, copying *Disgriad Arfau* (NLW MS 3032 (Mostyn MS 113)) and *Buchedd Martin Sant* (Cwrtmawr MS 530). The pool was augmented by the migration of some of the important medieval manuscripts of south Wales to north Wales during the sixteenth century. Apart from the Red Book of Hergest (*RBH* hereafter), the finest collection of literary and religious medieval prose-texts in Welsh is contained in *WBR*, written in south Wales, possibly at Strata Florida, *c.* 1350. There is evidence that this manuscript was for some time in the possession of Elisau ap Wiliam Llwyd (d. 1583) of Rhiwaedog, Llanfor, Merionethshire, and later owners included Jasper Gryffyth and John Jones, Gellilyfdy. The White Book of Hergest, said to have been written by the poet Lewys Glyn Cothi (*c.*1420–89), was another important manuscript from south Wales containing religious prose texts, which seems to have been in north Wales by the late sixteenth century. It was later acquired by the antiquarian William Maurice of Cefn-y-braich, Llansilin, but was probably destroyed in a fire at a bookbinders in Covent Garden, London, in 1810 before most of Maurice's collection of manuscripts were later burnt in the fire at Wynnstay near Ruabon in 1858. Both Thomas Wiliems and John Jones copied medieval religious prose texts. The former's main source was the White Book of Hergest, from which he transcribed, amongst other things, the *Elucidarium* and *Ymborth yr Enaid* including *Pryd Mab Duw* and *Nawradd Angelion Nef* (Peniarth MS 227). He also copied texts from *WBR*, for example *Y modd y dysgir i ddyn pa ddelw y dyly credu Duw* (BL Addl MS 31055). Many of the religious texts in *WBR* were copied by John Jones between 1604 and 1610 (Cardiff MS 2.633 (Hafod MS 23)), probably from transcripts made previously by Richard Langford of Trefalun.

Apart from Ieuan ap Wiliam, other humanists showed an interest in the medical and pseudo-scientific texts of the Middle Ages and the Renaissance. William Salesbury compiled a large collection of herbal recipes, partly based on learned works in Latin and English. Although the original manuscript is lost, transcripts of the text survive in the hands of Roger Morris (NLW MS 4581) and of the eighteenth-century scribe and collector of manuscripts, Evan Thomas of Cwmchwylfod near Bala (NLW MS 686). Thomas Evans of Hendreforfudd, who acquired some of Morris's manuscripts after his death, also compiled a volume of medical recipes (Cardiff MS 2.973). Thomas Wiliems's medical manuscripts are often given as the source of recipes in later compilations but no substantial collection of such recipes in his hand has survived, although his interest in the subject is apparent from the marginal notes in his hand found in some of the major medieval medical manuscripts, for example, BL Addl MS 14913 (*RMWL* 26). Welsh translations of printed medical books in other languages were made, for example, Thomas Paynel's *Of the wood called guaiacum that healeth the French pockes* . . . (London, 1536), itself a translation of a work by Ulrich von Hutten (NLW MS 5280). Texts relating to astrology, astronomy, palmistry, weather prognostication and the interpretation of dreams were also popular. The astrological/astronomical text *Rheol y Syr neu Wybryddiaeth* was copied by Thomas Wiliems (BL Addl MS 31055, NLW 3029 (Mostyn 110)), John Jones (NLW MS 5278) and Thomas Evans (Peniarth MS 187), and pseudo-scientific texts, some relating to palmistry and the interpretation of dreams, occur in the manuscripts written in the 1580s by the cleric 'Sir' Richard Jones (Peniarth MS 172 and Cwrtmawr MS 208).

The humanists' primary concern in the study of Welsh history was to defend the foundation myths, especially that of Brutus as recorded in Geoffrey of Monmouth's *Historia Regum Britanniae*, against such critics as Polydore Vergil. It is therefore not surprising that the various medieval Welsh versions of Geoffrey's work, *Brut y Brenhinedd*, were copied during the second half of the sixteenth and beginning of the seventeenth centuries. The *Brut* was often preceded in the same manuscript by *Dares Phrygius*, a text re-counting the exploits of the heroes at the destruction of Troy, and followed by the Welsh chronicle *Brut y Tywysogion*. Sometimes, these three texts were preceded by *Y Bibyl Ynghymraec*, a transla-tion of *Promptuarium Bibliae* attributed to Petrus Pictaviensis, thus presenting a continuous history from the creation of the world to more recent times. These texts were copied by both the poets and the humanists. *Dares Phrygius* and *Brut y Brenhinedd* were copied by Siôn Brwynog (NLW MS 3034 (Mostyn MS 115)), and *Brut y Brenhinedd* and *Brut y Tywysogion* by Wiliam Cynwal (Peniarth MS 212). The humanists who copied them include John Jones: *Y Bibyl Ynghymraec* (NLW MS 5277), *Dares Phrygius* (NLW MS 5277, Peniarth MSS 264, 265, 314), *Brut y Brenhinedd* (NLW 5277, Peniarth MSS 264, 265, 266, 314), and *Brut y Saeson* (NLW MS

5277); Edward Kyffin: *Dares Phrygius, Brut y Brenhinedd, Brut y Tywysogion* (NLW MS 13211) for Siôn Trefor, Trefalun; Llywelyn Siôn: *Y Bibyl* (Llanstephan MS 164); Rhisiart ap Siôn: *Brut y Tywysogion* (Llanstephan MS 172) copied from NLW MS 3035 (Mostyn MS 116); Siôn Dafydd Rhys: *Y Bibyl* (Llanstephan MS 55), and *Brut y Brenhinedd* (Peniarth MS 118) from *RBH*; Thomas Wiliems: *Y Bibyl* (BL Addl MS 31055) from the White Book of Hergest, and *Brut y Brenhinedd* (NLW MS 5281) from a lost manuscript of Maurice Wynn of Gwydir. An anonymous scribe, who collaborated with Anthony Powel of Llwydiarth in copying the religious texts in Hafod MS 22 (see below), made two copies of *Brut y Tywysogion* (Llanstephan MSS 61, 62). Other historical texts copied include *Buchedd Gruffudd ap Cynan*, a version of Randolph Higden's *Polychronicon* and various short chronologies.

The Welsh native tales *Pedair Cainc y Mabinogi* (The Four Branches of the Mabinogi) and the Arthurian romances are noticeably absent from the inventory of prose texts copied by the bards. Furthermore, there was very little interest shown in these stories by the humanists. The only known full transcript of the *Mabinogi* by a humanist is that made by Roger Morris in NLW MS 3043 (Mostyn MS 135) from *WBR*, a feat not repeated until the beginning of the eighteenth century when the *RBH* text was copied. Apart from copies made by south-Walian scribes of *Owain a Luned* in which the language was modernized (see below), *Historia Peredur* was the only other Arthurian romance to be copied, by an unidentified mid-sixteenth-century scribe in a manuscript which belonged to Edward ap Rhoesier (BL Addl MS 14967), and by Roger Morris (NLW MS 3043), John Jones (NLW, J. Gwenogvryn Evans MS 1A), John Davies of Mallwyd (NLW MS 5269) and his amanuensis, Rowland Lewis (Cardiff MS 2.25 (*RMWL* 17)). Roger Morris and John Jones also copied into their respective manuscripts the *WBR* text of *Ystorya Bown o Hamtwn*. The native tale *Breuddwyd Macsen Wledig* was copied by Thomas Wiliems (BL Addl MS 31055, NLW MS 3029 (Mostyn MS 110)) and John Jones (Peniarth MS 267), and *Ystorya Siarlmaen* by Perys Mostyn (Cwrtmawr MS 2) and the poet Wiliam Cynwal (Peniarth MS 183). Both Roger Morris (NLW MS 1553) and John Jones (Peniarth MS 111) copied *Chwedl Taliesin* which is better known from the version that Elis Gruffydd, 'The Soldier of Calais' (*c.* 1490–*c.* 1552), included in his Chronicle of the World (NLW MS 5276). Other literary texts copied by the humanists include the rhetorical texts *Areithiau Prôs*, for example, by Robert Vaughan and Thomas Wiliems (NLW MS 3029 (Mostyn MS 110)), and prophecies, for example, by John Jones (NLW MS 3041 (Mostyn MS 133)).

The humanists' interest in bardic learning and the rules of Welsh prosody brought them into direct conflict with the bards, whom they criticized for their reluctance to share the secrets of their craft. The first successful attempt to bridge the gap between the ideals of humanism and the esoteric learning of the bards was the co-operation between the humanist William Salesbury and the poet Gruffudd Hiraethog, even though Salesbury says that the proverbs he published in *Oll Synnwyr Pen Kembero Ygyd* in 1547 were 'stolen' from one of Hiraethog's manuscripts. However, both men had respect for each other and Salesbury dedicated his *Llyfr Rhetoreg* (1552) to the bard, referring to him as his chief ally in his efforts to save and maintain the Welsh language. Although Salesbury recognized the importance of the press for promoting the Welsh language, this work was not intended for publication but for circulating in manuscript among a small circle, and a copy in his hand survives in Cardiff MS 2.39 (*RMWL* 21). Hiraethog was also ready to share his bardic learning with those outside the bardic order, as exemplified by his compilation of proverbs and bardic lore known from its opening words *Lloegr drigiant . . .*, which he dedicated to Richard Mostyn, a gentleman whose family had long taken an active interest in Welsh literary life. No autograph copy of this work survives, the earliest being in the hand of Mostyn's kinsman, Rhisiart Phylip (b. 1535) of Picton, Pembrokeshire (Peniarth MS 155).

The bardic grammar associated with Einion Offeiriad of Gwynedd and Dafydd Ddu Athro of Hiraddug, Flintshire, was eagerly sought after by the humanists and many copies were made by them, for example, by Thomas Evans (Peniarth MS 157), John Jones (several versions in Cardiff MS 2.634 (Hafod MS 24)), Robert ab Ifan of Brynsiencyn (Peniarth MS 158), Roger Morris (Peniarth MS 169), Sir John Prys of Brecon (Balliol College, Oxford MS 353), Siôn Dafydd Rhys (Llanstephan MS 55), and Thomas Wiliems (NLW MS 3039 (Mostyn MS 110), Peniarth MSS 62, 77)). Gruffudd Hiraethog is credited with having imposed a final order on this bardic grammar, and his work came to be known as *Y Pum Llyfr Cerddwriaeth*. No copy exists in Hiraethog's hand but several copies survive in the hands of his pupils, the fullest being Simwnt Fychan's (Jesus College MS 15 (*RMWL* 9)), to which he added a treatise on figures of speech, an adaptation made by William Salesbury of Petrus Mosellanus' *Tabulae de schematibus et tropis* and dedicated (as we have seen) to Gruffudd Hiraethog, in which examples from Welsh poetry have been substituted. Wiliam Cynwal's copy (Cardiff MS 1.16 (*RMWL* 38)) omits Salesbury's treatise. By the second half of the sixteenth century, whatever barriers had existed between bard and humanist were breaking down and texts were exchanged freely between them. The *Pum Llyfr Cerddwriaeth* is a good example of how a bardic text was copied and circulated outside the bardic order. Simwnt Fychan's copy seems to have been in the possession of Dafydd Salesbury of Dolbadarn, when it was copied by Roger Morris (BL Addl MS 15047, Peniarth MS 169) and by Rhisiart ap Siôn (Peniarth MSS 159, 160), another gentleman who maintained close contact with the bards of the Vale of Clwyd. Peniarth MS 160 was copied in 1606 by John Jones (NLW MS 7007), which in turn was copied in 1664 by William Maurice (manuscript burnt 1858; see NLW MS 2016 (Panton MS 48)). Another text copied by both bards and humanists was the so-called *Statud Gruffudd ap Cynan*, a document probably drawn up at the time of the first Caerwys Eisteddfod of 1523, in order to regulate the poetic and musical crafts. The earliest copy is an incomplete one in Gruffudd Hiraethog's hand (Peniarth MS 194), but a complete copy appears in his *Lloegr drigiant* . . . Other copies include those by the poets Wiliam Llŷn (NLW MS 3025 (Mostyn MS 87)) and Rhys Cain (BL Addl MS 19711) and by the humanists John Jones (Cardiff MS 2.634 (Hafod MS 24), Peniarth MS 295), Robert ab Ifan of Brynsiencyn (Peniarth MS 158), Roger Morris (Peniarth MS 168), Siôn Dafydd Rhys (Llanstephan MS 55, Peniarth MS 270), Thomas Wiliems (Peniarth MS 77), which includes a copy of William Salesbury's preface, and William Dafydd Llywelyn (Peniarth MS 147). Other texts associated with bardic learning copied by the humanists include the historical triads *Trioedd Ynys Prydain*, by William Salesbury (Cwrtmawr MS 3), Thomas Wiliems (BL Addl MS 31055, Peniarth MS 77), and by John Jones and Robert Vaughan who both compiled collections of triads from a number of sources (Peniarth MSS 267 and 185 respectively); *Pedwar Marchog ar Hugain*, by Thomas Wiliems (BL Addl MS 31055, Peniarth MS 77) and Robert

Vaughan (Peniarth MS 185); *Pedwar Brenin ar Hugain a farnwyd yn gadarnaf*, by John Jones (Peniarth MSS 215, 267); and *Tri Thlws ar Ddeg Ynys Prydain*, by John Davies, Mallwyd (NLW MS 5269), Rowland Lewis of Mallwyd (Cardiff MS 2.25 (*RMWL* 17)), John Jones (Peniarth MSS 216, 295), Llywelyn Siôn (NLW MS 13075), and Thomas Wiliems (Peniarth MS 77).

Although manuscripts containing poetry written by the bards themselves first made an appearance in the second half of the fifteenth century, no manuscript survives containing holograph poetry by Lewys Morgannwg and only four poems or fragments of poems by his pupil Gruffudd Hiraethog survive in the poet's hand (Peniarth MSS 86, 153). However, from the second half of the sixteenth century onwards and through the seventeenth century, the number of surviving manuscripts written totally or partially by the poets increases. Lewys Morgannwg's pupil in Glamorgan, Meurug Dafydd, copied his own poetry together with some by other poets in NLW MS 13066, and Dafydd Benwyn did the same in Llanstephan MS 164 and Cardiff MS 2.1 (*RWML* 10). NLW MS 13068, which contains poetry mostly in the hand of Sils ap Siôn and includes some of his own compositions, also includes possible holograph poetry by Thomas Lewis. Edward Dafydd of Margam (*c.* 1600–78?) and Dafydd Williams, vicar of Pen-llin near Bridgend, are two of a number of seventeenth-century poets who have copied their work in NLW MS 13078. Likewise, in north Wales, a substantial body of poetry survives in the hands of Hiraethog's pupils and other poets who succeeded him, for example Wiliam Llŷn (Cardiff MS 2.103 (*RMWL* 8), Cardiff MS 5.167 (Thelwal MS), Peniarth MS 84), Simwnt Fychan (Peniarth MS 64), Wiliam Cynwal (Christchurch College, Oxford MS 184, Bodewryd MS 101B), Siôn Brwynog (BL Addl MS 14978, ff. 155ᵛ–219ᵛ, 223–46ᵛ, Cwrtmawr MSS 23, 312), Lewys Dwn (NLW MS 5270, Peniarth MS 96), Rhys Cain and Siôn Cain (Peniarth MSS 116–17).

The preservation of much of the strict-metre poetry of the fourteenth, fifteenth and sixteenth centuries is the fruit of the labours of gentlemen and clergymen and others outside the bardic order, who, during the late sixteenth and early seventeenth centuries, compiled large collections of the works of the *cywyddwyr*, often on behalf of other gentlemen. The most important 'professional' scribe in Glamorgan, Llywelyn Siôn, compiled a number of manuscripts of strict-metre poetry, some volumes in a characteristic 'long book' format such as Cardiff MS 5.44 (The Long Book of Llanharan), and in 1674 Thomas ab Ieuan of Tre'r-bryn, Llangrallo, compiled a large collection of poetry (NLW MS 13069), much of it copied from Llywelyn Siôn's manuscripts. In north Wales, the gentlemen and clergy of the Vale of Clwyd were prominent in producing large collections of poetry. A notable example is BL Addl MS 14866 (*RMWL* 29), written by Dafydd Johns, vicar of Llanfair Dyffryn Clwyd, for John Williams, a London merchant. In this, Johns provides copious marginal notes on the characters of Welsh legend referred to in the poems and on the metres of the *awdlau*. Another clergyman who has left behind him several large volumes of poetry is Humphrey Davies (d. 1635), vicar of Darowen (Llanstephan MSS 35, 118, NLW MS 3056 (Mostyn MS 160), Bodewryd MS 1, and Brogyntyn MS 2, the latter copied for Theodore Price, sub-dean of Westminster). In a poem asking for copies of a hundred poems by Dafydd ap Gwilym for Lewys Gwyn of Dolau-gwyn, the poet Rhisiart Phylip refers to Dafis's collections of Welsh poetry, maintaining that there was not a Welsh poem of which he did not have a copy (NLW, Bodewryd MS 1, pp. 390–3). John Jones, Gellilyfdy, transcribed large collections of Welsh poetry arranged into volumes according to type, for example *englynion* (NLW MS 3039 (Mostyn MS 131), Peniarth MS 313) and the works of the *cywyddwyr* (Peniarth MSS 72, 312). Several volumes of strict-metre poetry were compiled by John Davies of Mallwyd. These include BL Addl MSS 14871 (*RMWL* 20) (mainly poetry by Lewys Glyn Cothi), 14971 (*RMWL* 21), and 14976 (*RMWL* 22), and Peniarth MS 49 (poetry by Dafydd ap Gwilym). In a letter, dated 19 May 1639, to Owain Wynn of Gwydir, he refers to his collection of Dafydd's poems and his desire to obtain from William Mathew of Llandaff Castle 'a booke written in paper wth an ould hand w[ch] had many of them, whereof I gotte copie of the one half when I dwelt in those parts' (NLW MS 14529, ff. 12–13).

Free-metre poetry was also copied. It often took the form of the carol or the more localized *cwndid* popular in Glamorgan and Gwent and *halsing* in Carmarthenshire, south Cardiganshire and north Pembrokeshire, which were religious or moralistic in tone. An early collection of carols was made by John Jones, Gellilyfdy (Cwrtmawr MS 203) and of *cwndidau* by Llywelyn Siôn (NLW MS 13070). *Halsingod*, although composed during the seventeenth century, are mostly preserved in eighteenth-century manuscripts. An exception is a small collection composed and copied by James Phillippes, probably a Carmarthenshire man, about 1673–4 in NLW MS 12071. Many seventeenth-century poets, such as Huw Morys, Edward Morris, Wiliam Phylip, and Siôn Dafydd Laes, composed poetry in strict- and free-metre, and both forms are found in the manuscripts copied during the seventeenth century. Roman Catholic devotional poetry in free metre was also composed and copied, notable examples being in the two volumes (NLW MSS 4710, 13167) copied by Gwilym Pue (*c.* 1618–*c.* 1689) of Penrhyn Creuddyn, Caernarfonshire, in which he includes not only his own devotional poetry but also that by other recusant poets including the martyr Richard White. Also to the category of free-metre poetry belong the metrical versions of *Troelus a Chresyd*, copied in 1622 by John Jones (Peniarth MS 106), and *Siôn Mawndfil*, copied by Thomas Evans (NLW MS 1553) and by John Jones (Peniarth MS 218) from a copy (now lost) written by Rhisiart ap Siôn in 1586; the Welsh religious plays *Y Tri Brenin o Gwlen* (The Three Kings of Cologne) and *Y Dioddefaint* (The Passion) copied by, among others, Roger Morris (Cwrtmawr MS 530) and the dialogue *Yr Enaid a'r Corff* (The Soul and the Body) by Owen John (Peniarth MS 65), a late-sixteenth-century scribe, probably of Glamorgan or Gwent.

Certain humanists were interested in the early Welsh poetry of the *cynfeirdd* and *gogynfeirdd*. In 1573, Richard Langford copied *Englynion Marwnad Geraint ab Erbin* from leaves now missing in *WBR*. Roger Morris transcribed poetry from the Black Book of Carmarthen (*BBC* hereafter) in Peniarth MS 173. Both Langford's and Morris's transcripts were copied in 1607 by John Jones (Peniarth MS 111). A verse from Aneirin's *Gododdin* was copied by Dafydd Johns (BL Addl MS 14866, f. 257) from which another copy was made by Jasper Gryffyth (Bangor, Gwyneddon MS 3, f. 157). The fullest transcript of the *Gododdin* by any humanist is that made by Thomas Wiliems (BL Addl MS 31055, ff. 138–43, 161ᵛ–3). Both Robert Vaughan and William Maurice made copies but they are now lost. John Davies copied in NLW MS 4973 the contents of the Book of Taliesin, and the saga *englynion* including those of the Llywarch Hen Cycle probably not directly from *RBH* but from a manuscript whose readings were close to it. The Hendregadredd MS (NLW MS 6680), one of the most important sources of *gogynfeirdd* poetry, was in north Wales in the latter part of the sixteenth century, having been acquired by Huw Llŷn after the death of Gruffudd Dwn of Ystrad Merthyr near Llanelli in about 1570, and quotations from the poetry in it appear in Wiliam Llŷn's vocabulary in Cardiff MS 3.12 (*RMWL* 82). It was also seen by Thomas Wiliems who quoted from it in his vocabulary in Cardiff MS 4.330 (Hafod MS 26), and transcribed some poetry from it in BL Addl MS 31055. The *gogynfeirdd* poetry in *RBH* was copied by Siôn Dafydd Rhys (Peniarth MS 118). John Davies, Mallwyd, compiled at least two collections of *gogynfeirdd* poetry: BL Addl MS 14869 (*RMWL* 19), a transcript of the Hendregadredd MS, and NLW MS 4973, probably copied from a source now lost, containing some poetry found in *RBH* but also including poetry not found in any of the surviving medieval collections. Davies later saw *RBH* in 1634 and added variant readings from it in the margins.

An important aspect of Welsh humanism was the desire on the part of some humanists to provide Welsh translations of English or other foreign-language texts and, in some cases, to create original prose compositions. On the whole, these works were not intended for publication but were written either for the gratification of the writer or for circulation in manuscript. The texts chosen for translation varied in subject matter. Siôn ap Hywel ab Owain (d. 1627) of Cefn Treflaeth, Llanystumdwy, translated part of Cicero's putative work on rhetoric, *Rhetorica ad Herennium*, of which only an incomplete transcript survives, written by Wiliam Bodwrda (NLW, Llanfair and Brynodol MS 2, 17–19), and translations of Seneca's *De Remediis Fortuitorum Liber* and of *Colloquium Adolescentis et Scorti*, one of Erasmus' colloquia, are found in Cardiff MS 2.615, an eighteenth-century manuscript containing copies of texts from a lost manuscript written by John Jones; Richard Langford and an amanuensis copied a translation made by one Richard Owen of Juan Luis Vives's treatise on the education of women, *De institutione feminae Christianae* (Peniarth MS 403); William Dafydd Llywelyn copied a translation of Humphrey Lhwyd's *The Treasury of Health* (several editions published between 1550 and 1560), which in turn was a translation of *Thesaurus Pauperum* attributed to Petrus Hispanus (BL Addl MS 15078); and an anonymous scribe copied in BL Addl MS 14921 (*RMWL* 27) a translation of *The Voiage and Trauayle of Syr John Maundeuile* (London: Thomas East, 1568).

A significant proportion of the Welsh humanists were Roman Catholics. Government control and the physical dangers which recusants could expect to suffer if detected added to their difficulties in seeing Catholic literature in print. Instead they found that the more effective and less hazardous way of circulating their texts was in manuscript and for this purpose they often employed professional scribes of a similar persuasion. A large collection of saints' lives, being translations mainly from the 'Golden Legend', were copied by Roger Morris (Llanstephan MS 34). He also copied a translation of *Sacra Historia Sulpicius Severus*, from an edition published by Victor Giselinus in Antwerp, 1574 (NLW MS 1553), and the Jesuit John Hughes (1616–85) copied the translation made by his father, Huw Owen (1575–1642), Gwenynog, Anglesey, of Robert Persons's *Christian Directorie* (1585) (Cardiff MS 4.193). However, the greatest contribution to this genre was made by the recusants of south Wales and by the Glamorgan scribes Llywelyn Siôn (1540–1615?), Ieuan ab Ieuan ap Madog (*fl.* 1547–87), and the Breconshire scribe William Dafydd Llywelyn. In Glamorgan, there was an interest among recusants in reading the religious and secular prose texts of the Middle Ages as found in such south-Walian manuscripts as the Book of the Anchorite of Llanddewibrefi (Jesus College, Oxford, MS 119 (*RMWL* 2)), *WBR*, and *RBH*, and to meet this need they took advantage of the literary skills of one or more talented prose-writers who rewrote many of the traditional medieval texts in the Welsh language of their day. Important collections of medieval texts, the language of many of them such as *Ystoria Saith Doethon Rhufain* and *Owain a Luned* having been modernized, were copied by Llywelyn Siôn in NLW MS 13075 and by Ieuan ab Ieuan in Llanstephan MS 171. On linguistic and stylistic grounds, it would seem that the same 'school' of prose-writers was responsible for translating into Welsh a number of religious and moralistic texts popular in England or on the Continent. These include translations of Henry Parker's *Dives et Pauper* (first published in 1493), two copies of which are in Llywelyn Siôn's hand (Cardiff MS 2.618 (Hafod MS 4), Cardiff MS 3.240); of *Gesta Romanorum*, also in the latter's hand (NLW MS 13076); of William Goodyeare's *The Voyage of the Wandring Knight* (London, 1581), an allegorical text which is in turn a translation of Jean de Carthenay's *Le Voyage du Chevalier Errant*, in Ieuan ab Ieuan's hand (Llanstephan MS 178); of part of *Liber*

Festialis by John Mirk, prior of Lilleshall, Shropshire (first printed by Caxton in 1483), in the hand of an associate of Anthony Powel of Llwydiarth, Llangynwyd (Cardiff MS 2.632 (Hafod MS 22)).

The scribes Llywelyn Siôn and William Dafydd Llywelyn also copied original works in Welsh by contemporary Catholic writers, especially those by Robert Gwyn (*c.* 1540/50–1592/1604). Despite the printing of part of it secretly in a cave on the Little Orme, Caernarfonshire, the only complete copy of *Y Drych Cristianogawl* (The Christian Mirror), a work concerning 'the Four Last Things' and attributed to Gwyn, survives in the hand of Llywelyn Siôn (Cardiff MS 3.240). The same scribe made two copies of *Coelio'r Saint* (Cardiff MSS 2.82, 2.620 (Hafod MS 6)), a work also attributed to Gwyn. William Dafydd Llywelyn copied the manuscript known as the *Lanter Gristnogawl* (NLW MS 15542) which incorporates the texts *Nad oes vn Ffydd onyd y wir Ffydd* and *Gwssanaeth y Gwŷr Newydd*, written by Gwyn between 1571 and 1575, and which like *Coelio'r Saint* is a response to Bishop John Jewel's *Apologia Ecclesiae Anglicanae* which Maurice Kyffin translated into Welsh as *Deffynniad Ffydd Eglwys Loegr* in 1595. William Dafydd Llywelyn also copied a translation of *A Manvall or Meditation* (1580–1) by his contemporary Richard Bristowe (Llanstephan MS 13, Swansea Public Library MS A 1.57). The preceding chapter deals in more detail with many of the works mentioned in this paragraph.

Although the printing of Protestant literature in Welsh was not illegal, Welsh Protestants faced other difficulties in seeing their work through the press, such as printing costs, the ignorance of London printers of the Welsh language, and the size of the Welsh reading public. The result was that they often fell back on the manuscript for preserving, and possibly disseminating, their works. An interesting late-sixteenth-century original text, *Llefr o'r Eglwys Crhistnogedd* by Rowland Puleston, dealing with the state of religion under the law and the Gospel with an account of the Church down to the reign of Elizabeth I, written from the Anglican point of view, still remains unpublished in manuscript (NLW MS 716). Many of the texts are translations from English. Welsh translations of two early Protestant works, namely parts of Thomas Cranmer's first litany published in *An exhortation vnto prayer* . . . (1544) and his *The order of the Communion* (1548), were copied into Hafod MS 22 by Anthony Powel of Llwydiarth and by the same anonymous scribe who copied such Catholic texts as *Liber festialis* in the same manuscript. Other translations into Welsh of popular Anglican works include Leonard Wright's *A Summons of Sleepers* (1589) translated by Siôn Conwy (*c.* 1546–1606) of Botryddan near Rhuddlan for Robert Salesbury of Rug (BL Addl MS 14920) and Bishop Joseph Hall's *The Balme of Gilead or Comforter* (1646) by Robert Jones, curate of Gyffylliog near Ruthin, in 1659 for William Salesbury of Rug (Llanstephan MS 110); Christopher Sutton's *Disce Mori: Learne to Die* . . . (London, various editions between 1600 and 1662) by David Rowlands, vicar of Llangybi, in 1633 (NLW MS 731); and John Mayer's *The English Catechisme Explained* . . . (London, various editions between 1621 and 1635) by Wiliam ap Howell, minister of Wrexham, in 1636 (Peniarth MS 231). At the end of the seventeenth century, Samuel Williams, vicar of Llandyfrïog, translated James Ussher's *Immanuel, or the Mystery of the Son of God Unfolded* (London, 1638) (Llanstephan MS 22), and several works were translated in the 1680s by Nathaniel Jones, including *The Husbandman's Calling*, a sermon preached by Richard Steele in 1688 (NLW MS 10254), and Jeremy Taylor's *Daily Rule* (Llanstephan MS 109). Also, a Welsh translation of the prayers of the Lutheran theologian, Johann Gerhard (1582–1637), probably from Ralph Winterton's English translation of them published in 1631, occurs in a late seventeenth-century manuscript in the hand of Ffoulk Wynne of Nantglyn (NLW, Plas Nantglyn MS 5).

The finest collection of medieval and Renaissance Welsh manuscripts assembled during the seventeenth century was that made by Robert Vaughan at Hengwrt near Dolgellau. The manuscripts of John Lewis, Llynwene, the greater proportion of Siôn Cain's valuable collection of bardic and other manuscripts, some of John Davies, Mallwyd's manuscripts, and the bulk of John Jones, Gellilyfdy's manuscripts all found a home on the shelves of his library. These included some of the most important manuscripts in the Welsh language such as *BBC*, *WBR*, and the Book of Taliesin. Vaughan's contemporary, William Maurice, Cefn-y-braich, Llansilin, also assembled a valuable collection of Welsh manuscripts, many from the library of the Thelwall family of Plas-y-ward, which included the works of the bards of the Vale of Clwyd. After Maurice's death, his daughter sold them to Sir William Williams of Llanforda for £60 and most were destroyed in the

Wynnstay fire of 1858. Other important collections of Welsh manuscripts formed during the seventeenth century included those of the Mostyn family of Mostyn Hall, Flintshire, and of Robert Davies (*c*. 1658–1710) of Llannerch and Gwysaney in Denbighshire and Flintshire respectively.

Robert Vaughan was one of the foremost antiquarians of his day and corresponded with other antiquarians outside Wales such as James Ussher, archbishop of Armagh, William Camden and John Selden, supplying them with information from his manuscripts. He could also hold his own with the herald bards Rhys and Siôn Cain, who often sought his help in verifying facts on Welsh genealogical and heraldic matters. Both Vaughan and Maurice shared the same antiquarian interest in Welsh literature, history and law, and manuscripts were exchanged between them. Both sought to defend the early history of Britain as given by Geoffrey of Monmouth against critics, and Maurice sent Vaughan a copy of his 'History of Bellinus and Brennus defended'. He also compiled in 1659 '*Organum Britannicum*, being a catalogue of authors treating of the History of Britain written in Welsh, Latin, and English' (copies of both works occur in NLW MS 2036 (Panton MS 71)). Both took great interest in Welsh native law. Vaughan owned many of the important medieval manuscripts of the Laws of Hywel Dda, including both the earliest Latin text (Peniarth MS 28) and the earliest Welsh text, namely that in The Black Book of Chirk (Peniarth MS 29), and he made a number of transcripts from his collection. Maurice was the first antiquarian to attempt a classification of the texts of the Laws of Hywel Dda in his *Corpus Hoelianum* or *Y Deddfgrawn* (Wynnstay MSS 37–8), based mainly on manuscripts belonging to Robert Vaughan and on a manuscript, now lost, which the antiquarian Meredith Lloyd (*c*. 1620–95) of Welshpool gave him in 1678.

Robert Vaughan and William Maurice were probably the last of the great Welsh humanists, although manuscripts continued to be collected and copied by such men as James Davies (Iaco ab Dewi) (1648–1722), Humphrey Humphreys (1648–1712), successively bishop of Bangor and Hereford, Thomas Wilkins (1626–99), rector of St Mary Church, Glamorgan, and Samuel Williams (*c*. 1660–*c*. 1722), vicar of Llandyfrïog, later rector of Llangynllo, Cardiganshire, father of the antiquarian Moses Williams (1685–1742). At the close of the seventeenth century and the beginning of the eighteenth century, there was renewed interest in Welsh manuscripts and the texts they contained amongst a group of men who came under the influence of the philologist and scientist Edward Lhuyd (1660?–1709), keeper of the Ashmolean Museum, Oxford. Lhuyd and his small band of helpers recognized the necessity of first locating the manuscripts, listing their contents, and producing library catalogues of the more extensive collections. This was part of a wider programme of research which involved the systematic recording of the history, antiquities, folklore, traditions, language, and literature of Wales, as well as its geology, fauna, and flora, and for this purpose, questionnaires were sent out to incumbents and other gentlemen in parishes throughout Wales seeking information on these subjects. This investigation led to the discovery of manuscripts previously unknown to the humanists such as the Red Book of Talgarth (Llanstephan MS 27) which contains a valuable collection of medieval religious texts. However, their most enduring contribution to Welsh literature was the significance they attached to the prose texts in the Red Book of Hergest, in particular the 'Four Branches of the Mabinogi' and the Arthurian romances, which had been so neglected by the humanists, but which from now on were to attract great interest amongst successive generations of Welsh scholars and *literati* and were to reach an even wider audience when Lady Charlotte Guest published her English translation of them in 1846.

ABBREVIATIONS

BBC: Black Book of Carmarthen (Peniarth MS 1).
RBH: Red Book of Hergest (Jesus College Oxford MS 111).
RMWL: J. Gwenogvryn Evans, *Report on Manuscripts in the Welsh Language* (Historical Manuscripts Commission, London, 1899–1910).
WBR: White Book of Rhydderch (Peniarth MS 4 and 5).

BIBLIOGRAPHY

Peter C. Bartrum, 'Further Notes on the Welsh Genealogical Manuscripts', *Transactions of the Honourable Society of Cymmrodorion* (1976), 102–18.

Idem, 'Genealogical Sources Quoted by Gruffudd Hiraethog', *National Library of Wales Journal*, 26 (1989–90), 1–9.

Idem, 'Notes on the Welsh Genealogical Manuscripts', *Transactions of the Honourable Society of Cymmrodorion* (1968), 63–98.

Idem, 'Tri Thlws ar Ddeg Ynys Prydain', *Études celtiques* 10 (1962–3), 434–77.

Idem, 'Y Pedwar Brenin ar Hugain a Farnwyd yn Gadarnaf (The Twenty Four Kings Judged to be the Mightiest)', *Études celtiques*, 12 (1968–71), 157–94.

D.J. Bowen, 'Gruffudd Hiraethog ac Argyfwng Cerdd Dafod', *Llên Cymru*, 1 (1951), 259–68; 2 (1952), 71–81.

Idem, *Gruffudd Hiraethog a'i Oes* (Caerdydd, 1958).

Geraint Bowen, 'Gweithiau Apologetig Reciwsantaidd Cymru (Dau lyfr yn ateb John Jewel, esgob Salisbury a'r Diwygwyr)', *National Library of Wales Journal*, 12 (1961–2), 236–49.

Idem, 'Llanstephan 13 (A Manvall or Meditation)', *National Library of Wales Journal*, 10 (1957–8), 51–8.

Idem, 'Llyfr y Resolusion neu Directori Christianogol Huw Owen o Wenynog', *National Library of Wales Journal*, 11 (1959–60), 147–51.

Idem, 'Yr Halsingod', *Transactions of the Honourable Society of Cymmrodorion* (1945), 83–108.

R. Bromwich, 'Pedwar Marchog ar Hugain Llys Arthur', *Transactions of the Honourable Society of Cymmrodorion* (1956), 116–32.

Eadem, *Trioedd Ynys Prydein* (second edition; Cardiff, 1978).

R. Alun Charles, 'Teulu Mostyn fel Noddwyr y Beirdd', *Llên Cymru*, 9 (1966–7), 74–110.

W. Beynon Davies, 'Siôn Mawndfil yn Gymraeg', *Bulletin of the Board of Celtic Studies*, 5 (1929–31), 287–327.

Idem (ed.), *Troelus a Chresyd o Lawysgrif Peniarth 106* (Caerdydd, 1976).

Hywel D. Emanuel, 'The Gwysaney Manuscripts', *National Library of Wales Journal*, 7 (1951–2), 326–43.

Patrick K. Ford (ed.), *Ystoria Taliesin* (Cardiff, 1992).

R. Geraint Gruffydd, 'Dau Destun Protestannaidd Cynnar o Lawysgrif Hafod 22', *Trivium*, 1 (1966), 56–66.

Idem, 'The Renaissance and Welsh Literature', in Glanmor Williams and Robert Owen Jones (eds), *The Celts and the Renaissance: Tradition and Innovation* (Cardiff, 1990), 17–39.

Lemuel J. Hopkins-James, *Hen Gwndidau, Carolau, a Chywyddau* (Bangor, 1910).

Garfield H. Hughes, '"Dysgeidiaeth Cristnoges o Ferch"', in T. Jones (ed.), *Astudiaethau Amrywiol* (Caerdydd, 1968), 17–32.

Daniel Huws, 'Canu Aneirin: the other manuscripts', in Brynley F. Roberts (ed.), *Early Welsh Poetry Studies in the Book of Aneirin* (Aberystwyth, 1988), 43–56.

Idem, *Llyfrau Cymraeg, 1250–1400* (Darlith Syr John Williams 1992) (Aberystwyth, 1993).

Idem, 'Llyfr Gwyn Rhydderch', *Cambridge Medieval Celtic Studies*, 21 (Summer 1991), 1–37.

Branwen Jarvis, '"Dysgeidiaeth Cristnoges o Ferch" a'i gefndir', *Ysgrifau Beirniadol*, 13 (Dinbych, 1985), 219–26.

Eadem, 'Note on a Welsh Version of the Thesaurus Pauperum', *Studia Celtica*, 10–11 (1975–6), 256–60.

Dafydd Jenkins, 'Deddfgrawn William Maurice', *National Library of Wales Journal*, 2 (1941), 33–6.

Bedwyr L. Jones, 'Siôn ap Hywel ab Owain a'r Rhetorica ad Herrenium yn Gymraeg', *Llên Cymru*, 6 (1960–1), 208–18.

Evan John Jones, *Medieval Heraldry* (Cardiff, 1943).

Francis Jones, 'An Approach to Welsh Genealogy', *Transactions of the Honourable Society of Cymmrodorion* (1948), 303–466.

Gwenan Jones, *A Study of Three Welsh Religious Plays* (Bala, 1939).

Gwendraeth Jones, 'Siôn Conwy III a'i waith', *Bulletin of the Board of Celtic Studies*, 22 (1966–8), 16–30.

R. Brinley Jones, *William Salesbury* (Cardiff, 1994).

Thomas Jones, *Y Bibyl Ynghymraec* (Cardiff, 1940).

Idem, 'Cyssegredic Historia Severus Swlpisws', *Bulletin of the Board of Celtic Studies*, 8 (1935–6), 107–20.

Aneirin Lewis (ed.), *Agweddau ar Hanes Dysg Gymraeg: detholiad o ddarlithiau G.J. Williams* (Caerdydd, 1969).

Ceri W. Lewis, 'Einion Offeiriad and the Bardic Grammar' in A.O.H. Jarman and Gwilym Rees Hughes (eds), *A Guide to Welsh Literature*, 2 (Swansea, 1979), 58–87.

Idem, 'Syr Edward Stradling (1529–1609)', *Ysgrifau Beirniadol*, 19 (Dinbych, 1993), 139–207.

Nesta Lloyd, 'Cyfieithiad o Ran o *Colloquium Adolescentis et Scorti* Erasmus i'r Gymraeg', *Bulletin of the Board of Celtic Studies*, 25 (1972–4), 32–46.

Eadem, 'Cyfieithiad o Ran o *De Remediis Fortuitorum Liber* Seneca i'r Gymraeg', *Bulletin of the Board of Celtic Studies*, 24 (1970–2), 450–8.

W. Alun Mathias, 'Rhai Sylwadau ar Robert Gwyn', *Llên Cymru*, 3 (1954–5), 63–73.

Idem, 'Wiliam Salesbury—Ei Fywyd a'i Weithiau', in Geraint Bowen (ed.), *Y Traddodiad Rhyddiaith* (Llandysul, 1970), 27–53.

Gerald Morgan, 'Testun Barddoniaeth y Tywysogion yn llsgr. NLW 4973', *Bulletin of the Board of Celtic Studies*, 20 (1962–4), 149–50.

Prys Morgan, 'Glamorgan and the Red Book', *Morgannwg*, 22 (1978), 42–60.

Morfydd E. Owen, 'The Prose of the *Cywydd* Period', in A.O.H. Jarman and Gwilym Rees Hughes (eds.), *A Guide to Welsh Literature*, 2 (Swansea, 1979), 338–75.

T.H. Parry-Williams, *Canu Rhydd Cynnar* (Caerdydd, 1932).

Jenny Rowland, *Early Welsh Saga Poetry: a Study and Edition of the Englynion* (Cambridge, 1990).

Eadem, 'The Manuscript Tradition of the Red Book *Englynion*', *Studia Celtica*, 18/19 (1983/4), 79–95.

E.I. Rowlands, 'Y Tri Thlws ar Ddeg', *Llên Cymru*, 5 (1958–9), 33–69.

Michael P. Siddons, *The Development of Welsh Heraldry* (three volumes; Aberystwyth, 1991–3).

G.J. Williams, 'Traddodiad Llenyddol Dyffryn Clwyd a'r Cyffiniau', *Transactions of the Denbighshire Historical Society*, 1 (1952), 20–32.

Idem, *Traddodiad Llenyddol Morgannwg* (Caerdydd, 1948).

G.J. Williams and E.J. Jones (eds.), *Gramadegau'r Penceirddiaid* (Caerdydd, 1934).

Glanmor Williams, 'The Achievement of William Salesbury', *Transactions of the Denbighshire Historical Society*, 14 (1965), 75–96.

Idem, 'Religion and Welsh Literature in the Age of the Reformation' (Sir John Rhys Memorial Lecture), *Proceedings of the British Academy*, 69 (1983), 371–408.

Gruffydd Aled Williams, *Dyffryn Conwy a'r Dadeni* (Llanrwst, 1989).

J.E. Caerwyn Williams, *Geiriadurwyr y Gymraeg yng Nghyfnod y Dadeni* (Caerdydd, 1983).

Idem, 'Gutun Owain', in A.O.H. Jarman and Gwilym Rees Hughes (eds.), *A Guide to Welsh Literature*, 2 (Swansea, 1979), 262–77.

Idem, 'Thomas Wiliems, y Geiriadurwr', *Studia Celtica*, 16/17 (1991/2), 280–316.

FROM MANUSCRIPT TO PRINT
II. PRINTED BOOKS

CHARLES PARRY

It is widely acknowledged that the development of movable type was a major landmark in history. Gutenberg's invention in the mid fifteenth century made available a process whereby ideas could be interchanged much more easily than by the slow and laborious copying of texts. The part played by print in spreading the ideas of the Renaissance and the Reformation cannot be overestimated.

That William Caxton was England's first printer is well known, the first book coming off his press at Westminster in 1477. Two years earlier he had produced at Bruges the first book to be printed in English. Caxton was a successful businessman, but not all of the earliest English printing ventures succeeded. Several provincial ventures in places such as Oxford and York failed in the late fifteenth and early sixteenth centuries. Traditionally, the copying of manuscripts had been carried out in abbeys, and it is interesting to note that there were short-lived attempts to practise printing at three English abbeys. However, there is no evidence of printing in Wales before the 1580s; and even that was a brief episode on a Catholic secret press.

In 1557, eleven years after the appearance of the first Welsh printed book, a charter was granted to the Stationers' Company which contained a *de facto* ban on printing outside London. Exceptions were made in the case of the universities of Oxford and Cambridge, each of which was allowed a press by a decree of Star Chamber in 1586. The Stationers' Company had originally been a guild of those involved in manuscript production, but by the 1550s the printers had taken control. This state of affairs continued until 1695, and thus all but a small handful of sixteenth- and seventeenth-century Welsh books were printed in London. The remainder were printed at Oxford, at Dublin, at secret Welsh presses, at four continental centres, and, after 1695, at Shrewsbury. No Welsh books are known from Worcester although a printer

named John Oswen, operating there between 1549 and 1553, was
granted a seven-year royal privilege in January 1549 to print service
books and religious treatises for Wales and the Marches. Since
Welsh church services were not allowed at this time, it seems likely
that the privilege refers to English books. One or two of Oswen's
books state, 'They are also to sell at Shrewsburye', indicating that
he had an outlet in that town. Perhaps it was problems of
distribution from London that led to the granting of the 1549
privilege. No more is heard of Oswen after 1553.

The complete absence of printing in Wales in the period
preceding the 1557 Stationers' Company ban on provincial printing
is not difficult to explain. Wales was a thinly populated country of
small scattered communities. There were no large centres of
population, universities, or courts to foster native culture. It was
geographically isolated and distant from centres like London and
the European cities where the new ideas of the Renaissance and
Reformation had taken hold. Illiteracy was the norm, with possibly
as few as 10 per cent of the population being able to read Welsh.
Life for the majority was a constant struggle and the acquisition of
books in any language was not a priority. Some englynion by Lewis
Gethin, rector of Llandegla and Llanferres, date from 1529 and
express a desire for Welsh printed books, but this would have
reflected the feelings of a very small minority of the population. In
the first half of the sixteenth century there was no capital in Wales
to set up a printing press and no demand for what it might print.

That said, it is important to stress that the society was not a
philistine one. Welsh scholars distinguished themselves at Oxford
and Cambridge, and Latin and English books by Welsh-born
authors were published from quite early on in the sixteenth century.
A rich corpus of literature in the vernacular was to be found in
manuscript, but very little interest in the potential of printing for its
dissemination was shown by copyists, collectors, or writers.

It is to a small minority of scholars, men influenced by the
Renaissance and Reformation, that Wales is indebted for its earliest
printed books. Mostly Protestant, these humanists desired to see
Protestantism firmly established. In addition, they cherished a
desire to see Welsh literature and scholarship flourish and become
known to a wider world through print. The books they produced in
1546 and later were intended to help achieve these two aims and
thus enable them to be divided into two main subject groupings. On

the one hand, there are translations of the Scriptures, of Anglican liturgy and Protestant religious treatises and, on the other, humanist works, predominantly grammars and dictionaries of the Welsh language. Behind their publication were men like William Salesbury, Siôn Dafydd Rhys, Gruffydd Robert and Sir John Prys, mainly Protestants. Gruffydd Robert, however, was a Roman Catholic, while the religious affiliations of Siôn Dafydd Rhys fluctuated.

Sir John Prys, scholar and royal administrator, was the compiler of the first Welsh book, *Yn y lhyvyr hwnn*. Consisting of translations of the Creed, the Lord's Prayer, the Ten Commandments, and other matter it was printed by Edward Whitchurch who held the monopoly for printing prayer-books. Some eighteen years earlier in 1528 the earliest printed item with a Welsh connection had appeared in the form of a Latin indulgence printed for Strata Marcella Abbey by Richard Pynson, London.

Though Prys's book was the first off the press, the leading Welsh humanist and bibliographically the most productive was Denbighshire-born William Salesbury, whose printed books, all from London presses, include both religious and humanistic works. In the former category are his *Kynniver llith a bann* (1551) and his Welsh translations of the New Testament and Book of Common Prayer (both 1567). Salesbury's humanistic works include *A dictionary in Englyshe and Welshe* (1547), *A briefe and playne introduction, teaching how to pronounce the letters in the British tong* (1550, with another edition in 1567) and the posthumous *Eglvryn phraethineb* (1595), begun by Salesbury and completed by Henri Perri. *Oll synnwyr pen Kembero*, a collection of proverbs made by Gruffudd Hiraethog and edited by Salesbury, appeared in 1547 with a second, enlarged, edition in 1567.

Other important humanist works of the late sixteenth and early seventeenth centuries include William Midleton's *Bardhoniaeth, neu brydydhiaeth* (1593), the grammars of Siôn Dafydd Rhys and Henry Salesbury (1592 and 1593), and the grammar and Welsh–Latin/Latin–Welsh dictionary of Dr John Davies of Mallwyd (1621 and 1632). A small number of late sixteenth-century works on Welsh history by humanist scholars such as Humphrey Lhwyd, David Powel, and the aforementioned John Prys are of considerable importance but are either in English or Latin, and there is no comparable Welsh-language printed volume in the pre-

1701 period. All are from London presses except for Humphrey
Lhwyd's *Commentarioli Britannicae descriptionis fragmentum*
(1572), which was printed at Cologne.

In 1588 a long-held dream of Welsh humanists was realized with
the publication of the complete Bible in Welsh, translated by
Bishop William Morgan. There were to be further editions before
1701, all but one printed in London. The first edition intended for
family as opposed to church use was a conveniently sized octavo
issued in 1630. Two separate and distinct versions of the metrical
Psalms appeared in 1603, those of William Midleton and Edward
Kyffin and, most popular by far, that of Edmwnd Prys, published
with the Book of Common Prayer, followed in 1621. A Welsh
version of the Primer under the title *Llyfr Plygain* was published
quite regularly from the late sixteenth century onwards as were
further editions of the Book of Common Prayer in the decades
between William Salesbury's 1567 version and the end of the
seventeenth century. In addition to Welsh translations of the
Scriptures and standard Anglican liturgical works, some Welsh
versions of well-known English theological and devotional treatises
came off London presses at quite early dates, for example Maurice
Kyffin's 1595 translation of John Jewel's *Apologia Ecclesiae
Anglicanae* and a 1629 version of Lewis Bayly's *The Practice of
Piety*.

Religious works printed in London dominated the meagre output
of Welsh printed books for the century and a half after the
appearance of *Yn y lhyvyr hwnn* in 1546. Classic English religious
works continued to be translated in the late seventeenth century—
works such as Allestree's *Whole Duty of Man*, published in a Welsh
version in 1672, and Bunyan's *Pilgrim's Progress* appearing as *Taith
neu siwrnai y pererin* in 1688. The preponderance of religious
material at this time was, if anything, even more marked than in
earlier decades for the publication of scholarly humanist works had
to all intents and purposes ceased with the appearance of John
Davies's *Dictionarium Duplex* in 1632. The humanists were replaced
as authors and translators in the closing decades of the seventeenth
century by pious, godly clerics more concerned for the salvation of
people's souls than for nourishing their minds along with their
spirits. Men like Charles Edwards, Stephen Hughes, and Thomas
Gouge worked tirelessly to provide a supply of devotional and
improving texts. The cost of printing and dissemination was borne

by philanthropic individuals and particularly, after its founding in 1674, by the Welsh Trust. It was at the very end of the century that the SPCK came into being. Consequently its involvement with the publishing of Welsh books belongs to the eighteenth and nineteenth centuries. Much of this material, intended for comparatively unlearned, possibly newly literate, people, consisted of translations but there were original works also, one of the most notable being the religious verse of Rhys Prichard, vicar of Llandovery.

Before considering those early Welsh titles printed at centres other than London, it is as well to note the fact that in the years before 1701 there are entries in the Stationers' Company registers for at least fourteen Welsh books which are not extant. From 1557 onwards a stationer was required to enter each 'copy' or book which he proposed to print in the register of ownership of copies kept by the Stationers' Company. The likelihood is that some of these fourteen items were never printed. In the case of the others, all copies have perished. A study of the entries in the registers suggests that several works of considerable interest may have disappeared completely.

Of the quite small number of pre-eighteenth-century Welsh books printed outside London, the majority derive from Oxford. Printing began again at Oxford in 1585, just over a century after another printing venture there had failed. Official permission for printing was granted the following year. One of the arguments used to support the new press was its potential usefulness for supplying the needs of Wales, the west of England, and Ireland. Although this might refer to English books for the Welsh market, Oxford could be considered an appropriate place to print Welsh books. It had more Welsh students than Cambridge, scholars who could proof-read and might be purchasers. The first Welsh book printed at Oxford was *Perl mewn Adfyd*, a 1595 translation by Huw Lewys of Miles Coverdale's English version of a work by Otto Werdmüller. The seventeenth century saw the printing of several important Welsh volumes at Oxford, for example three editions of an important original work by Charles Edwards, *Y Ffydd Ddi-ffuant*, and a 1690 folio Bible.

The earlier of two Welsh books printed in Dublin in the seventeenth century is now lost. However, there is good reason for believing that the first edition of Morgan Llwyd's *Gwaedd Ynghymru* was seen through the press in that city in 1653 by the regicide Colonel John Jones of. Maesygarnedd. In 1700 a Welsh version of the *Testament of the Twelve Patriarchs* was printed in the Irish capital. Welsh books printed at Loreto, Milan, Paris, St Omer, and on secret presses in Wales all have Roman Catholic connections, most with the Counter-Reformation movement. The Loreto item is a broadside account of the famous Marian shrine in that town. It dates from 1635. It was in 1567 that the Catholic humanist Gruffydd Robert published the first part of his famous Welsh Grammar, *Dosparth Byrr* at Milan, probably printed by Vincenzo Girardone. This is the earliest of the handful of Welsh books printed abroad. Further parts of *Dosparth Byrr* appeared before the century's end, printed at either Milan or Paris.

Books published as part of the Counter-Reformation efforts to return England to the Catholic fold had to be printed abroad or on secret presses in Britain since Catholic printing was prohibited. The earliest Welsh book belonging to this movement is Morris Clynnog's translations of Johannes Polancus' *Dottrina Christiana* printed at Milan in 1568 under the title, *Athravaeth Gristnogavl*. No other sixteenth-century Welsh Catholic books from continental presses are known although Anglesey-born Owen Lewis, later bishop of Cassano, appealed to the Pope in 1578 for a contribution towards the cost of printing three Welsh books in Milan.

Rhosier Smyth, a priest based on the Continent, translated several well-known Catholic works and arranged for their printing in Paris in the early seventeenth century. Welsh versions of works by Petrus Canisius appeared in 1609 and 1611 and a translation of Pierre Boaistuau's *Théâtre du mond* in 1615. However, it is suggested in Rees's *Libri Walliae* that the latter's imprint may be fictitious and that the book may have been printed in London. A translation by Smyth of part of a work by Robert Southwell was printed in Paris in 1612. This work was unknown until 1992 when a copy came to light at the Bibliothèque Mazarine, Paris. St Omer in France was an important centre for printing English Counter-Reformation books. One Welsh book is known from St Omer, a translation by Richard Vaughan, printed in 1618, of a work by Roberto Bellarmino.

The alternative to smuggling Catholic books printed abroad into the country was to print them secretly on illegal presses in Britain. One Welsh book, Robert Gwyn's *Y Drych Cristianogawl* is known to have been printed in 1587 by the printer Roger Thackwell in a cave on a Catholic-owned estate near Llandudno. Its completely fictitious imprint states that it was printed at Rouen in 1585. The intention, of course, was to mislead the authorities. No other Welsh book has the type used in the *Drych*. In addition to the cave press, there is evidence for a secret press in the house of the grammarian Siôn Dafydd Rhys in Brecon and of another in 1590 somewhere in the Overton area of Flintshire. It is likely that Gruffydd Robert's *Ynglynion ar y Pader* (*c*. 1590) and Richard White's *Carolau* (1600) were printed on secret presses in Wales. Despite the small number of Welsh Catholics and tight control of the press, the faithful succeeded in printing at least four Catholic works between 1618 (the date of the St Omer volume) and the end of the century. One, *Allwydd neu Agoriad Paradwys i'r Cymru* (1670), compiled by the Jesuit John Hughes, is of bibliographical as well as theological interest. Like the 1587 *Drych*, it bears what it generally agreed to be a false imprint. The title-page states that it was printed in Liège, but the probability is that it came off a London press.

Decade by decade the increase in the number of Welsh books printed in the years after 1546 was very slight though the late seventeenth century did see a more marked rise. However, the end of the century saw two developments that were to revolutionize the world of Welsh publishing. The first was the emergence in the 1670s of Thomas Jones (1648–1713), the man who has been called the father of Welsh publishing; the second was the end in 1695 of the ban on provincial printing.

Merioneth-born Jones, settled in London since about 1666, was at first a tailor but subsequently took to bookselling and publishing, with his name appearing in imprints, including those of English books, from 1676 onwards. Thomas Jones was a born pioneer and entrepreneur and appears to have known what he wanted to achieve from his earliest days in the book trade. His dream was to supply cheap Welsh-language books of good technical quality. Achieving this aim, however, was another matter. The London trade, on the one hand, was very loath to involve itself in ventures which were financially risky and, on the other, had a longstanding reputation for unreliability and fraudulent practices. Stephen Hughes, the indefatigable editor and translator, complains of the latter in his prefaces to parts three and four of the works of Rhys Prichard. Nevertheless, Thomas Jones succeeded in publishing a fair number of Welsh books in London in the 1680s and 1690s prior to his move to Shrewsbury on the repeal of the Licensing Act in 1695. Although he achieved much in London, it is with Shrewsbury that his name is usually linked. His London books include some secular volumes as well as religious works, for he saw the need for cheap, popular secular books, a type of publication hitherto unavailable. Among these is his well-known popular dictionary, *Y Gymraeg yn ei Disgleirdeb* (1688).

Thomas Jones's most famous secular publication by far is his almanac, the first of its kind printed in Welsh. It was printed every year between 1680 and 1712, with ample contemporary evidence of its great popularity. At the beginning of 1679 Jones was granted a royal patent giving him the sole right to write, print and publish a Welsh-language almanac. Transferring his business to Shrewsbury was a wise, and no doubt, profitable move by Thomas Jones. He was now far closer to his public, based in a town that had been a trading-centre for north Wales for generations. Here he took to printing, producing not fine printing on good-quality paper, but what he wished to achieve: inexpensive adequately printed reading matter for the common man. Thomas Jones established Shrewsbury as the main centre for the printing of Welsh books until well into the eighteenth century. Ballads also were destined to come off Shrewsbury presses in very large numbers, with Thomas Jones once again pioneering the printing of this particular genre. He printed ballads in his almanac, but the first-known separate publication is a small collection of four ballads advertised in his 1699 almanac.

Though so many of Thomas Jones's ventures proved successful, there is one notable exception. A Welsh-language news-sheet advertised in his almanac of 1691 and 1692 failed and there are no copies now extant. Nevertheless, Jones is truly important on account of the wide range of his publications, his abilities as a businessman, and, quite simply, the fact that he was the first individual to make a living in the Welsh book trade, being involved during his career in bookselling, publishing, printing, authorship and translation.

In estimating the number of pre-eighteenth-century Welsh books it is usual to count all printed items, both single sheets and folio bibles. Lost works for whose existence there is apparently firm evidence are counted, as are all the Stationers' register books no longer extant though some of this group may never have been printed. R. Geraint Gruffydd in *Argraffwyr Cyntaf Cymru:*

gwasgau dirgel y Catholigion adeg Elisabeth estimates the number of Welsh books from this period as approximately two hundred. The paucity of early books is a disappointment despite the fact that the various compelling reasons that account for it are known.

The author or translator's distance from the press, type fonts unable to do justice to the Welsh language, and printers to whom the latter was incomprehensible, inevitably mean that the earliest Welsh books are not examples of particularly fine printing. However, English printing at this time does not compare favourably with the finest continental work. Apart from the problem of misprints, pre-1701 Welsh books are generally no more badly printed than thousands of their English contemporaries. The one exception is the group of books printed by Thomas Jones at Shrewsbury in the late 1690s. These are typographically inferior to the London and Oxford output, but were perfectly acceptable to Jones's readers. Subject matter and cost precluded illustrations, of course.

Apologies for the excessive number of misprints are found in the introductions to many early Welsh books with the blame laid at the door of printers unacquainted with the language. Such complaints can be found, for example, in the Welsh New Testament of 1567, in John Edwards's translation of *The Marrow of Modern Divinity* (1651) and in Thomas Jones's *Y Gymraeg yn ei Disgleirdeb* (1688). The correction of proofs by the author at the press was the normal practice until the beginning of the eighteenth century, but it is clear that several authors and translators of early Welsh books were not present for this vital work. William Salesbury, William Morgan, and Charles Edwards are important figures known to have spent periods in London supervising the printing of their work. The above-mentioned John Edwards, on complaining to his printers about the misprints, was told that it was well-nigh impossible to find a Welshman in London who could proof-read and advise the English workers. This claim was inaccurate for there is evidence for the existence of Welsh-born men in the London book trade in sources such as the apprentices' lists of the Stationers' Company. Before the emergence of Thomas Jones, the most important London-Welsh stationer involved in the production of Welsh books is Thomas Salisbury of Clocaenog, Denbighshire. A man of some learning himself, he published Henry Salesbury's *Grammatica Britannica* (1593), metrical translations of the Psalms by William

Midleton and Edward Kyffin (both in 1603) and a Welsh translation of part of James I's *Basilikon Doron*. In addition, the Stationers' registers reveal his intention to print two other works, neither now to be found. Evidence from other sources suggests that he had plans for further books but nothing was to come of them. Despite the presence of Welsh-born men in the London book trade, all the evidence indicates that most Welsh books were printed by printers to whom the language was a foreign tongue. The reoccurrence of certain printers' names is an indication, perhaps, of their moderate prices rather than a reputation for quality work. The books printed at Oxford from the late sixteenth century onwards, though far fewer in number, have, on the whole, a higher standard of accuracy than London works.

Monoglot English printers also had difficulties with the Welsh alphabet with its additional letters such as *dd* and *ll* and its use of *w* and *y* as both consonants and vowels. These differences put a strain on type fonts never designed to accommodate the Welsh alphabet. There were not sufficient characters since their incidence in Welsh is quite different from that in English. Sixteenth-century authors moreover had varying theories on orthography. The 1567 Welsh Book of Common Prayer is an example of a shortage of particular characters influencing orthography. The reader is told that *c* is being used for *k* since the printers lack the number required by the Welsh. In some words *c* is used for *g*. A shortage of the letter *w* was often overcome by the use of two *v*s, especially in capitals.

Although most are typographically unremarkable, one early Welsh book has attracted the interest of printing historians. Siôn Dafydd Rhys's *Cambrobrytannicae . . . Linguae Institutiones*, printed by Thomas Orwin in 1592, is the first book printed in England to make extensive use of Hebrew type. Letters were specially cast to cater for the Welsh alphabet's added requirements. They were specially cast also for Henry Salesbury's grammar of 1593. There is evidence from several other volumes of the late sixteenth and early seventeenth century of a serious attempt to cater for the Welsh language typographically.

The concept of copyright derives from a practice begun shortly after the printing of the first Welsh book. As stated above in the context of non-extant books, from 1557 the stationer was required to enter each 'copy' or book which he proposed to print in the Stationers' register, to ensure that he had an official licence which permitted publication. By the end of the sixteenth century an entry was taken to mean that the person in whose name the entry was made had the sole right to print that particular copy. From the sixteenth century onwards, certain printers were also on occasion granted the sole right by the Crown to print certain classes of books. Among examples of patents or privileges granted by the Crown for the printing of Welsh books is that which appears to have been granted by Elizabeth I in 1563 to William Salesbury and John Waley. They were given the sole right for seven years to print the Bible, the Book of Common Prayer, the Book of Homilies 'or any other books of godly doctrine in the British or Welsh tongue'. When, however, the Welsh New Testament and the Book of Common Prayer were printed in 1567, Waley's name did not occur in the imprint. The works were printed by Henry Denham 'at the costes and charges of Humphrey Toy'. The complete Welsh Bible of 1588 has an imprint stating that it was printed by the deputies of Christopher Barker, the king's printer who held the patent to print bibles. The imprint of William Morgan's Bible is a good example of how the unwary can be misled by publication details as given in some early books. While it is made clear that the patent holder, Christopher Barker, is ultimately reponsible for its appearance, the suggestion is that it was printed by his deputies. Barker's deputies in 1588 were George Bishop and Ralph Newbery neither of whom was a printer. They presumably followed the practice of the time and engaged a master printer, possibly Henry Denham, to print this most famous of Welsh books. Similarly, four works by William Salesbury claim to have been printed by Robert Crowley. Crowley was a clergyman, author and publisher, but not a printer. There is reason for believing that the four Salesbury books were printed by Robert Grafton. Piracy, that is the printing and publishing of books by persons other than the copyright owner, was common from the earliest period and dealt with by the Stationers' Company. Copyrights could be bought and sold, as evidenced by the various London printers who figure in the complicated printing history of the work of Rhys Prichard.

Printing Welsh books in London in the sixteenth and seventeenth centuries was not a profitable activity. There was therefore little temptation to pirate them. An exception was Thomas Jones's almanac. As already stated, Jones had been awarded the royal patent for a Welsh almanac in early 1679, one he was to defend to the point of obsession in later years. Several piracies were printed in the period between the 1680s and the first decade of the eighteenth century. There is also a reference in a Bodleian Library manuscript to William Lloyd, bishop of St Asaph, urging John Fell, effective founder of the Oxford University Press, to accept a draft sheet almanac in Welsh so as to provide profitable work for the Welsh press at Oxford.

With some exceptions, little is known of the size of print runs of early Welsh books. The earliest volumes came off the press at a time when the potential readership was very small and an effective distribution system largely undeveloped. Such circumstances suggest editions limited to a small number of copies. Formidable difficulties put in the way of Catholic printing must have had a similar limiting effect. In the context of the Welsh Bible, details of numbers of copies printed, where known, are given in John Ballinger's *The Bible in Wales* (1906). About a thousand copies of the 1588 Bible were printed, this being dwarfed by the edition of 1677–8 and 1689–90, with some 8,000 and 10,000 copies respectively. It is known that Sir Edward Stradling paid for the printing of 1,250 copies of Siôn Dafydd Rhys's grammar of 1592. The 1677–8 Bible was largely financed by the Welsh Trust. Printed accounts of the Trust from the 1670s give details of the print runs of a few non-biblical works published by it.

An effective distribution system for Welsh books appears to have evolved in the seventeenth century, more particularly towards its end, with the rise in the number of books printed, the formation of the Welsh Trust and the emergence of Thomas Jones. It is clear that by the 1670s general dealers or mercers in many Welsh towns were selling books. A list of several towns where Welsh books were available for sale at this time may be found in the imprints of books by Charles Edwards and John Jewel (a reprint). Somewhat later, Thomas Jones's famous almanac lists vendors of the almanac in various parts of Wales, often in very small communities. Chapmen and peddlars must have been selling popular material by the end of the century. Many books were published by subscription, though the first titles to include a list of the subscribers' names date from the first decade of the eighteenth century.

Some twenty-five to thirty of the most important early Welsh printed books have been reprinted, usually in facsimile, since the end of the nineteenth century. The University of Wales Press has reprinted several notable titles; in recent years some of the Catholic and linguistic books have also been issued in well-known facsimile reprints series such as *English Linguistics* and *English Recusant Literature*. In 1988 the National Library of Wales issued a handsome facsimile of the most outstanding early Welsh book, Williams Morgan's 1588 Bible. No other book of the early period combines religious and linguistic significance to the same extent as Morgan's masterly translation.

BIBLIOGRAPHY

Edward Arber (ed.), *A Transcript of the Registers of the Company of Stationers of London: 1554–1640 AD* (five volumes; London and Birmingham, 1875–94).

John Ballinger, *The Bible in Wales* (London, 1906).

Bernard Capp, *Astrology and the Popular Press: English Alamanacs 1500–1800* (London, 1979).

Harry Carter, *A History of the Oxford University Press: Volume I. To the year 1780* (Oxford, 1975).

W.Ll. Davies, 'A Argraffwyd Llyfr Cymraeg yn Iwerddon cyn 1700?', *Journal of the Welsh Bibliographical Society*, 5 (1937–42). This periodical contains many relevant articles on early Welsh publishing.

George E.B. Eyre and C.R. Rivington (eds), *A Transcript of the Registers of the Worshipful Company of Stationers from 1640–1708 AD* (two volumes; London, 1913–14).

John Feather, *A Dictionary of Book History* (London, 1986).

Idem, *A History of British Publishing* (London, 1988).

R. Geraint Gruffydd, *Argraffwyr Cyntaf Cymru: gwasgau dirgel Catholigion o adeg Elisabeth* (Caerdydd, 1972).

Idem, 'Thomas Salisbury o Lundain a Chlocaenog: ysgolhaig-argraffydd y Dadeni Cymreig', *National Library of Wales Journal*, 27 (1991–2), 1–19. This periodical contains other relevant articles on early Welsh publishing.

Garfield H. Hughes (ed.), *Rhagymadroddion, 1547–1659* (Caerdydd, 1951).

Geraint H. Jenkins, *Hanes Cymru yn y Cyfnod Modern Cynnar, 1530–1760* (Caerdydd, 1983).

Idem, *Literature, Religion and Society in Wales, 1660–1730* (Cardiff, 1978).

Idem, *Thomas Jones yr Almanaciwr, 1648–1713* (Caerdydd, 1980).

Ifano Jones, *A History of Printing and Printers in Wales to 1810* (Cardiff, 1925).

D.F. McKenzie (ed.), *Stationers' Company Apprentices, 1605–1800* (three volumes; Charlottesville Va and Oxford, 1961–78).

Eiluned Rees, *Libri Walliae: A Catalogue of Welsh Books and Books*

Printed in Wales, 1546–1820 (two volumes; Aberystwyth, 1987). The most comprehensive bibliography of early Welsh printed books. Copious and valuable book trade and other indexes in volume 2.

Eadem, *The Welsh Book Trade Before 1820* (Aberystwyth, 1988). Also printed in volume 2 of *Libri Walliae*.

Eadem 'Welsh Publishing Before 1717', in D.E. Rhodes (ed.), *Essays in Honour of Victor Scholderer* (Mainz, 1970), 323–36.

INDEX